THE GREAT FAMINE AND THE IRISH DIASPORA IN AMERICA

THE GREAT FAMINE AND THE IRISH DIASPORA IN AMERICA

Edited by ARTHUR GRIBBEN

Introduction BY RUTH-ANN M. HARRIS

UNIVERSITY OF MASSACHUSETTS PRESS   Amherst

This book is published with the support and cooperation of the University of Massachusetts Boston and the California Branch of the American Irish Historical Society

Printed in the United States of America
LC 98-8432
ISBN 1-55849-172-4 (cloth): 173-2 (pbk)

Designed by Dennis Anderson
Set in Monotype Dante by Graphic Composition, Inc.
Printed and bound by BookCrafters

Library of Congress Cataloging-in-Publication Data

The great famine and the Irish diaspora in America / edited by Arthur Gribben ; introduction by Ruth-Ann Harris.
    p   cm.
    Includes bibliographical references (p.) and index.
    Contents: Women and the great famine / Patricia Lysaght — A Tory periodical in a time of famine / Wayne Hall — Alexis Soyer and the Irish famine / Jillian Strang and Joyce Toomre — The transfer of land and the emergence of the graziers during the famine period / David S. Jones — The great famine / Gearóid Ó hAllmhuráin — Grosse Île / Michael Quigley — The famine beat / Neil Hogan — Revenge for Skibbereen / Kerby Miller — The pauper and the politician / Kerby A. Miller and Bruce D. Boling — The famine and collective memory / Mick Mulcrone — The great famine / Christine Kinealy.
    ISBN 1-55849-172-4 (cloth : alk. paper). — ISBN 1-55849-173-2 (pbk. : alk. paper)
    1. Famines—Ireland—History—19th century.   2. Ireland—Emigration and immigration—History—19th century.   3. Ireland—History—1837–1901.   4. Irish Americans—History   I. Gribben, Arthur.
DA950.7.G735   1999
941 508—DC21   98-8432
                                                                                          CIP

British Library Cataloguing in Publication Data are available.

This volume is dedicated to the memory of all who suffered and died because of the Great Hunger and to those who labored on their behalf during that great calamity. May the lessons learned from a reading of these essays inspire generosity and constructive intervention from those who can make a difference when and wherever tragedy strikes.

Contents

Preface

"THE GREAT FAMINE 1845–1850: A Commemoration" was the theme of a symposium held at Loyola Marymount University, Los Angeles, on October 2, 1993. The symposium was a project of the California American Irish Historical Society. In the course of that day, papers were presented; a rough cut of Paul Wagner's documentary film *Out of Ireland* was screened with accompanying commentary from the director; a member of the Choctaw Nation chanted and performed a religious song in memory of the Famine victims; and actress/director Fionnula Flanagan led a group of performers in dramatic readings recalling Ireland's historic struggle for freedom from colonial domination by Britain. Throughout the day, Dr. Philip O'Carroll's traditional music and song heartened the proceedings. Inspired by the success of the symposium, this interdisciplinary volume of essays presents a set of Famine scholarship that leads from Ireland to the United States and demonstrates the engagement of both countries that resulted from the Famine.

Since much of the drive for renewed investigation into the Great Famine over the past decade or more came from a variety of academic disciplines, the idea for an interdisciplinary volume of essays seemed highly appropriate. In addition, most edited collections of Famine essays to date have focused almost exclusively on the Famine in Ireland. This volume reaches beyond island boundaries by including essays addressing the implications and ramifications of the Famine for the Irish-American experience.

Without the gracious assistance of individuals and organizations, this book would not have been possible. First, I must thank colleagues such as Meg Brady of the University of Utah, Salt Lake City; Ginger Farrer of California State University, Chico; Michael Gillispie of the American

Conference for Irish Studies; and Shalom Staub of the American Folklore Society, who helped place the call-for-papers in various academic newsletters across the country. As a result of their good deed, upwards of sixty manuscripts were either proposed or submitted, from which the essays appearing here were chosen. I sincerely wish to thank everyone who showed interest in contributing to the project, especially those whose work did not make the final cut. Congratulations to the final contributors whose work is presented here, especially those who bore with me over the course of many trying revisions.

The assistance and encouragement of other individuals must also be acknowledged. In this connection, I would like to thank Kerby Miller, Bill Williams, Jim Duran, Chris Mooney, Judy McCulloch, and Catherine Pierce, all of whom provided invaluable feedback on the manuscript. I would also like to express my gratitude to Mary Ferguson and the 1992 board of directors of the California American Irish Historical Society for their generous grant in support of publication of the project. No doubt, there are some other friends and supporters whose names I have misplaced in the course of five years of notes and memos. To them also, thank you so much! Finally, to Paul Wright of the University of Massachusetts Press, who kept faith in the project through thick and thin, *Go Raibh Míle Maith Agat!*

ARTHUR GRIBBEN
California State University, Northridge

THE GREAT
FAMINE AND
THE IRISH
DIASPORA
IN AMERICA

RUTH-ANN M. HARRIS

Introduction

MICHAEL SULLIVAN, a laborer from Cork, was one of a thousand witnesses who testified before the Devon Commission, which in 1843 collected evidence on conditions in the Irish countryside.[1] His story may be taken as typical of the situation experienced by the very poorest families of Ireland, those persons most vulnerable to the devastation of the Famine. When asked how much property he held, his reply was that he held no ground. "I am a poor man. I have nothing but my labour." He rented his house and an acre of ground from a farmer called Daniel Regan—undoubtedly the undertenant of a larger landlord—at a rate of three pounds; two for the acre of ground and one for the lease of the house. Working as a day laborer for Regan for a wage of sixpence a day and meals, he said that when that work wasn't available he went farther south in Cork or north to Tipperary or Limerick for the harvest or digging potatoes. When asked how he supported a family of seven on sixpence a day, he said that he could occasionally make a little more from road making. His wife supplemented their income by selling eggs, "or [she] makes up a skein of thread in the market, she may take home with her a pen'orth or two pen'orth of something to nourish the children for that night; but in general I do not use 5s. of kitchen[2] from one end of the year to the other." Of schooling for his children he said, "A better labouring man than what I am cannot afford his children any schooling." Even the farmers of his district were badly off. Of them he said,

> One out of 100 cannot drink a pint of sour milk among five in family from about Christmas until about the 17th of March or so; and then generally they are forced to sell the sour milk in order to meet the rent, or pawn their clothes. I know in different places three women in one house trusting to one cloak, and for a time, perhaps, it might be in the pawn office.

Did people of his class ever emigrate to America? Sullivan replied that he knew of few that had emigrated. Would they be willing to emigrate, he was asked. He replied, "It is hard for a man to account for another man's mind, but of course they would."

By present standards Michael Sullivan's life seems incredibly bleak, yet he still aspired to have his children educated and would have considered going to America if he could receive assistance. His aspirations mirror the social changes transforming life in Ireland in the decades prior to the Famine, changes that paralleled the changing economic conditions of the country. Michael Sullivan and his family of wife and five children, the eldest of whom was only twelve, were typical of those who would disappear within the next five years. Their bodies, weakened by years of an inadequate diet, would have succumbed fairly quickly when their acre of potatoes, their only bulwark against disaster, rotted as the potato blight swept over Ireland in late September of 1845.

The Great Famine has been the unseen guest at every Irish dinner table since the mid-nineteenth century. Despite long familiarity with famine conditions—there were five periods of major famine conditions in the eighteenth century and eight in the nineteenth century prior to 1845— the Great Famine stands by itself as one of the worst catastrophes of modern Irish history.[3] While the suffering of the poor could have been ignored in earlier times, this was no longer possible in mid–nineteenth century Britain, an age marked by growing public debate on issues of social policy. Public reaction to the phenomenon of widespread suffering in an age that considered itself enlightened was the consequence of the increased humanitarianism of the age. Clashing ideologies between Romanticism, with its emphasis on feelings, and the harshness of the new political economy, which put its faith in capitalism, led to intense debates among the informed public. And just at a time when technology and commerce promised boundless increase in the general well-being of mankind, disaster arrived which would forever poison relations between the Irish people and the British government.

The Great Famine of 1845 to 1850 was caused by the failure of the potato through blight, an irresistible fungus *Phytophthora infestans,* which found its way into Ireland from North America. The crisis was far worse in Ireland than anywhere else the potato was grown, owing to its role as an important part of the diet for 66 percent of the population and the sole article of diet for one third of the population. The blight was a particular disaster for the agricultural laborer and cottier classes, which were hardest hit because they were most dependent on the nutritious and prolific potato for their survival. Few had the resources to flee the disaster, and the scene of their emaciated dying bodies lying by the roadsides remains vivid in the folk memory to this day.

The Famine was a catastrophe also for the British government, ill prepared as it was to cope with the gigantic challenge of administering relief on such a scale. In an earlier famine of 1816–17, relief was the responsibility of the Irish chief secretary, a young politician called Sir Robert Peel, who developed a successful project of public works. From that date until 1845, the government continued the program of public works designed to relieve poverty by creating access to remote areas of the country, eventually spending an estimated one million pounds in loans and grants to local authorities for development of isolated regions. Earlier experience of famine relief may have misled the authorities into thinking they could marshal relief measures that had been effective in the past.

When in September of 1845 the blight first appeared, it was noted in local newspapers. Brief paragraphs appeared in the *Waterford Freeman* and the *Dublin Evening Post* on September 6, but most public reaction was influenced by political or sectional allegiances, which tended to minimize or exaggerate its intensity or extent. No unusual alarm was expressed, except by the editors of the *Gardener's Chronicle,* who delayed publication of their September issue to announce the arrival of the blight. Public discussion ensued and there was considerable debate as to which group—medical, commercial, or administrative—was competent to deal with the outbreak.[4]

Peel, who had been the prime minister of Britain since 1841, set in motion a train of relief measures to alleviate the worst effects of food shortage. Ignoring the political risk inherent in failure to obtain cabinet approval, Peel arranged for one hundred thousand pounds worth of cornmeal (which became known scathingly as "Peel's brimstone" when it proved hard to digest for a population accustomed to the mild potato diet) to be imported from the United States. This first effort came to an end when his government fell in June of 1846 after repeal of the Corn Laws. Lord John Russell, succeeding Peel as prime minister, came to government handicapped in dealing with the crisis by his commitment to free trade and laissez-faire economic principles, which caused him to believe that food was not to be sold below the market price so as not to interfere with normal trade. While Russell did not stop the distribution of free soup ordered by Peel, he ordered the closure of the public works which had provided some measure of relief to distressed districts, claiming that financial crisis in England made it impossible to provide aid for Ireland.[5] Policies of drift prevailed, exacerbated by an English bias in favor of capitalist farming and the belief that overpopulation was at the root of the problem that had resulted in the Famine.

During the second half of the eighteenth century, Irish farmers were gradually converting from grazing to tillage agriculture, a process that increased between 1810 and 1845, when the formerly protected English market was opened to Irish grain after 1806.[6] Between 1811 and 1815 the price of Irish wheat rose 61 percent and oats 59 percent.[7] The transition from grazing to agriculture, which included the cultivation of the potato, tended to lessen the natural checks on population when farming land became more easily available.

Ireland's social history cannot be written without focusing upon the role of the potato economy in the development and eventual deterioration of the physical well-being of the Irish people. Louis Cullen has demonstrated that while possibly too much stress has been placed upon the potato as an active agent of change, the potato diet played a significant role. In his view, its adoption was a response to population increase, though not necessarily the cause of it.[8] The potato had obvious advantages contributing to its initial adoption by a land-hungry population: food production per acre of potatoes was approximately four times greater than that of grain crops, and that, along with the fact that potatoes could also be consumed without further processing, made a winning combination. During this period, changes in the cultivation of the potato that lengthened the interval between planting and harvest allowed seasonal migrants to leave their home plots earlier and return later in the agricultural season, which led to an increase in seasonal migration to work elsewhere, either in Ireland or in England. A writer in 1794 observed that cottiers were planting their potatoes earlier in the season because of their obligations to their landlords and their desire to seek work elsewhere.[9] The shift to production for an export market changed the relationship between tenants and laborers and their landlords. Grazier landlords needed few tenants, but tillage required more labor. As the importance of rural laborers increased, this lessened the restraints on population growth prevalent under the previous system of subsistence agriculture. Relations within the family also changed. Until the 1760s a father's control of the land ensured his dominant position, both in the household and in the prevailing farming system; a son only obtained his share at his father's death. But by the mid–eighteenth century, the source of patriarchal power had been eroded with the expanding number of males who could earn income through wage labor without directly controlling land. This broke a socially necessary preventive check on marriage and thus on population growth. After 1760, a young man with only a laborer's income could rent land to grow potatoes and, subsisting on them, pay rent as high as or higher than his father. In this way the ability to pay rent conferred on the son the same right to the land as the father. The shift in the son's role vis-à-vis that of his father undoubtedly contributed to the release of traditional restraints on physical movement, which in turn facilitated an energetic and ambitious young person's desire to migrate when opportunity offered.[10]

Landlords regarded their Irish properties as sources of revenue rather than opportunities for long-term investment. In addition to this, the spirit of the Penal Laws, enacted in the late seventeenth century to prevent Catholics from being disloyal citizens, also exacerbated differences between the usually Protestant landlord and his usually Catholic tenant, with the result that relationships between different classes in Irish society were often acrimonious. Alexis de Tocqueville, who journeyed to Ireland in July and August of 1835, called attention to the tainted relations between classes in Ireland when he said, "Here it happens that those who want to get are of one religion, and those who want to keep of another. That makes for violence."[11] It was in this poisoned atmosphere, in which popular discontent was directed at the landlord class, that the famine-tried people of Ireland were in 1845 faced with yet another catastrophe.

Ireland was scarcely an isolated country in the first half of the nineteenth century, so that conditions there did not go unnoticed. Travel was a popular form of recreation, and travelers in Ireland have left at least 106 accounts of Irish tours and journeys between the years 1800 and 1849.[12] Parliamentary investigations of conditions abound. Three contemporary accounts by persons who experienced the Famine years at first hand are noteworthy. Asenath Nicholson, an American woman who traveled throughout Ireland in 1844 and 1845, investigated the condition of the Irish poor.[13] In her book *Annals of the Famine in Ireland in 1847, 1848, and 1849*, Nicholson did not let her missionary effort to bring the Bible to the Irish blind her to their greater need for sustenance. Teacher, reformer, abolitionist, and writer, her work suffered the fate of that of many other women: she was more or less ignored until recently, when her writings were republished and evaluated in a critical article by Maureen Murphy, who regards Nicholson as performing a valuable service by informing the American public of the extent of the calamity taking place in Ireland.[14] Alexander Somerville was a Scottish journalist whose *Letters from Ireland during the Famine of 1847* sought to convince a skeptical British public of the extent of the disaster that was occurring.[15] Like most others, he laid the blame for Ireland's difficulties at the feet of the landlord class, regardless of their faith and politics. Nicholson and Somerville were alike in having a valuable eye for detail—for rents, wages, rates, regional types of farming, the way people armed and conducted themselves, and how the Famine affected particular individuals. In other words, both writers brought the Famine down to a human level that a reading public could comprehend.

John Mitchel provided the first really crucial explanation of the Famine, and for those seeking a nationalist interpretation of the period he provided the classic exposition.[16] In his newspaper, *The United Irishman*, he advocated extreme measures for the starving peasantry to take against their landlords and the authorities. His fury expended itself in the splenetic prose evidenced in his *Jail Journal*, which first appeared in 1854 in the New York newspaper he founded after escaping to America from penal servitude in Van Diemen's Land (Tasmania). Kevin Nowlan, in his introduction to Edwards and Williams's classic study of the Great Famine, suggested that the imprecations of Young Irelanders Charles Gavan Duffy and Mitchel, who described the Famine as nothing less than "a fearful murder committed on the mass of the people," were an exaggerated response. Those seeking a more organic explanation for the origin of the Famine have turned to the writings of James Connolly, the early twentieth-century socialist and labor union organizer, who stated that "No man who accepts capitalist society and the laws thereof can logically find fault with the statesmen of England for their acts in that awful period."[17]

For the facts about the Famine one goes to sources such as the contemporary newspapers, the 1851 Census tables, which tell a graphic story of loss of population, and to the reports of the Society of Friends (Quakers). As the desolation of the Famine years subsided, a relative silence about the subject descended until Father John O'Rourke's *The Great Irish Famine of 1847* appeared in 1874 and presented one of the first Catholic interpretations of Irish history.[18] Again silence followed. With the foundation of the Irish Historical Society and the journal *Irish Historical Studies* in the 1940s, the scene was set for new and more objective approaches to the study of Irish history and to the topic of the Famine in particular. The need for an authoritative study of the Great Famine was first proposed by the then *Taoiseach*, Eamon de Valera, in 1944. The resulting volume was published in 1956 as *The Great Famine: Studies in Irish History*, edited by R. Dudley Edwards and T. Desmond Williams. Cormac Ó'Gráda, in his introduction to the new edition of this classic, says that despite its critics, "The book confronted an important if distressing subject with unprecedented academic rigour, and overall its contents have worn very well indeed."[19] When the first edition finally appeared after a rather unhappy history of delay and dispute and was presented to De Valera, he did not much care for it. He preferred instead Cecil Woodham-Smith's evocative *Great Hunger*, which is still the best-known source for the reading public.[20] That book was ignored or ridiculed by scholars who viewed it as the product of an amateur historian, but as Kevin Whelan has recently said, "It is hard not to detect certain tones of chauvinism [toward Woodham-Smith] in their attitude."[21]

In the last three decades we have seen an extraordinary outpouring of scholarship building on, although not replacing, subjects covered by the Edwards and Williams volume.[22] The best overall surveys of the Famine are by Mary Daly, Cormac Ó'Gráda, and Christine Kinealy. Daly's *The Famine in Ireland* and Cormac Ó'Gráda's *Ireland before and after the Famine: Explorations in Economic History, 1800–1930*, are excellent general introductions to the subject.[23] Ó'Gráda's postrevisionist version of the Famine blends academic rigor with an unusual sensitivity to the human dimension of the disaster. Daly's work has focused on the operations of governmental programs during the Famine years, calling for the network of blame to include the Irish themselves. She has been harshly criticized for this extreme revisionist position, to which she has partly responded by concluding that "It is easy to be wise after the event."[24] In her recent book, *This Great Calamity: The Great Irish Famine, 1845–1852*, Christine Kinealy emphasizes the aim of key members of the government to utilize the Poor Laws as tools to transform Ireland's backward economy.[25] Meanwhile, administrators most closely associated with the Poor Laws were increasingly dubious about their efficacy in achieving this aim. The result was that after 1847 the provision of relief broke down with consequent increased—and unnecessary—suffering.[26]

There has been a notable lack of studies covering the impact of the Famine in the northern counties, and thus a general impression that this region suffered very little. If population loss is any measure of distress, county Fermanagh with a 26 percent population loss ranks as high as county Clare (26 percent) and almost as high as Galway (27 percent) and Mayo (29 percent).[27] Fortunately, a recent volume, *The Famine in Ulster,* edited by Christine Kinealy and Trevor Parkhill, will go some way toward correcting this oversight.[28]

While for some years the Famine was not a popular subject for professional historians, it did attract scholars from other professions. Preeminent among these was agricultural meteorologist and plant biologist Austin Bourke, who focused on the role of the potato in Irish history. His work, recently published as *'The Visitation of God?' The Potato and the Great Irish Famine,* is a selection of his published and unpublished essays which presents a highly readable and valuable overview of the importance of the potato in the Irish economy.[29] Margaret Crawford draws on her extensive knowledge of the subject of nutrition to examine aspects of diet and disease during the Famine period. In her recently published examination of the relationship between food and famine, Crawford agrees with Bourke's argument that the level of devastation was unavoidable.[30] Economist Joel Mokyr's provocative *Why Ireland Starved: A Quantitative and Analytical History of the Irish Economy, 1800–1850,* asks the basic question as to why Ireland was poor.[31] His work emphasizes the overall underdevelopment of the economy during the decade preceding the Famine. Factors such as low productivity of labor and insufficient physical capital, conflicts between landlords and tenants, and the rigidity of Irish economic institutions were at the basis of causative factors resulting in the Famine. Peter Solar's "The Singularity of the Great Irish Famine" poses the question of why the repeated crop failures of the Famine period led to so much misery, so many deaths, and so much emigration.[32] He sees the Famine as an "extremely cruel manifestation of a major regression in the conditions of agricultural production." Solar's overall conclusion is that there was a lack of political will at the top to solve the problems posed by the disaster.[33]

As nationalist explanations for the Famine began to be replaced by emphasis on more scientific and objective examinations of the Irish past, these interpretations too came under increasing attack. James Donnelly Jr.'s article "The Great Famine: Its Interpreters, Old and New" challenges the revisionist historiography of the Famine, insisting that the judgment of Mitchel and other nationalists should not be dismissed out of hand.[34] In his article, Donnelly draws on Brendan Bradshaw, who questioned the emphasis of revisionist school scholars on value-free examination of Irish history, asserting that "the revisionist historians have not honestly and squarely confronted 'the catastrophic dimensions of the Irish past.'"[35] Roy Foster has come under criticism for what is believed to be an attempt to marginalize the Famine in Irish history in his magisterial *Modern Ireland, 1600–1972*.[36] In turn, in a recent interview, Foster claims that in the work of Ó'Gráda and Mokyr, their view of Famine administration is closer to that of Cecil Woodham-Smith than that of Edwards and Williams.[37]

During the quiet years after the Famine when Ireland was becoming more and more conservative, literature played a significant role in preserving and shaping the memory of the Famine for succeeding generations.[38] In an important study of images in Famine literature, Margaret Kelleher explores the development of the image of famine as female.[39] The horrors of famine were represented through hunger-ravaged female bodies, half-naked and starving mothers cradling children to their breast—images akin to Madonna and Child, but in which the mother offers no nourishment or sustenance. This is the image in two of the most famous Famine novels, Anthony Trollope's *Castle Richmond* (1860) and William Carleton's *The Black Prophet* (1847).[40] Subsequently, other fictional treatments of famine emerged, a majority of which were by women such as Mary Anne Hoare (*Shamrock Leaves* in 1851) and Mary Anne Sadlier (*New Lights* in 1853). Famine poetry appeared in periodicals such as the *Dublin University Magazine*, *The Nation*, and Mitchel's *United Irishman*. Christopher Morash has published an anthology of famine poetry in *The Hungry Voice: Poetry of the Irish Famine*.[41] For a study of Irish-American literary accomplishment, see Charles Fanning's *The Exiles of Erin: Nineteenth-Century Irish-American Fiction*.[42]

What sets the Irish Famine apart from most modern famines is that emigration provided a safety valve for those who could afford to flee. Modern famines often force people to move, but with few exceptions this has meant temporary internal displacement rather than emigration.

The best overview of emigration during the Famine is still Oliver Mac-Donagh's "Irish Emigration to the United States of America and the British Colonies during the Famine," in Edwards and Williams's *The Great Famine*.[43] A more recent, and excellent, overview of emigration is *Irish Emigration, 1801–1921*, by David Fitzpatrick.[44] Among the best of the published works on eighteenth-century immigration to North America is *Ireland, Irishmen and Revolutionary America, 1760–1820*, by David Noel Doyle.[45] Older but still sound surveys are *Ireland and Irish Emigration to the New World, from 1815 to the Famine*, by William Forbes Adams, and Arnold Schrier's *Ireland and Irish Emigration, 1850–1900*.[46] Kerby Miller's monumental, densely documented *Emigrants and Exiles: Ireland and the Irish Exodus to North America* has been influential, albeit controversial, in depicting Irish immigrants as suffering a sense of loss.[47]

The first book to deal with the world population movement of the Irish diaspora is Donald Harmon Akenson's *The Irish Diaspora, a Primer*.[48] Akenson has waged an almost single-handed battle for recognition of the Canadian Irish in the immigration stream to North America. He claims that Canada was (and still is) more Irish than is the United States. For example, in 1860, when the population of Irish-born persons in North America was at its peak, the proportion of Irish-born in the U.S. population was 5.12 percent; while in Ontario (Canada's most populous province), Irish-born were 18.5 percent of the population.[49] In a methodologically innovative study linking immigration, settlement, and subsequent internal migration, Bruce Elliott followed the lives of 775 families of Irish immigrants who arrived in Canada between 1815 and 1855 in his book *Irish Migrants in the Canadas: A New Approach*.[50] *The Irish in Atlantic Canada, 1780–1900*, edited by Thomas P. Power, is an excellent collection of essays that brings together new findings on the experience of the Irish in Atlantic Canada.[51]

This volume seeks to present a balanced overview of responses to the Great Famine by drawing on contributors from many disciplines dealing with the consequences of the Famine from a variety of viewpoints. Each of the contributors is actively involved in research that challenges or contributes to other work on the period. Their contributions vary in the sources they draw upon and their interpretations.

Patricia Lysaght's essay, "Women and the Great Famine: Vignettes from the Irish Oral Tradition," examines the oral traditions of the Famine as they relate to women.[52] Lysaght's work reflects a growing sophistication in the field of women's folklore and the field of women's studies in general.[53] She found the picture of women emerging from the oral tradition as one of great power. Women were perceived as powerful, confronting injustice by drawing on ancient weapons of the oppressed such as ritual cursing.

Wayne Hall's essay, "A Tory Periodical in a Time of Famine: The *Dublin University Magazine*, 1845–1850," focuses on the *Dublin University Magazine* (*DUM*). This monthly literary journal, founded by Isaac Butt, reflected for the most part the political insensitivity of the loyalist Protestant Ascendancy class for which it was founded. Despite frequent examples of this insensitivity to the distress caused by the Famine, Hall concludes that through stories such as William Carleton's *The Black Prophet*, first serialized in the *DUM*, and pieces such as Butt's "The Famine in the Land," published in April 1847, the magazine provided some powerful metaphors through which to understand the conflict and tensions evoked by the Famine years.

Famine relief, which ultimately was something of a debacle, is the topic of the essay by Jillian Strang and Joyce Toomre, "Alexis Soyer and the Irish Famine: 'Splendid Promises and Abortive Measures.'" In February 1847, the worst year of the Famine, a French-born chef, Alexis Soyer, offered his services to feed the starving Irish. When Soyer left London for Dublin, he left the most industrially advanced country of the nineteenth century and entered the backyard of this nation, one of the most impoverished regions of Europe. Soyer's brief was to concoct a palatable, cheap, nutritious soup, which was to be distributed by the most modern technology then available. One can see in this famous chef all the confidence of the age, an age of individuals that believed science and faith could solve all human ills—in what the authors call a "heroic entrepreneurial style." In a supreme paradox, one scientist found that Soyer's most expensive broth was the least nourishing, while the cheapest was the most nutritious.[54] The authors conclude that Soyer mirrors the unjustified faith in technology that left social welfare to the private sector.

The growth of grazier farming in the west of Ireland in the aftermath of the Famine is the subject of David Jones's essay, "The Transfer of Land and the Emergence of the Graziers during the Famine Period." As landlords set their faces against a multiplying tenantry in the years after the Famine, the large-scale grazier tenant became the preferred option. Jones concludes that while ranching was made possible by a land market created by the Famine, it also depended upon the conjunction of other conditions, the most important of which was the availability of capital and a market that promised profitable returns. In the game of winners and losers, the human catastrophe of devastation stands in stark contrast to the strengthened position of these strong grazier farmers.

The Famine was a catalyst for Irish traditional music, according to Gearóid Ó hAllmhuráin in his essay, "The Great Famine: A Catalyst in Irish Traditional Music Making." His argument that the climate of change for traditional musicians was already under way at least a decade before the effects of the Famine began to undermine traditional culture is consistent with what we know of other aspects of Irish life. By the late 1830s, Father Mathew's sobriety movement was filling small towns with the brass bands of the Temperance Societies. Observers of Irish life witnessed the changed habits of people as early as the 1830s; and while some were elated by the decreased drunkenness, they were able to mourn the loss of a world in which the uilleann piper could no longer live by his music. In the aftermath of the Famine, the world of the *clochan* settlement virtually disappeared, replaced by a materialistic world of profit-seeking economics and conservative social mores. The political ballad and the emigrant song, once peripheral, now became commonplace. What Ó hAllmhuráin calls "the unquiet ghosts of the Great Famine" continued to haunt the communal psyche of rural Ireland, extending a far-reaching impact on the musical culture of its people at home and abroad.

The history of the first memorial to victims of the Great Famine appears in this volume in the essay by Michael Quigley, "Grosse Île: Canada's Famine Memorial." Illustrative of the complexity of reactions to the Famine was the delayed appearance of any Famine memorials. In contrast to the absence of nineteenth-century memorials to the Great Famine are two monuments erected in the aftermath of an eighteenth-century famine (1740–41)—an obelisk on the top of Killiney Hill, just outside Dublin, and a 140-foot-high structure between Celbridge and Maynooth.[55] No public monuments in Ireland or North America were erected until the twentieth century; the first was the Celtic Cross erected in 1909 on the Canadian island of Grosse Île in the St. Lawrence River, downriver from Quebec. The island, only three miles long, was chosen as a quarantine station in 1832 to isolate cholera victims arriving from Ireland and England. In 1847, the flight from famine brought hundreds of thousands flocking to Canada, only to overwhelm the meager facilities available. Today two monuments preserve the memory of the approximately fifteen thousand persons who lie buried there. The first memorial was erected on what was once the site of the immigrant cemetery by Dr. Douglas, medical superintendent of the quarantine station, to memorialize the four doctors who died in their efforts to ease the sufferings of the unfortunate people. The second monument, erected in 1909 by the Ancient Order of Hibernians, is a Celtic Cross bearing inscriptions in English, French, and Irish. In 1996 the site was recognized as a National Historic Site telling the story of the Irish tragedy and of the mass grave of the Irish Famine victims.

Newspapers are a relatively underutilized resource for most historians. One of the most significant stories of the nineteenth century for Canadian and United States newspapers was the story of the Irish Potato Famine. North American newspaper coverage of this story is the topic of Neil Hogan's essay, "The Famine Beat: American Newspaper Coverage of the Great Hunger." The first news arrived when the British Royal Mail Ship *Cambria* steamed into Halifax, Nova Scotia, on the first of October 1845 with a load of European newspapers. Halifax's weekly newspaper, the *Nova Scotian,* announced the news as follows: "As in other parts of the United Kingdom and on the European Continent, the potatoe [sic] crop has suffered an epidemic, and the effect of such a disaster to Ireland will be very serious." [56] This story was the first of many on the Great Famine. The author finds that the newspapers attempted to play to their Irish-American readership by featuring the back-home news. The *Boston Atlas* reported in November 1847 that those leaving were of the class known as "snug people," able young fellows of the laboring classes, "whose energies do not seem to have been much impaired by the prevailing destitution." Papers put correspondents to good use by focusing on particular aspects of the Famine story. The Boston *Pilot* deputized a correspondent to travel throughout the western parts of the United States and write glowing reports in the hope that immigrants would leave the crowded eastern cities and move westward.

In his analysis of the motif of revenge among the Famine immigrants, Kerby Miller examines the desire for "revenge for Skibbereen" which animated large numbers of Irishmen and -women to hold bitter memories of the reasons why they were forced to leave. In "'Revenge for Skibbereen': Irish Emigration and the Meaning of the Great Famine," Miller makes innovative use of emigrants' letters to demonstrate the anomaly of a people apparently so grateful for help during the crisis, but who in the aftermath found comfort in politicized explanations of governmental and landlord cruelty. Drawing on the work of MacDonagh, Miller interprets the disintegration of personal relationships and the social dislocations that occurred after 1845 as reflecting not just a failure of the potato crop but "a failure of morale as well." [57] A demoralized people, often able to save themselves only at the expense of family and neighbors, frequently displayed what one observer called "the most unscrupulous . . . Knavery, cunning & falsehood." [58] Adding fuel to the fires of resentment, unrealized prospects were often the Famine emigrants' compensation in America, he says, concluding that all too often the reward was "bitter disillusion and profound homesickness among those who once fondly imagined they had escaped from poverty and Protestant prejudice."

In "The Pauper and the Politician: A Tale of Two Immigrants and the Construction of Irish-American Society," Miller and Bruce Boling counterpoise the lives of two very different immigrants to America. The first is Mary Rush, who in September 1846 wrote a desperate letter of entreaty from county Sligo to her parents, settled since the 1820s in a township north of Montreal. The letter, poignant in its appeal, found its way into the British Parliamentary Papers after Mary's father used it to petition for funds to bring his daughter's family to America. He was unsuccessful in obtaining funds to bring her to Canada, but there is evidence in ship passenger lists that Mary and her husband, Michael, arrived in New York in May 1847, only to disappear without further trace in that city's nearly 176,000 Irish-born inhabitants. Mary's story ends on the New York docks. More is known of Richard O'Gorman, an example of an idealistic Irish revolutionary turned pragmatic American politico. Between the two they represent the complexity of Catholic culture in Ireland: Mary Rush, a peasant married to a cottier farmer in poor circumstances in county Sligo, and O'Gorman, the son of a prosperous woolen merchant and Catholic politician in Dublin, educated at Trinity College and trained in London to become a barrister. O'Gorman fled Ireland to escape capture after abortive revolutionary activities as a Young Irelander, arriving in New York in June 1849. Admitted to the New York bar through the patronage of the distinguished Thomas Addis Emmet family, O'Gorman soon became a successful businessman and Tammany Hall operator. Ten years after arriving he wrote to his friend Smith O'Brien, who was back in Ireland after penal servitude and contemplated visiting New York. The price of O'Gorman's assimilation into American life was to become like his fellow countrymen, of whom he wrote,

It is refreshing however to find that in this effervescing process [of corruption], our Countrymen have their share—in all political proceedings—primary Elections—smashing Ballot boxes—[im]personating citizens—filling minor offices of all kinds, and plundering the Public for the Public good. . . . The honest fellow, I left behind me in Ireland a "cheque clerk" on the road, is now owner of a corner grocery in new York and covets the post of alderman, and scents plunder from afar.

Boling and Miller conclude that bourgeois Irish Americans such as Richard O'Gorman endeavored to break the cycle of alienation and conflict which ground down the likes of Mary and Michael Rush, and to unite them politically behind middle-class leadership and "uplift" them socially and culturally toward middle-class norms.

In "The Famine and Collective Memory: The Role of the Irish-American Press in the Early Twentieth Century," author Mick Mulcrone examines the growing self-definition of Irish immigrants. The author draws on a sample of four weekly papers exclusively devoted to Irish issues—two New York papers, a Chicago and a San Francisco paper. By the early twentieth century Ireland was emerging from its long colonial past. In the author's words the offspring of the immigrants were still uneasy exiles in search of a secure self-definition, and bitter memories of the Famine were used as a clarion call to rally support for the independence struggle in Ireland.

Anniversary commemorations of the Great Famine have proliferated in the past decade, as Christine Kinealy reminds us in the final essay, "The Great Irish Famine—A Dangerous Memory?" In this essay, Kinealy examines the implications of Famine memorial endeavors. In defining a research agenda for future Famine studies, she says that some of the larger defining issues of the Famine remain underexplored, and archives in both Ireland and Britain remain underutilized.

The vivid memory of the Famine has given rise to a long tradition of generosity by the Irish in contributions to relieve distress in the Third World. Former Irish president Mary Robinson, in her many appeals for helping present-day victims in Africa, emphasized this generosity. She sought to make evident the continuing relationship between the Irish in Ireland and their countrymen who had been thrust abroad by the circumstances of the Famine. In her words, while the failure of the potato was a "natural disaster" across Europe, "in Ireland it took place in a political, economic and social framework that was oppressive and unjust."[59] On

December 3, 1990, in her inaugural address, Mary Robinson drew all the people of the Irish diaspora to her when she said: "There are over seventy million people living on this globe who claim Irish descent. I will be proud to represent them." [60]

This collection of essays fills many gaps that remain in the literature and sheds light on the diverse effects of the Great Famine on the society and economy of Ireland, the images that reflect and create Irish identity, and on the emergence of a distinctive Irish-American culture. Thus, this volume enhances our current understanding of the long-term impact of the Famine. The contributors are a group of active participants in a vigorous new body of scholarship, and it is inevitable that this knowledge will be widened and extended further by them in coming years.

Notes

1. See *Devon Report (Occupation of Land in Ireland)*, 4 vols. For the testimony of Michael Sullivan see *Devon Digest*, in J. P. Kennedy, ed., *Digest of Evidence on the Occupation of Land in Ireland* (Dublin: Alexander Thom, 1848), 488–90.

2. "Kitchen" was a term referring to flavorings such as salt, buttermilk, or salted fish.

3. There were major failures of the food crop in 1728, 1739–41, 1756, 1766, 1798, 1800, 1817, 1821, 1825, 1831, 1835, 1839, and 1840, according to William Wilde's annalistic compilation of Irish famines from 900 to 1850 which appeared in the introduction to the 1851 Census of Ireland. An abridgement of the entries gathered by Dr. Wilde appears in *Famine: The Irish Experience, 900–1900*, ed. E. Margaret Crawford (Edinburgh: John Donald Publishers Ltd., 1989), 3–27.

4. For a discussion of the onset of the blight, see P. M. Austin Bourke, "The Emergence of Potato Blight, 1843–6," in Bourke, ed., *'The Visitation of God'? The Potato and the Great Irish Famine*, edited for *Irish Historical Studies* by Jacqueline Hill and Cormac Ó'Gráda (Dublin: The Lilliput Press, 1993), 140–49.

5. See Peter Gray, "Ideology and Famine," in Cathal Póirteír, ed., *The Great Irish Famine* (Dublin: Mercier Press, 1995), 86–103.

6. The subject of David Jones's essay in this volume is the accelerated conversion to grazing as a consequence of the Famine.

7. See E. R. R. Green, "Agriculture," in *The Great Famine: Studies in Irish History, 1845–52*, ed. R. Dudley Edwards and T. Desmond Williams (Dublin: Brown and Nowlan, 1956, 1994), 90.

8. L. M. Cullen, "Irish History without the Potato," *Past and Present* 40 (July 1968): 72–83. For the counterargument to Cullen, see Joel Mokyr, "Irish History with the Potato," *Irish Economic and Social History* 8 (1981): 8–29.

9. Breandan MacAodha, "A Booley Place Name in County Tyrone," in *Ulster Folklife* 2 (1956): 61–62.

10. See Anne O'Dowd, *Spalpeens and Tattie Hokers: The History and Folklore of*

the *Irish Migratory Agricultural Worker in Ireland and Britain* (Dublin: Irish Academic Press, 1991). See also Ruth-Ann M. Harris, *The Nearest Place That Wasn't Ireland: Early Nineteenth Century Irish Labor Migration* (Ames: Iowa State University Press, 1994).

11. Alexis de Tocqueville, *Journeys to England and Ireland*, ed. and trans. Emmet Larkin (New Haven: Yale University Press, 1958), 155.

12. For a discussion of Irish tours as a source of information for historians, see C. J. Woods, "Irish Travel Writings as Source Material," in *Irish Historical Studies* 28, no. 110 (Nov. 1992): 171–83.

13. Asenath Nicholson, *Annals of the Famine in Ireland in 1847, 1848, and 1849* (New York: E. French, 1851); and *Ireland's Welcome to the Stranger, or, Excursions through Ireland in 1844* (London: 1847).

14. Maureen Murphy, "Asenath Nicholson and the Famine in Ireland," in *Women and Irish History: Essays in Honour of Margaret MacCurtain*, ed. Maryann Gialanella Valiulis and Mary O'Dowd (Dublin: Wolfhound Press, 1997), 109–24.

15. Alexander Somerville, *Letters from Ireland during the Famine of 1847*, ed. K. D. M. Snell (Dublin: Irish Academic Press, 1994).

16. John Mitchel, *The Last Conquest of Ireland (Perhaps)* (Dublin: Sadlier, 1861).

17. As quoted in Edwards and Williams, *Great Famine*, viii.

18. John O'Rourke, *The Great Irish Famine of 1847, with Notices of Earlier Famines* (Dublin: M'Glashan & Gill, 1875, republished 1989).

19. R. Dudley Edwards and T. Desmond Williams, *The Great Famine: Studies in Irish History* (Dublin: The Lilliput Press, Ltd., 1994), xviii. See Cormac Ó'Gráda, "Making History in the Ireland of the 1940s and 1950s: The Saga of the Great Famine," *The Irish Review* 12 (Spring/Summer 1992): 87–107.

20. Cecil Woodham-Smith, *The Great Hunger* (New York: Harper & Row, 1962).

21. Kevin Whelan in keynote lecture before the New England Conference of Irish Studies, Boston, November 15, 1997.

22. See Ó'Gráda, "Introduction," in Edwards and Williams, *Great Famine*, xxi.

23. See Mary Daly, *The Famine in Ireland* (Dundalk: Dublin Historical Association, 1986); Cormac Ó'Gráda, *Ireland before and after the Famine: Explorations in Economic History, 1800–1930* (Manchester: Manchester University Press, rev. ed. 1993), and Ó'Gráda, *The Great Irish Famine*, (London: Macmillan, 1989).

24. See Mary Daly's chapter on Famine relief, "The Operations of Famine Relief, 1845–47," in Póirtéir, *Great Irish Famine*, 123–34.

25. Christine Kinealy, *This Great Calamity: The Great Irish Famine, 1845–52* (Dublin: Gill & McMillan, 1994).

26. See Joan Vincent, "A Political Orchestration of the Irish Famine: County Fermanagh, May 1847," in *Approaching the Past: Historical Anthropology through Irish Case Studies*, ed. Marilyn Silverman and P. H. Gulliver (New York: Columbia University Press, 1992), 75–98.

27. See Joan Vincent, "People, Place and Time: An Anthropological Perspective on the Great Irish Famine," unpublished paper presented at the Great Famine Commemoration, "An Gorta Mor 1845–1850," at Dublin Castle, May 9–10, 1997.

28. Christine Kinealy and Trevor Parkhill, eds., *The Famine in Ulster* (Belfast:

Ulster Historical Foundation, 1997). See also David W. Miller, "Irish Presbyterians and the Great Famine," forthcoming in *Historical Studies*, papers read before the 23rd Irish Conference of Historians, St. Patrick's College, Maynooth, May 16–18, 1997.

29. Bourke, *Visitation*.

30. E. Margaret Crawford, ed., *Famine: The Irish Experience 900–1900*, (Edinburgh: John Donald Publishers, Ltd., 1989). See also her "Food and Famine" in Póirteír, *Great Irish Famine*, 60–73.

31. Joel Mokyr, *Why Ireland Starved: A Quantitative and Analytical History of the Irish Economy, 1800–1850* (London: Allen and Unwin, 1983, rev. ed. 1985).

32. Peter Solar, "The Singularity of the Great Irish Famine," in Crawford, *Famine*, 112–31. See also Kevin O'Rourke, "Did the Great Famine Matter?" *Journal of Economic History* 51 (1991): 1–22.

33. Solar, "Singularity," 128.

34. James S. Donnelly, Jr., "The Great Famine: Its Interpreters, Old and New," *History Ireland* 1, no. 3 (Autumn 1993): 27–33. See also Donnelly, "The Administration of Relief, 1846–7," in W. E. Vaughan, ed., *A New History of Ireland*, vol. 5 (Oxford: Oxford University Press, 1989), 294–99.

35. Brendan Bradshaw, "Nationalism and Historical Scholarship in Modern Ireland," *Irish Historical Studies* 26 (1989): 329–51. As quoted in Donnelly, "Interpreters," 27.

36. R. F. Foster, *Modern Ireland, 1600–1972* (London: Allen Lane, the Penguin Press, 1988).

37. See an interview with Foster by Peter Gray in *History Ireland* 1, no. 3 (Autumn 1993): 9–12. Foster says of revisionism and Irish history, "we are coming back to views of, say, the famine which the people of the 1960s would have thought were being replaced," 10.

38. Margaret Kelleher, "Irish Famine in Literature," in Póirteír, *Great Irish Famine*, 232–47.

39. Margaret Kelleher, *The Feminization of Famine* (Cork: Cork University Press, 1997).

40. See also Trollope's *The Irish Famine: Six Letters to the Examiner 1849–50*, reprinted as L. O'Tingay, ed., *The Irish Famine* (London: Silverbridge Press, 1987).

41. Christopher Morash, *The Hungry Voice: Poetry of the Irish Famine* (Dublin: Irish Academic Press, 1989).

42. Charles Fanning, ed., *The Exiles of Erin: Nineteenth-Century Irish-American Fiction* (Notre Dame, Ind.: University of Notre Dame Press, 1987).

43. Oliver MacDonagh, "Irish Emigration to the United States of America and the British Colonies during the Famine," in Edwards and Williams, *The Great Famine*, 319–88.

44. David Fitzpatrick, *Irish Emigration, 1801–1921* (Dundalk: Dundalgan Press Ltd., for the Economic and Social History Society of Ireland, 1984).

45. David Noel Doyle, *Ireland, Irishmen and Revolutionary America, 1760–1820* (Dublin: Mercier Press, 1981).

46. Arnold Schrier, *Ireland and the Irish Emigration, 1850–1900* (Minneapolis:

University of Minnesota Press, 1958), and W. F. Adams, *Ireland and Irish Emigration to the New World, from 1815 to the Famine* (New Haven: Yale University Press, 1932). Adams remains the only scholar who has gone carefully through the primary sources on Irish migration to British North America and to the United States, according to D. H. Akenson in *The Irish Diaspora, a Primer* (Belfast: The Institute of Irish Studies of the Queen's University of Belfast, 1993), 293.

47. Kerby A. Miller, *Emigrants and Exiles: Ireland and the Irish Exodus to North America* (New York: Oxford University Press, 1985).

48. Akenson, *Diaspora.*

49. Ibid., 256–57. In a large-scale survey of immigration patterns, Harris has shown that some 65 percent of Irish immigrants to North America, prior to 1850, arrived through the Canadian ports. See R. A. Harris, "Introduction" to *The Search for Missing Friends: Irish Immigrant Advertisements Placed in the* Boston Pilot, ·vol. 1, 1832–50 (Boston: The New England Historic Genealogical Society, 1989), i–lxii. An increasing amount of materials concerning the Irish diaspora is now accessible through websites. A UK-based Irish Diaspora Studies Center website at the University of Bradford is maintained by Dr. Patrick O'Sullivan. The URL is *http://www.brad.ac.uk/acad/diaspora*. In Ireland, Dr. Piaras Mac Einri, director of the Irish Centre for Migration Studies at University College, Cork, maintains a diaspora website for which the URL is *http://www.ucc.ie/icms*.

50. Bruce S. Elliott, *Irish Migrants in the Canadas: A New Approach* (Kingston and Montreal: McGill-Queen's University Press, 1988).

51. Thomas P. Power, ed., *The Irish in Atlantic Canada, 1780–1900* (Fredericton, N.B.: New Ireland Press, 1991).

52. Folklorist Roger McHugh was one of the first scholars to utilize the oral history memories of the Famine from a questionnaire circulated in 1945 collecting the oral traditions of the Famine. Roger J. McHugh, "The Famine in Irish Oral Tradition," in Edwards and Williams, *Great Famine*, 391–436. The Irish Folklore Commission was founded in 1927 to collect and preserve the oral traditions of the people at a time when a continued hemorrhage of emigration threatened to sap the lifeblood of the nation. The archives of the IFC are at University College, Dublin.

53. For an innovative use of the IFC archives as source material for female emigration, see Grace Neville, "Dark Lady of the Archives: Towards an Analysis of Women and Emigration to North America in Irish Folklore," in *Chattel, Servant or Citizen: Women's Status in Church, State and Society*, ed. Mary O'Dowd and Sabine Wichert (Belfast: The Institute of Irish Studies of The Queen's University of Belfast, 1995), 200–214.

54. As quoted in Crawford, "Food and Famine" from *The Times*, February 8, 1847, 69. As the Famine distress deepened, nutritional levels also deteriorated. Potatoes are rich in vitamin C, and with their disappearance from the general diet, widespread cases of scurvy developed. Margaret Crawford has drawn attention to why scurvy developed so quickly once the potatoes failed. Vitamin C is not storable and so people cannot build up reserves. Added to this is the fact that this was a population conditioned to high levels of the vitamin and thus ex-

tremely vulnerable with the withdrawal of that foodstuff. See Crawford, "Subsistence Crises and Famines in Ireland: A Nutritionist's View," in Crawford, *Famine, the Irish Experience,* and "Food and Famine," in Póirteír, *Great Irish Famine,* 60–73.

55. For a discussion of the earlier famine, see David Dickson, "The Other Great Irish Famine," in Póirteír, *Great Irish Famine,* 50–59.

56. "The English Mail," *The Nova Scotian* (Halifax, N.S.), Oct. 6, 1845, as reported in Hogan, "The Famine Beat," in this volume.

57. MacDonagh, "Irish Emigration," 329, as quoted in Miller, *Emigrants.*

58. R. D. Webb, *Narrative of a Tour through Erris in 1848,* as quoted in Miller's essay in this volume.

59. Address by former president Mary Robinson at Grosse Île, Quebec, August 21, 1994. Department of Foreign Affairs.

60. As quoted in Akenson, *Diaspora,* 15.

2

PATRICIA LYSAGHT

Women and the Great Famine

Vignettes From the Irish Oral Tradition

> *Let darkness and the shadow*
> *of death stain that day when*
> *first the potato was planted*
> *in this green isle of the sea . . .*

Asenath Nicholson, "Lights and Shades of Ireland" (1850)

Brighde . . . suffered great trouble and distress at the start of her days. She was married in the Coum [Coumeenole, Parish of Dunquin, county Kerry] in Famine Times; eight in family she had, but indeed, not one of them survived. Hunger killed some of them—not all of them to be sure, but what followed the hunger, God between us and all harm. Brighde had buried seven of the family and their father, and all she had left alive then was herself and her eldest daughter, the loveliest and finest girl seen in Kerry for generations. To crown her misfortune, God save us, the daughter died too.

That was no great novelty in those days; Brighde had no one to give her a helping hand because all the people were dispirited so she herself had to carry her daughter's body to the graveyard—a bitter experience for the poor woman. She got a *súgán* rope [woven straw rope] and tied it around the daughter's waist; then she tied the rope around her own waist and placed the dead daughter's two hands on her own shoulders from behind. That's how she brought the corpse to Ballinahow graveyard, walking and resting, every second turn.

A woman from Ballinglanna saw her passing—her name was Nóra Landers. "May God look down on you, Brighde," she said in her own mind, "your heart is crushed this day and you're played out with hunger. If only I could do something for you!"

She turned into her room and brought out six potatoes from a handful of seed potatoes she had stored; she put the potatoes roasting under live embers so that she'd have them ready when Bríghdín would be passing back again.

When Bríghde reached the churchyard with her load, she hadn't the strength to open the grave; four men from Ballinahow arrived and covered the daughter for her with sods of earth.

As soon as the last sod was on the grave, Bríghde cried out in a loud voice: "Sleep peacefully in eternal rest, beloved family and gentle husband! There's no fear that you'll ever awaken until the ocean pours from the north and the dark raven turns snow white. Have no fear now, dear ones, that you will ever again suffer hunger or thirst. You have plenty in the Stream of Glory to quench your thirst this day. I leave you now to rest in the grace of God until the angel sounds his trumpet on Judgement Day."

Bríghde was right, for a sod hasn't been turned on that grave ever since. She faced for home but, if she did, Nóra stood before her on the road.

"Come in with me, poor Bríghde," she said. "You have the evening long for walking west."

"Wisha, Nóra, I have no business walking west any more for what I owned of the west I've buried in God's ground this day."

"Never mind that, Bríghde! Come in; I have a fistful of potatoes under the embers for you. Come on in and eat them and it'll give you courage for the long road."

"God grant you never know trouble like mine!"

Bríghde sat by the fire and Nóra brought her a drop of milk and put the roast potatoes before her. Bríghde caught one of the potatoes in her hand and said in a loud voice: "Thanks be to God that it isn't you for a potato I have left in Ballinahow."

That drew a tear from Nóra's eye for she knew right well that Bríghde needed the potatoes at that time. . . . She lived to be ninety years of age. . . .

THIS EXTRACT from Peig Sayers's autobiography (1936)[1]—like the other excerpts from the oral traditions of the Famine presented here—is a powerful human document and an attempt to comprehend and express the tragedy of the Great Famine of the mid–nineteenth century. It is a stark and startling reminder of the enormity, complexity, and implications of the calamity on a number of levels, which befell many parts of Ireland at that time and which has, to a greater or lesser degree, affected the Irish psyche ever since. Although focusing on a remote peninsular area in the southwest of Ireland, it serves almost as a touchstone in attempting to assess the Great Famine experience of the rest of Ireland. It mentions the virtual depletion of entire households, not only through starvation, but also from the various diseases arising from Famine conditions, a phenomenon not unique to west Kerry, but rather a commonplace result of the Famine in many areas along the western seaboard of Ireland. It points also to the erosion of social customs and norms, especially in relation to the burial of the dead, to which both the literature and folklore of the Famine testify. The severe strain which the scale of Famine mortality and the fear of disease placed on the age-old custom of neighborliness, especially in relation to the burial of the dead, which found almost universal mention in Famine literature, is also underlined—the depiction of a woman bearing a corpse to the cemetery for burial in the foregoing extract is evidence of this. In addition, the image of the corpse-bearing woman is indicative of fundamental changes in attitudes toward the traditional roles of women during the Famine period, not only in relation to the care of a deceased person, but also in terms of family support and maintenance. It is also abundantly clear from the extract, however, that not all women or families were similarly affected, and often a balance is struck, as in this and other excerpts from the oral traditions of the Famine, between the woman who, as heroic victim, confronts the Famine conditions in order to support her family and, when necessary, to bury the family dead, and the compassionate generous woman who recognizes her situation and supports her.

The pragmatic comment in relation to food ascribed to the woman in the text also raises the issue of women's influence on the incidence of survival and mortality within the family during the Famine, as, traditionally, the division of food between parents and siblings was usually the prerogative of the woman of the house. These and other aspects of oral traditions of the Famine as they pertain to women—such as the reaction of women to injustice, especially in relation to eviction—and hitherto not specifically dealt with by scholars will be considered here.

This essay is based on the substantial corpus of oral traditions of the Famine collected by the Irish Folklore Commission from the 1930s onward, especially as a result of a questionnaire (see Appendix) circulated by the commission on the hundredth anniversary of the Famine in 1945.[2] A few of the tradition bearers who contributed were born during the Famine, but most of the recollections come from the children or grandchildren of those who witnessed the Famine. As is to be expected, the scope of the material is influenced by the range of queries in the questionnaire, but the replies of the full- and part-time collectors of the commission—who supplied most of the material[3]—are both wide-ranging and varied. Naturally, Famine recollections were particularly rich in the west of Ireland where Famine conditions were most pervasive and serious, and especially, therefore, in the Irish language. In this essay, I have endeavored, where possible, to present Irish language traditions of the Famine (in translation), as these have not always been accessible to, or used by, scholars who have considered this material in the past.[4]

As there was no specific query in the questionnaire about the role of women during the Famine, such information as there is has been included incidentally by tradition bearers. While the position of women during the Famine must be viewed in the context of overall Famine conditions, it is evident from the material that the circumstances of women (and children) are referred to again and again in order to represent the Famine's worst consequences. It is also apparent that it is, by and large, exceptional circumstances or incidents—of hunger, generosity, distress, or degradation—in relation to women during the Famine which have been particularly remembered. Much of the material on women also belongs to traditions of the Famine handed down in various families, which often offers much scope for extolling the generosity and compassion of the woman of the house—a grandmother or mother—who is said to have shared her resources with a less fortunate woman who, because of Famine circumstances, is forced to beg for herself and her children, or who is unjustly treated by some members of the community in which she is seeking alms. Although some of the accounts of the Famine are told with an almost contemporary freshness, even a century after the event, and could indeed be referring to events that actually occurred, much of the narrative has become schematized, and groups of popular legends, some of which have only local relevance, while others are more widely distributed, have developed around certain themes. Indeed, age-old motifs, such as that charity and generosity are rewarded, stemming from a biblical source, have been attracted to the Famine complex of traditions, particularly in relation to women, and have given rise to an *exemplum*-type narrative found widely in the Famine context in Ireland.[5] In the light of such source material, it is not the purpose of this paper, therefore, to test the veracity or historicity of the various incidents and circumstances mentioned; rather it is to seek to ascertain perceptions of, and attitudes toward, the circumstances and role of women during the Famine.

Women and the Provision of Food during the Famine

An unmistakable impression one gets from the oral traditions of the Famine is that of people on the move in search of food: darting figures of the night stealing sheep or bleeding animals on the mountainside, creeping figures stealthily entering turnip fields or rooting seed potatoes from drills of a newly planted crop in search of a meal, helpless figures of the day ceaselessly journeying in search of alms, in an attempt to remain alive.[6] Then there is the impression of local communities, some just managing to survive, others in reasonable or even in good circumstances, being called upon to provide food, not only for themselves and often hungry neighbors, but also for starving people wandering through the countryside. It is clear from the folklore material that the provision of food for the hungry or starving was considered to have essentially depended on the generosity of those families in the countryside who had provisions. Even when official or semiofficial relief became available, the difficulties often experienced in getting access to the food, its perceived association with proselytism in some areas, and the negative social attitude toward accepting *min déirce*, "charity food," served to maintain pressure on local resources and families to provide for the hungry. The perception of the manner in which communities—or various sections of communities—met this challenge differs throughout the country. Variations on the statement "Anyone that had anything to give, gave it with a good heart always regretting that they had not more to give"[7] to describe people's reaction to the hungry who called at their doors looking for food are both supported and qualified in the oral traditions of the Famine. Documenting the local situation, these traditions point both to a willingness to give and to share food where possible—though of course accounts of acts of generosity during the Famine period are more likely to be handed down in families than the reverse, especially as they also provide an opportunity for the teller to boast about the family's favorable circumstances (usually mentioning the variety of foods in their diet)—and to attitudes toward the poor even during the Famine and its aftermath. A narrative (translated from Irish) told by Seán Ó Criomthain (Cillmaolchéadair, Dingle Peninsula, county Kerry), referring to his father's generosity one Easter Sunday—when traditionally large quantities of eggs were eaten—in giving his share of boiled eggs to beggars who called to the house looking for food, is also pointing out the normality of the situation in their household despite Famine circumstances.[8] In response to his mother's remark that he has "no sense" to be giving away all the eggs, he is said to have replied: "I have sense enough . . . because I have sufficient to eat without them, and that is not the situation with those poor creatures." He had potatoes and he had bread.[9]

Instances of almsgiving during the Famine period in circumstances considered exceptional for one reason or another are part of the Famine memory and are highlighted in family and local recollections. Some of these almsgiving occasions are remembered in a body of narrative that documents the sometimes fatal consequences of generosity, especially the danger of giving a starving person a generous helping of food unsupervised—the person is said to have been found dead shortly after the kind act and often close to the house that provided the food. The following story from west Kerry linked to a local place-name originating in the Famine period vividly refers to such an incident:

> I used to hear my father say—it was before he married at all that it happened—that they were eating the dinner [midday meal]—of potatoes and milk I suppose—when this person came in to them. He had a bag but there was nothing in it. They told him to sit down and to eat a potato with them, but he wouldn't. One of them—it doesn't matter which one—said that he'd best to take a few potatoes with him as he might eat them after a while.
>
> He was given a handful of potatoes—I suppose they weren't given sparingly or meanly—he got sufficient. He left, and I suppose they didn't pay any more attention to him. They went out after eating, each one going about his own business in a different direction.
>
> They found the bag and there were no potatoes in it—he had left the bag behind him when he had eaten them. And they found him dead on a patch of untilled ground, a very rushy patch called "Tadhgeen's corner." His grave is there, the grave of Tadhgeen O'Brien, because that was his name. . . . [10]

The overwhelming picture of the quest for food presented by the oral material is that it was those without resources to purchase supplies who were involved—an aspect dealt with below. But another category of almsseeker also features in a number of narratives. These narratives usually involve strangers—an individual or family—calling to a house for alms during the Famine period. They are generously dealt with, and, some years later when a member of the erstwhile benefactor's family is visiting another town, he is recognized by one of the recipients of the charity. The generosity shown to him or to his family during the Famine is sincerely acknowledged and returned. As the following narrative (related by an elderly woman born in the 1850s) indicates, this group of legends concerns people understood to have been in comfortable circumstances prior to the "bad times" but who were forced to take to the road and seek alms during the Famine. Probably avoiding their own community because of the shame of begging, they are perceived as strangers in the areas where the story is set:

> I heard my mother saying that a woman and her three children called in to her one day. They were after walking from Cahirciveen—they belonged to Skibbereen.[11] She came in to my mother and asked her permission to boil a few heads of cabbage which she had. My mother gave them bread and tea[12] and she gave her a cake of bread and some flour for the road. My brother James was nine years [old] at the time.
>
> Himself and my father went to Skibbereen some years afterwards—my father had a sloop and he used to trade along the Cork coast. When they landed in Skibbereen James went up to the town for milk and he met a young boy in the street with a churn of milk—himself and his mother. The boy recognized him and drew his mother's attention to him. The mother told the story then—how they had called to his father's house in the bad times, etc. She had the grass of sixteen cows in Skibbereen. She sent down a keeler of prints of butter the following day to the boat.[13]

While the positive aspects of almsgiving and of attitudes toward the poor and hungry are expressed in the oral traditions of the Famine, also referred to are instances of injustice and inhumanity among, and toward, the poor and hungry. Indeed, it is arguable that this is, perhaps, the most emotive aspect of the Famine memory. In the extreme circumstances that prevailed during the Famine period, stealing food for survival had popular sanction, even though ordinary families, as well as the large farmers and landowners, were targets of this activity. Indeed, accounts of ingenious thieving methods used in the quest for food remained a feature of the oral traditions of the Famine,[14] as well as the strong-arm tactics adopted by some of the larger farmers and landowners in protecting their newly planted or maturing crops. Acts of violence toward those stealing or searching for food are also part of the Famine memory, and the abhorrence with which such acts were viewed is evident from accounts collected from oral tradition in the 1940s. Details of such an incident said to have occurred in county Limerick (given here in translation from Irish) were recalled by a man born about a decade after the onset of the Famine:

> About three miles from us here on the northern side of the parish a sad thing happened in Famine times. A poor man who was in distress went into a farmer's haggard where a heap of roots [turnips] were stored. He started to eat as well as he was able. Somehow the man of the house found out that he was there, and out he went in a rush. He took up a spade, and with a blow of it killed the man at the mouth of the heap. He was never brought to justice for that ugly deed, but if he wasn't, a curse was pronounced on him and his people, which affected them from that on. They were prosperous at that time; there isn't a trace of them in the place now.[15]

In accordance with the gender division of labor in Irish rural society, the production and provision of food was essentially the task of the man of the house, while the woman of the house was largely concerned with the management of the food supply—that is, preserving and preparing it, and sharing it among the members of the family. Giving food to the poor and those who called to the door seeking alms was also at the discretion of the housewife. In the oral traditions of the Famine, however, aspects of the woman's role in relation to food that are especially highlighted are procuring or providing food (in contrast to the normal situation in non-Famine times) and sharing it with family and neighbors, and especially with the poor.

Exceptional efforts by some women to procure food for their families find mention in the oral accounts of the Famine. Thus, we hear of a Donegal mother who walked many miles barefoot across the hills to sell wool in order to buy meal to make porridge for her family.[16] What makes accounts of this kind memorable, however, is not just the details of the distance traveled by the women in question to buy food, but also because for some the journey is said to have been in vain, or even dangerous, as the food was stolen, and could even have been the cause of the woman's death. From county Limerick tradition we hear of a widow who first walked over ten miles to town to buy bread or flour or oatmeal, only to have her parcel of goods snatched off the shop counter by another woman. She then had to set out for another town in search of provisions, and eventually arrived home with two loaves of bread and a little milk for her son, having journeyed more than forty miles for this amount of food.[17] We also hear about a Mayo woman who walked the thirty-mile return journey to Westport only to have the two stones of yellow meal (maize) she brought back with her stolen from her as she rested in a neighbor's house before going home: "She left the little bundle she was carrying on the end of the table near the door. When she arose to go to her own house the little bag and everything in it was gone. . . ."[18]

Being in possession of food during the Famine period is shown to have been risky, as in the case of a Mrs. Brien of Kilfeacle, county Tipperary, who is said to have been brutally murdered for the one pound of meal she had carried home from the meal-distribution center in Golden. Although this case seems untypical, and the perpetrator of the crime is identified as "a local ruffian,"[19] nevertheless it raises the issue of violence against women attempting to procure food during the Famine—something that also features in oral traditions of the Famine.

The women mentioned in the previous section had some substance to buy basic food items, or had access to food, meager though it was. But the oral tradition also refers to less fortunate women—often destitute mothers trying to provide food for their hungry children. It is against this background of extreme want that narratives concerning the miraculous provision of food—which are a prominent feature of oral traditions of the Famine—are best understood. In the Famine context in Ireland, these narratives, representative of medieval European tradition and involving an element of wishful thinking, may also have had the role of seeking to restore faith in God's mercy after the tragedy of the Famine. The following narrative emphasizes that a mother's trust in God was rewarded:

In the height of the Famine a poor woman lived in Doon. She was a widow with four young children about the house and they were very poor all the time. One winter's morning she was completely out of food and the children were crying from hunger. She had nothing for them to pacify them. She put down the pot over the fire as usual though there was nothing in it but water. But when the water in the pot was boiling she had no meal and when the children used to say, "Why don't you put in the meal in the pot?," she used to say the old Irish saying *Is giorra cabhair Dé ná an doras*, "God's help is nearer than the door." Out about twelve o'clock in the day the children were wild with hunger and the pot of water was still boiling over the fire. At that time a man came in to the house, saying in Irish, "God save all here!" "God save you kindly, sir, and welcome!", said the poor widow. The man sat down on the chair she offered him and talked.

After a while he asked why were the children crying or was it how they were sick. "Yerra," said the mother, making an effort to deny the real cause, "the blackguards, it is easy to make them cry and there's nothing ails them!" They talked on and again the children started crying. After being again questioned she told him that they had plenty cause to cry, poor things, as they had nothing to eat since this time yesterday. "What have you in the pot?" questioned the visitor. "Nothing," said she, "but water!" "Are you sure?" said the man. "I am and very sure," said she. "What else could be in it, it is long ago today I put it down." "Look at it again," he said. "Didn't you say that 'God's help was nearer than the door.'"

He persuaded her to lift the cover. And when she did she was surprised to see it full of big bones of beef and they boiling and simmering away. She was greatly surprised. "Now," said he, "would it not be nice if you put couple of quarts of oatmeal down on that and you'd have fine porridge for yourself and the children." "I have no meal in the house," said the widow. "Try your little bin," said the visitor, "there may be some grain of meal in it." "God help us," said she, "there isn't. I cleaned it out well yesterday." "Try again," said he. She lifted the cover of the bin and lo! it was full to the top of fine oatmeal. "God be praised and glorified," said she, turning round, but the visitor had gone.

She went out to see where he was or where he was going to, but though there was nothing around the house to hide him; he had completely disappeared. She made many enquiries after among the neighbors—whether anyone had seen such a man, but she never got trace or tidings of him again. She had no doubt, nor had any of the people she told her story to, but that her visitor was sent by God to aid her in answer to her hope "That God's help was nearer than the door." [20]

What was in fact the stark reality of the Famine situation, however, namely, that women were forced through circumstances of hunger to attempt to steal food, is also strongly attested in the oral tradition. [21] Even a century after the events, oral tradition in various parts of Ireland, in referring to acts of injustice—even brutality—against such women by some farmers attempting to prevent them stealing food still preserved memories of that situation. What must rank as one of the most graphic accounts of brutality against women during the Famine—even allowing for the dramatic ability of the narrator, Peig Sayers—is an incident she heard of from her father concerning a traveling woman who was physically assaulted by a farmer for taking potatoes brought to the surface of the soil in a field he was ploughing. [22]

In the following narrative a male narrator is full of indignation at the callousness of the farmer who locked a lactating mother in his turnip shed overnight:

Down at Nohoval lived at that time a man nicknamed "old Shoulder" and his wife Moll. I remember their daughter. He had no work and she used earn a few pence per day drawing stones on her back for drains in boggy lands where no horse could travel. They were miserably poor and had no

food. One night they came to the conclusion that they'd go to a neighboring farmer's barn and bring a turnip from there that they'd eat. She
went (oh! was it stealing?), but the farmer's dog gave tongue and she was
caught in the act, and what did the man do but turn the key in the lock,
and kept her in the barn all night till morning, although he knew very well
that she was suckling a baby. Her breasts were bursting with milk, I often heard, and her baby crying with hunger, and poor old "Shoulder" at
home with his finger in the baby's mouth, and the poor baby sucking the
finger. . . . [23]

Wild cabbage or charlock was a plant much sought after by the poor
and hungry during the Famine; they flocked to fields where it grew, took
it home in baskets and boiled it like domestic cabbage.[24] In normal times
this was a plant of little or no consequence to the farmer or housewife,
but the scarcity of food, including vegetables, during the Famine years
caused people to resort to it again, thereby reducing its availability to the
poor. Even in such strained circumstances, however, the lack of charity
and neighborliness said to have been shown by a farmer to a neighboring
widow is recalled in the following story (translated from Irish):

> There was a woman in Cillcúile called Nóra Dubhdha. Her mother was a
> widow. Her mother went one day to pick a basket of charlock in order to
> boil it for her children. She had picked it in a neighbor's land. What do you
> say about the man who came and took the pannier of charlock off her back
> and sent her home empty?[25]

Almsgiving by generous women is a recurring theme in the oral traditions of the Famine and, as is evident from this article, it finds expression
in a variety of narratives. Especially common in the Famine context is a
legend about the miraculous replenishment of food given by a charitable
woman to the poor, and the earthly reward that follows such an act. In
many versions of the legend a contrast is drawn between the generosity
of the woman and the pragmatism of her husband, who is concerned
about the family's supply of food. The following version is from Castle-
townbere, county Cork:

> To the west of Castletownbere there is a place called Drom. . . . At the
> time the Famine was in Ireland a man of the Hurleys lived here. He had a
> small farm and was married to a small charitable woman. This farmer was
> a hard worker and he always tried to be up to time with his crops and to
> have everything done *blasta* ["tasty" or "neatly"]. He could not bear to hear

anyone say that he was a lazy or untidy man. That was an *asachán* [taunt] he could not stand.

Well, the Great Famine came in 1848. Times got very bad entirely. The potatoes all blackened, and other crops, too, especially oats was very bad the same year. This poor man was struck very hard for he had only enough potatoes that would feed a few pigs, and he had only two bags of oats, as he thought.

When he had everything gathered in the first thing he did was to fill a firkin[26] of potatoes and put them aside as seed for the coming year. Then he sieved the oats and found that it was all chaff with only a grain here and there. He gathered chaff and grain all into one bag and put that aside also.

That was alright until the winter came, and the hunger and the cold. The place was full of poor people going around looking for something to eat. Again and again they came to the farmer's house. His good wife never left them go empty. She could not bear to refuse a thing to anyone who asked for it in God's name. Soon she found that her store was getting very small. Yet, the numbers of poor people who came to the house increased daily. In the end she was up against it as she hadn't left but the firkin of potatoes and a few bags of chaff. Often and often the husband told her not to meddle with the seed whatever else she would do.

Now the poor people who came to the house had to go away empty-handed. Still they continued to come day after day. The poor woman was very troubled when she had to put them off day after day. She thought it very wrong to be refusing when they asked for it "for God's sake," and when she had a little still left. In the end it came so hard on her that she commenced giving out the potatoes now and again.

When the spring came her husband went to examine the seed one day, and when he found that the firkin of seed potatoes was half empty, he became very angry. He abused his wife left and right. He said they would be shamed forever before the neighbors when they would have no crop in the fall or harvest, a thing he said never happened in their family before. The only answer the wife made him was to leave it to God, that He was strong and that He had a good mother.

About St. Patrick's Day when the farmer had the field ready for the *sceallán* [seed potatoes], he went again to the firkin to get as much seed as he could out of what remained. He was amazed this time when he saw that the firkin was full of fine potatoes. When he told his wife she was more surprised. They cut them into *sceallán* and planted them.

The farmer thought the oats he had was no good and was not going to sow it at all. His wife made him plough the field and made him shake it anyhow.

When the harvest came round again the talk and wonder of that neighborhood was the crops that were grown by the farmer. Their likes were never before or, perhaps since, seen.[27]

This legend[28] is especially common in the oral tradition of the Famine in the province of Munster, but it is also found in other contexts in Irish tradition. A version occurs in a seventh-century life of St. Brigid,[29] and also in the Old Testament—the story of the "Miracle of the flour and oil" in the Elijah Cycle in the first book of Kings (1 Kings 17:7–16).

Women and Children during the Famine

The plight of women and children is highlighted again and again in the oral traditions of the Famine. From the Rosses of Donegal we hear that a daughter, out of terror of Famine sickness, deserted her mother, leaving her to die on her own and to be buried by neighbors in the nearby moor.[30] By and large, however, the traditions are, not surprisingly, mainly concerned with the lack of food and the consequences arising therefrom for women and children. While stories of the miraculous provision of food in this connection—similar to that quoted above—are found in many parts of the country, virtual depletion of some families through starvation or disease is the more common and realistic scenario mentioned in oral traditions of the Famine, as an account from west Kerry, based on the recollection of an elderly man who lived through the Famine, indicates:

> My uncle Mick [Calahane]—he was nearly ninety-five when he died—(he is dead with twenty-seven years), remembered a family of the Caseys that lived up at the bottom of the mountain—at the top of the farm; the ruin [of the house] is there still. There were seven or eight of them there, a neat little family, and they had white heads. My uncle Mick used to cry when he used to be telling the story.
>
> The oldest girl went the six days of the week to Sneem for soup and came [back] empty. On the seventh day five of them died. The *olagón* which they raised on the sixth day when she came without any food was something dreadful.
>
> I remembered one of them—she was a withered old little woman then. The name of the place where they lived was Cúm an Chárthainn. Years after my father was ditching [fencing] near the ruin and he found the bones—an old man and a child; the arm of the old man was around the child.[31]

Perhaps the most vivid and powerful representations of the consequences of the Famine occurring in the oral tradition are those found in a group of narratives about the hungry women and children who journeyed through the countryside in search of food. Incidents concerned with exceptional deprivation or degradation are prominently mentioned, often because they form part of the Famine recollections of individual families, and usually because one or more family members are said to have witnessed the circumstances and sought where possible to relieve them.

The women in this group of narratives are variously depicted. One of the strongest images is of the mother striving against almost overwhelming circumstances to provide sustenance for her starving children. Another image is that of a compassionate generous woman who tries to alleviate her distress by offering her some food. This scenario is found in a number of legends that focus on the type of food the poor mother has found and which she seeks to prepare for her children and herself. Occasionally, in the oral traditions of the Famine, mention is made of people—adults and children—competing with animals—with pigs at a feeding trough, for example—for fodder. In the following two narratives from county Kerry (translated from Irish), offal—frequently the food of dogs—is the food in question:

> I heard an old woman, now dead, say that a poor woman with seven children called at her mother's house at nightfall, and she had a cow's stomach in her apron. The poor woman was crying. She asked the woman of the house for permission to boil it for the children. "Throw it away," said the housewife to her, "and I will give you a mug of meal to make a little porridge." She threw away the intestines then and made a pot of porridge for the children.[32]

In a narrative with a similar theme, an elderly woman born around 1855 attributes the following experience to her mother during the Famine:

> Nothing ever affected her so much as the day a poor woman with children came into her. She was cleaning the fish and the entrails were on the floor; she was cleaning the fish, *a chroí*,[33] and the poor woman asked her for the entrails. "O, God be with us and Mary His mother, you can have them," said she, "but what good are these to you?" "O I'll boil them and give them to the children," said she. It is often I heard her say that if you had the best roast in the world it would do you no good when you'd see the want and distress around you.[34]

It is evident from official as well as folklore sources that for some mothers the struggle was in vain, and overcome by circumstances they fell dead by the wayside. A farmer born around 1870 remembered his mother, who lived through the Famine, telling that one snowy night she and another little girl who had been sent on a message found a mother and daughter, who had been around the area the day before, dead on a pathway, "locked in each other's arms." [35]

One of the best-known poems of the Famine, "The Dying Mother's Lament," was composed by John Keegan in December 1846, on reading the inquest report in the *Kilkenny Moderator* on the death of a mother and three children who had been wandering in the neighborhood of Corbetstown, county Kilkenny, "in a state of extreme destitution." The introduction to the poem continues:

> They had received charity at a cabin a couple of days before their melancholy death, the mother appearing in a state of unconsciousness, evidently the effect of extreme mental anxiety. On the same evening (Fri. Nov. 27th), they were seen on the road, near the spot where their dead bodies were found on the morning of the following Monday. It is supposed they sat down to shelter themselves from the weather, which on that evening was very severe, and that from exhaustion they were unable to proceed until overtaken by the darkness and loneliness of the night. When found, the hand of one of the children, and the foot of another, were eaten away, it is supposed by dogs or swine. . . . [36]

But the image *par excellence* of the horror and injustice of Famine is that of the child at his dead mother's breast:

> With her friends or her kindred she'll never abide,
> On yonder pathway last night she died!
> Her infant lay close to her clay-cold breast;
> In the world to come they are both at rest.[37]

This image, frequently occurring in the literature of the Famine, is also found in the oral tradition and forms the central motif of a legend recorded from a number of areas of Ireland. The examples known to date are mainly from the *Gaeltacht* (Irish-speaking) areas of Kerry, Galway, Mayo, and Donegal.[38] The impact of most of the oral versions is heightened, however, in that the infant, when discovered, is said to be still alive and trying to draw sustenance from the dead mother's breast.[39] The legends, which are generally single-episodic, are usually short, and seldom identify the dead woman, giving the impression that she was a stranger in the area. The place of death, usually in the open air, however, is normally given, and this detail serves to anchor the legend in particular areas. Occasionally, also, the number of accompanying children—all of whom except for the infant being suckled by his mother are said to be dead—is mentioned. The following Donegal version of the legend, which is bi-episodic and also one of the longest, highlights an aspect of the nonprovision of food during the Famine mentioned in other contexts, namely, the reluctance of families to slaughter beef animals for food. A number of reasons can be posited for this reluctance. First of all, old food habits die hard, and in Irish rural society, salted pork rather than beef was a traditional element of diet. It must also be borne in mind that the preservation of a large beef animal would be beyond the capacity of most families. Apart from that, in normal times beef animals represented an important cash resource for the farmer, and the traditional view, *nár bheire sé orainn go ndíolfaimis aon ainmhí dár mbolg,* "May it never happen to us that we should sell an animal for our stomachs," [40] was transferred even into Famine circumstances:

> There was a man in this townland called Ned Ó Gallchobhair. One day he was going west to Sligo buying or selling or some business like that. There was a house on the way that he normally called in to when passing that way. On this day he went in and the woman was lying on the bed dying with hunger and a small child behind her and he crying. Ned asked her where the man of the house was. She said he died a while before them. There were two animals tied at the end of the house, "Great Scot," said Ned, "why don't you slaughter one of the animals. And while the meat lasts it will keep you alive?" "O Ned, my dear," said she, "I wouldn't like to kill any of my stock for as long as I can." "Well," said he, "I'm going west to Sligo and if I get any food at all, I will come back to you and I'll share it with you."
>
> He went to Sligo and a boat had come in with a cargo of yellow meal. He went towards the front with his bag and he got two stones of yellow meal. He made little delay until he returned to the woman who was dying when he left her. When he came in he found the woman lying dead in the middle of the house and the child sucking her. Ned went out and told the neighbors and some of them came in and took away the baby. Some sort of covering instead of a coffin was made for her and she was buried.
>
> Until the day he died Ned used to talk about that, and he used to say that of all he had ever seen, that was the sight that most affected him—the woman lying dead and the little infant sucking her and crying with hunger. [41]

A further development of the central motif of this legend in the oral tradition gives rise to what may be the most horrific image of the Great

Hunger—the infant eating the dead mother's breast. From county Kerry we hear:

> I heard my grandmother saying—she was from the Kenmare side—that the worst sight she ever saw—she saw the woman laid out on the street [in Kenmare] and the baby at her breast. She died of the Famine fever; nobody would take the child, and in the evening the child was eating the mother's breast.[42]

Although stories of heroic self-sacrifice by mothers on behalf of their families are the most abundant, there are also some discordant recollections in this connection in oral traditions of the Famine. These are depictions of mothers who were hungry almost beyond endurance and who could no longer care for their children. A tradition bearer born in the 1870s recalled his father telling about a woman who called to the house at nightfall and told him that she had left her son, who had "got weak and gave up," in a neighboring house to die and asked him to bury him. Then "she continued on her journey east the road . . ."[43]

There are also accounts that tell, with compassion, that mothers may have been driven by destitution to try to balance the greater good of the family against an individual member's needs, indeed even against an individual's life.[44] From Cape Clear Island, county Cork, we hear of a mother who is said to have snatched a potato from the child in her arms and to have eaten it herself, "because the hunger was too much for her." The child is said to have died some time later, but the narrator showed compassion for the mother by adding: "And it was said that from that day until the day she died the mother retained that memory, and it was also said that the matter shortened the poor woman's days."[45]

Women and the Care of the Dead during the Famine

Acknowledging that changes had taken place in death and burial ceremonial, one tradition bearer rather elegantly remarked that "there was a complete relaxation of customs and conventions associated with burials in many cases."[46] That this was also the case in relation to the dying is abundantly clear from a variety of sources both oral and literary; care of the spiritual, physical, and psychological needs of the dying, which was—and became again in post-Famine times—such an integral part of the death situation in Ireland, was no longer practiced on a large scale. Traditionally, it was women who dealt with the dying and saw to their special needs. The care of the deceased from the moment of death and for the duration of the wake was also traditionally assigned to women. Precautions were taken to ensure that the person was actually dead, and the period of about three hours after death during which the deceased was left undisturbed helped to ensure that death had in fact intervened. Due to the scale of Famine mortality and fear of disease, these practices were eroded during the Famine, probably giving rise to a widespread popular legend concerning the burial of people who were still alive. The legend is particularly associated with the men who were employed to collect and bury the dead, but in the following example (told by a narrator born in the 1850s) it is a father who is said to be taking his "deceased" daughter to the cemetery:

> My father [Sylvie Downey] came in to his dinner one day—two eggs and butter and potatoes. He sat down to the table but couldn't eat it. My mother asked him what was the matter with him. He said that he saw a man taking his daughter to Cillín [cemetery] in a wheelbarrow and that her toes were stirring. The father was hardly able to shove the wheelbarrow he was so weak, and he was saying to himself "Who'll bury me tomorrow?" [47]

It was the lack of attention to the dead—to the traditional burial rites and customs associated with the crisis of death—that most caught the public imagination. Again and again in literature and folklore, we hear of the shroudless and coffinless dead being buried without ceremony, often in mass graves, or even left abandoned by the wayside. Traditionally, it was the duty of the male members of the community to transport the coffin to the cemetery, and to effect the actual burial. In the following narrative, the man is attending to this task on his own, and his sister, who has not had the benefit of the washing and clothing rituals customarily · afforded the dead, is being transported on his back:

> . . . On his way [to the cemetery] at some point on the road he met a man from the island [Cape Clear Island]. He said the sight would never leave his heart. What did he see? He saw poor Tadhg Labhrás with a big basket on his back and his dead sister in it. Her head, he said, was hanging down over the mouth of the basket, and a fine long blonde plaitt was flowing down and brushing the road. It was a terrible sight, and the man who had that load on his back had great courage. But what could he do? There was no getting hold of a coffin or someone to bury her. But he took her down

to Cill Chiaráin and he placed her in the blessed clay with her ancestors and forebearers. And when he had that done he went home. . . . [48]

As the traditional gender division of labor became more and more modified during the social disruption caused by the Famine, women—even young girls—carried bodies, including those of children, to the cemeteries for burial. We hear of mothers taking their dead children on their backs to the cemetery, as in the initial extract from Peig Sayers quoted above, and of women carrying coffins. Usually four men "shouldered" a coffin, but in a Famine narrative from the Dingle Peninsula, county Kerry, we hear about four women and two men who carried the coffin of a relative who died in the poorhouse in Dingle on their shoulders to Ventry churchyard for burial, a distance of about eleven miles. [49]

Women of Power

So far we have heard traditions of women who confronted the Famine situation in a variety of ways: generous women who helped and showed compassion to the poor and hungry; poor women who struggled to provide food for their children and even buried the dead; women who in the attempt to survive probably made decisions in relation to their families that would be unthinkable in normal conditions. We have also heard of women who succumbed to death in circumstances of extreme privation and degradation. But there are a number of other situations in the Famine context in which women hit the headlines—in relation to land ownership and evictions, for example.

The vexing subjects of landlordism, evictions, and land-grabbing figure prominently in oral traditions of the Famine. Usually these activities are associated with the male members of the community reflecting the de facto situation, and women are often depicted as victims of these activities; occasionally also a woman is the protagonist, for example Bess Rice, who according to folk tradition was the apparently unloved "master" of part of the Dingle Peninsula. [50] We hear also, though rarely, of women who were land-grabbers and who took advantage of neighbors' distress to get possession of their lands. One such woman remembered in Mayo tradition was a widow with six sons whom she strove to put in possession of land during the Famine period. [51] The more usual role assigned to a woman—who is also occasionally said to be a widow—is that of someone who is at the mercy of the landlord or agent, and it is in this context especially that we occasionally see a flash of power from such women, usually in the form of ritual cursing.

The incidence of ritual cursing by women is mainly connected with the fraught topic of evictions during the Famine and its aftermath, and it is perhaps more widespread in Famine traditions than the available sources indicate. The women involved are depicted as fighting back on their own behalf or on behalf of their families against those who are turning them out of house and home. Their resistance in most cases is a symbolic one, however. As members of the poor and the oppressed sections of society, they are generally unable to avail themselves of the protection of law, but they are perceived, nevertheless, as women of power. According to popular belief they had at their disposal a powerful weapon, namely the power to curse those who sought to perpetrate what they considered acts of great injustice against them. The belief that one could cause physical injury to another by uttering hostile words is an ancient one,[52] and it continued until well into the nineteenth century and perhaps even later in some areas.[53] According to traditional belief still current in early twentieth-century Ireland, ritual cursing was something not to be undertaken rashly; frivolously calling down God's vengeance on another could have serious repercussions for the utterer since, according to the traditional wisdom, *is fá bhun chrainn a thuiteas a dhuilliúr,* "it is at the foot of the tree its leaves fall." The curse, once pronounced, must fall in some direction, and if it has been deserved by the person on whom it is evoked, it will fall on him sooner or later, but if it has not, then the unprovoked or unjust malediction will recoil on the person who pronounces it.[54] As eviction, or the threat of it—for an inability to pay rent as it fell due, or for other reasons, such as a desire on the part of the owners to clear the land for pasture—was generally perceived as unjust, it was considered particularly so in Famine times, and it is usually in this context in oral traditions of the Famine that women are depicted as sometimes resorting to ritual cursing.

Occasionally, the mere uttering of the malediction is sufficient to cause the landlord's agent to have a change of heart,[55] or the threatened eviction simply does not happen because he has died suddenly as a result of the curse that has already been invoked against him.[56] The more usual situation, however, is that the woman (or women) who pronounces the curse has just been evicted. Ritual cursing was often performed by the evicted woman on her knees in front of her erstwhile home, but instead of seeking benign recourse to God she calls down His vengeance on those responsible for the eviction.[57] It is to be understood from a number of accounts that the evicted woman's curse is also pronounced against the incoming tenants—by directing her curse at the house and lands she is said to rob them of prosperity. Only when she is reinstated in her home and when she lifts the curse, or when the terms of the curse are fulfilled, is prosperity restored. The following narrative from county Kerry deals with some of these issues:

> . . . On one occasion the landlord was demanding the rent and Muiris Ó Dearbhaí didn't have the money ready. He went out fishing with his brother, and this morning when he was coming near the house he heard the crying and lamenting. It wasn't long until he saw the pot of porridge which they had cooking on the fire thrown outside the door and everything else in the house being thrown outside by the bailiffs.
>
> When they had everything thrown out the woman went down on her knees, and moved from gable-end to gable-end of the house. She cursed the house, and prayed to God that there would be neither luck nor happiness in the house or place until one of his [Ó Dearbhaí's] descendants should live there again. That happened true enough. May all be safe and well where it is told!, there was no luck in the place from that on until one of the descendants of Muiris Dearbhaí married in there, and it has prospered in every way since then.[58]

Quenching the fire is a metaphor for eviction occasionally met with in the archival material, but it also reflects what was in fact an actual practice—"the fire was put out, the door locked and a piece of thatch pulled off the roof"[59]—and a recurring motif is that a pot of food cooking over the fire is thrown out by the bailiff. A bailiff on an estate was said to have "quenched" forty or fifty fires in the years 1840 to 1850 (and to have met a violent death through a fall from his horse as a result of the curses for these acts pronounced against him).[60] Quenching the fire had also a symbolic significance since the fire represented the life, vitality, and prosperity of the home. Consequently, the fire could be used in magical acts to bring ill luck to the house and lands. The ashes of the fire, for example, might be so used, according to the following account attributed to the Famine period; running water symbolically carries away the luck of the house and farm forever:

> In Coolaclaur, for instance, some forty tenants were evicted—as many as thirty in one day. It was on the latter occasion that six women proceeded to the river bank bringing the last ashes from the fires of their wrecked

homes. These ashes they threw into the flowing water. While on their knees they called down dire maledictions on the landlord and agents.[61]

Widows occasionally feature in eviction accounts during the Famine period—though not as frequently as one might expect, in view of the intensity of evictions especially in the immediate post-Famine period. The sentiment *Is mairg a thuilleann mallacht baintrí,* "woe to him who deserves the widow's curse"—expressed by a county Waterford tradition bearer[62]—aptly sums up popular perceptions of the power of the widow's curse.[63] From county Limerick we hear that "Nine widow women were evicted at Ballyboreen" and that they cursed Cloncurry, the landlord.[64]

Conclusion

Several years of starvation and food scarcity caused severe disruption in the fabric of rural Ireland in the mid–nineteenth century. This situation finds expressions in the oral traditions of the Great Famine which are so intimately concerned with the *petite patri*—with the townland and parish. Although descriptions of Famine experience have become schematized with the passage of time, and international themes and motifs have become part of the Famine complex of traditions, nevertheless, the oral tradition points to severe social disruption throughout the length and breadth of the areas worst affected by the Famine, and at times, it is astonishing in its particularity and the vehemence of attitudes to the Famine tragedy that it expresses. When reading the folklore accounts, one is struck by the tradition bearers' deep knowledge, both verbal and visual, of the effects of the Famine on the landscape: there are vivid recollections of land change, of settlements abandoned and erased from the countryside, but not from local memory, and of secular places made semisacred by the burial of the Famine dead, as tragedy etches their memory, perhaps forever, on the landscape. In just a couple of ill-fated years a new nomenclature, which was to survive in living memory for well over a century, emerged to identify particular features of the landscape resulting from the Famine experience, such as "Tadhgeen's corner," the patch of ground where Tadhgeen O'Brien, a Famine victim, was buried, as mentioned earlier in this essay.

Much of the oral traditions of the Famine belongs to family tradition. It is thus intimately focused on individual families, and tells of those who had resources and who were generous to the poor and those who were not. It tells also of those who were unable to pay the rent of their homes and potato plots and had to take to the road and wander through the countryside in search of food. Local grabbers who took advantage of neighbors' distress to gain possession of land are named, and local attitudes of abhorrence to their actions expressed.[65] Families and individuals who were forced by circumstances to abandon homes and farms from one day to the next to seek their fortunes in the New World, perhaps never to return, are also remembered. Above all, oral tradition tells of the incidence of death in families and communities, and the breakdown of traditional customs and practices concerning the care of the dying and the dead.

Women are accorded frequent specific mention in the oral traditions of the Famine. In the changed social and economic conditions of the time, many women's roles were fundamentally changed, some women becoming the breadwinners of the family and ultimately also, as necessity demanded, the bearers of the family dead to the cemetery for burial. In thus highlighting these aspects of the situation of women during the Famine, oral traditions eloquently stress the breakdown in traditional customs and modes of behavior.

The perception of a basic immorality in relation to the Famine situation in Ireland is expressed in those traditions about women who traveled through the countryside in search of food. The degradation caused by privation and hunger, the injustice, and, on occasion, even the brutality which they are said to have encountered highlights the perceived tyranny of the Famine situation. In folklore as well as in literature, the image of the starving mother and child is used to represent the Famine's most unjust consequences. The woman is usually perceived as a model of heroic self-sacrifice, but perhaps one of the most salient lessons to be learned from the oral traditions of the Great Famine in Ireland is about the dehumanizing effects of starvation. It indicates that situations can arise in which people—mothers—are forced to make choices unthinkable in normal circumstances; for example, where it might be perceived necessary to strike a balance between the survival of the individual and that of a majority. Perhaps the most vivid illustration of the strength of the instinct to survive is provided by the story of the baby who, when he can no longer get milk from his dead mother's breasts, is said to devour them in his effort to live. In civilized society, the baby is considered the most innocent of beings, yet in the legend he is a powerful symbol of basic and base instincts which could potentially surface in the circumstances of Famine.

Finally, in the oral traditions of the Famine, the women caught up in the Famine situation are also perceived as being ultimately women of power. They are depicted as widows or mothers of evicted families who confront injustice by resorting to ritual cursing, the age-old weapon of the oppressed, when they are turned out of house and home.

Appendix: Famine Questionnaire, 1945

Are there any local traditions about the manner in which the blight first appeared? How was the crop affected—while growing, before being dug, or when stored? Did the blight return on successive years at that time?

Please write down any stories or traditions you can find locally about the following: Famine deaths, burials, graves, graveyards. The Cholera in your district; local fever hospitals at that time.

Can you give any accounts of the dissolution of individual local families during the Famine—or soon afterwards—by death or migration—to other districts—or emigration—to other countries? Where did those who left the district go to? Passage money; emigrant ships.

Local evictions during or soon after the Famine. What was the attitude of the local landlords, merchants and shopkeepers, well-to-do families and priests to the people during the Famine; alms, credits, mortgages on land, seizures, evictions, etc. Local "poor-houses." Homeless individuals.

Food during the Famine: types of food available locally; uses made of special foods—herbs, etc. Food-centers set up by the Government and various societies; local soup-kitchens: how run: individuals associated with them; conditions—if any—attached to the receipt of food at some of those centers. Souperism and proselytism in your district during the Famine—it is necessary to distinguish between centers at which proselytism was carried on and those at which it was not. Any accounts of the forcible taking of food crops, cattle, etc., and of the means taken to counter it—man-traps, etc.

Accounts of local relief-schemes during the Famine—road-making, drainage, etc. Financing of these schemes, pay, stewards, choice of workers, value of the work done. Attitude of the people generally and of the well-to-do farmers to relief schemes.

Notes

1. From *Peig: The Autobiography of Peig Sayers of the Great Blasket Island*, trans. Bryan MacMahon (Dublin: The Talbot Press, 1973), 198–200. Original Irish text in *Peig .i. A Scéal Féin*, ed. Máire Ní Chinnéide (Baile Átha Cliath: Cló Talbóidigh, 1936), 234–36. See also Irish Folklore Collections, Department of Irish Folklore,

University College, Dublin 1070: 11–14 [hereafter cited as IFC] for another version of this account by Peig told to Seosamh Ó Dálaigh (full-time collector for the Irish Folklore Commission) in 1945, and IFC 1070: 146 for a version by Domhnaill Ó Criomthain, Coumeenole, Dingle, co. Kerry (1945).

2. This material is in the custody of the archive of the Department of Irish Folklore, University College, Dublin. The questionnaire replies, amounting to almost four thousand pages, were supplied by regular correspondents and the commission's own collectors. They are bound in vols. 1068–1075 of the archive's collections. For a detailed study of the circumstances of women and children during the Famine, based on this material, see Patricia Lysaght, "Perspectives on Women during the Great Irish Famine from the Oral Tradition," *Béaloideas* 64–65 (1996–97): 63–130.

3. Special volumes: IFC 1070–1075 were supplied by these collectors.

4. For example, R. J. McHugh, "The Famine in Irish Oral Tradition," in *The Great Famine: Studies in Irish History,* ed. R. Dudley Edwards and T. Desmond Williams (1956; rpt., Dublin: Lilliput, 1994); and Cecil Woodham-Smith, *The Great Hunger: Ireland 1845–1849* (London: Hamish Hamilton; New York: Harper & Row, 1962). About 40 percent of the questionnaire material on the Famine is in the Irish language. (Cf. Cormac Ó Gráda, *An Drochshaol* [Baile Átha Cliath: Coiscéim], 2. This booklet deals with the Irish language traditions of the Famine and is concerned mainly with the Irish language songs of the Famine period.)

5. For a study of this *exemplum* in Irish oral and literary tradition and its medieval European associations, see Patricia Lysaght, "Charity Rewarded: A Biblical Theme in Irish Tradition, with Glimpses of Medieval Europe," forthcoming in a festschrift for Leander Petzoldt, Innsbruck, Austria.

6. See also Ó Gráda, *An Drochshaol,* 23, in this connection.

7. IFC 1071: 252.

8. Seán Ó Criomthain's father was Tomás Ó Criomthain, author of the Blasket Island classic *An tOileánach* (Baile Átha Cliath: Oifig an tSoláthair, 1929); translated with introduction by Robin Flower as *The Islandman* (Dublin: The Talbot Press; London: Chatto and Windus, 1934).

9. IFC 1070: 157.

10. IFC 1070: 328–29.

11. This was one of the most distressed areas during the Famine. One of the most noted songs of the Famine period is "Remember Skibbereen!" See also in relation to the Famine in Skibbereen P. Hickey, "The Famine in the Skibbereen Union (1845–51)," in C. Póirtéir, *The Great Irish Famine* (Cork and Dublin: The Mercier Press, 1995), 184–203.

12. This is an instance of bringing later experience to bear on Famine traditions, as it was toward the end of the nineteenth century that tea became a common beverage in the Atlantic seaboard regions of Ireland—see Patricia Lysaght, "Innovation in Food—The Case of Tea in Ireland . . . ," *Ulster Folklife* 33 (1987), 44–71.

13. IFC 1070: 274–75. A "keeler" is a shallow stave-built wooden vessel in which milk was "set"; the cream was later skimmed off for butter-making. For other versions of this narrative, see IFC 1070: 241–46, 260–61 (co. Kerry).

14. IFC 1070: 101; IFC 1071: 87–88; see also Ó Gráda, *An Drochshaol,* 17–19, for further references to the incidence of stealing during the Famine.

15. IFC 1068: 91.

16. IFC 171: 318 (1936).

17. IFC 1071: 153–54.

18. IFC 1073: 168–69.

19. IFC 1068: 44.

20. IFC 1071: 95–97 (1945). "Mick Connor, Doon, aged 45, is my authority for the following which he heard from his father who is dead over 30 years and was over 80 when he died."

21. The stealing of seed potatoes by night by women is mentioned in a number of references, including IFC 1070: 34, 220–21, 286. Cf. also Ó Gráda, *An Drochshaol,* 17–19.

22. IFC 1070: 31–34.

23. IFC 1071: 81–82.

24. IFC 1070: 269; A. T. Lucas, "Nettles and Charlock as Famine Food," *Breifne* I (1959): 137–46.

25. IFC 1070: 139.

26. A wooden stave-built container formerly used for butter.

27. IFC 842: 39–42 (1942).

28. Although classified as a folktale (Type 750B*) in Antti Aarne and Stith Thompson, *The Types of the Folktale* (Helsinki, 1973, FFC 184; second revision), it has the characteristics of a popular legend. See also Frederick C. Tubach, *Index Exemplorum: A Handbook of Medieval Religious Tales* (Helsinki, 1981, no. 766, FFC 204; second printing).

29. Sean Connolly, "Cogitosus's *Life of St. Brigit:* Content and Value," *Journal of the Royal Society of Antiquaries of Ireland* 117 (1987): 14, 17.

30. IFC 1074: 191–92.

31. IFC 1070: 312–13.

32. IFC 1070: 384 (1944).

33. A term of affection meaning "dear heart."

34. IFC 1070: 345–46. See also IFC 1070: 264 (a woman calls to a house and asks permission to boil the skin of a sheep for herself and her children).

35. IFC 1070: 361.

36. Very Rev. J. Canon O'Hanlon, *Legends and Poems* (Dublin: Sealy, Bryers & Walker, 1907), 509.

37. Matthew Magrath, "One of Many," in *The Hungry Voice: The Poetry of the Irish Famine,* ed. Chris Morash (Dublin: Irish Academic Press, 1989), 45. See also William Carleton, *The Black Prophet. A Tale of Irish Famine,* (Shannon: Irish University Press, 1972), 344–45, (Photolithographic facsimile of 1899 edition; first published, 1947).

38. Co. Kerry: IFC 1068: 103–4, 136; IFC 1070: 305–6, 374; co. Cork: IFC 1071: 108–9; co. Galway—personal communication referring to Barna; co. Mayo: IFC 1072: 103; co. Donegal: IFC 1074: 294.

39. Only in one of the oral versions mentioned in the previous note (IFC 1068: 103–4), are both mother and child said to be dead.

40. IFC 1070: 163.

41. IFC 1074: 293–95. My translation from the Irish.

42. IFC 1070: 305-6. A similar happening is reported from Barna, co. Galway (personal communication). This version of the legend is probably more common than the available sources indicate.

43. IFC 107: 266–67.

44. IFC 1071: 145–47.

45. IFC 1071: 198–99. My translation from the Irish. For another version see IFC 1070: 349 (co. Kerry).

46. IFC 1072: 74 (co. Mayo).

47. IFC 1070: 273–74.

48. IFC 1071: 198–99. See also 1068: 198, Kilworth, co. Cork, 1945.

49. IFC 1070: 120–22; see also IFC 1070: 87–88 (eight women carry a corpse wrapped in a sheet to the cemetery for burial).

50. IFC 1070: 147.

51. IFC 1074: 169–71.

52. Keith Thomas, *Religion and the Decline of Magic: Studies in Popular Beliefs in Sixteenth- and Seventeenth-Century England* (Harmondsworth: Peregrine, 1978), 599–610.

53. Kevin Danaher, *Irish Country People* (Cork: Mercier Press, 1966), 15.

54. Cf. in this connection Thomas, *Religion and the Decline of Magic*, 602; W. G. Wood-Martin, *Traces of the Elder Faiths of Ireland*, vol. 2 (London: Longman, Greene, and Co., 1902), 57–58; Danaher, *Irish Country People*, 13.

55. IFC 44: 117–18, Bantry, co. Cork, 1933—in this account an old woman's curse in verse is said to have halted an eviction in progress.

56. IFC 1052: 414–15 (Iveragh, co. Kerry).

57. Thomas, *Religion and the Decline of Magic*, 605.

58. IFC 1068: 172–74.

59. IFC 1068: 143.

60. IFC 116: 144 (1935).

61. IFC 1068: 79.

62. IFC 85: 241 (1931). See Patricia Lysaght, "Is Mairg a Thuileann Mallacht Baintrí . . . ," *Sinsear* 8 (1995).

63. The widow's power is often compared to that of the priest—see, for example, IFC 1157: 368, and the section on *Mallachtaí*/Curses in the Subject Index in the Department of Irish Folklore.

64. IFC 1068: 85 (1945).

65. One such grabber was nicknamed *Donncha na gCúplaí*, "Denis of the Couples," from his practice of unroofing or demolishing houses on eviction. He is said to have been cursed by those he left homeless (IFC 1071: 112–13, 1945).

3

A Tory Periodical in a Time of Famine

The *Dublin University Magazine*, 1845–1850

I N ITS LEAD editorial for January 1835, the *Dublin University Magazine* (*DUM*) defined a typical Irish cabin as "a seminary for the education of pigs" and went on loftily:

> Much of the misery in Ireland is apparent, not real; and many of the priva-
> tions under which the people labour, and which, to a stranger, would seem
> to imply so much suffering, proceed from an utter indifference about com-
> forts and decencies, which, in England, would be deemed indispensible,
> and which a very ordinary effort of industry or ingenuity would be more
> than sufficient abundantly to supply.[1]

Nor did the beginning of the Great Famine in 1845 eliminate such insensitivity from the magazine's editorial repertoire. In February and again in
August 1846, for instance, fear of widespread hunger was dismissed as the
"potato panic." In the wake of the Famine, with the country still strug-
gling to shake off the effects of English neglect and denial during the
recent crisis, the *DUM* nonetheless reacted with enthusiasm to Queen
Victoria's visit to Ireland: "It delights us to dwell upon the manifestation
of love and duty which our country has just presented" (34 [Sept. 1849]:
254).

At one level, such let-them-eat-cake crassness may be expected. From
its outset in January 1833, the *DUM* had exhibited the ideological character
that R. F. Foster efficiently describes this way: in serving as "the organ of
intellectual Irish Toryism," the magazine asserted "an identity that was

Protestant, Unionist and Irish."[2] While the *DUM* occasionally veered toward a nationalist position on some issues, its political philosophy differed markedly from that of better-known Protestant elements, such as Young Ireland and *The Nation*. The Catholics, and not the English, were perceived as the main threat to Irish stability and progress, and so the *DUM* attacked Catholicism relentlessly during these decades as "a superstition which is the nightmare of Ireland" (33 [Jan. 1849]: 117). During the Famine years, moreover, the magazine expanded even further beyond its usual anti-Catholic conservatism to add an almost aggressive triviality, a tone set by its new editor John Francis Waller. Assuming the editorship from Charles Lever in the latter half of 1845 and then continuing to guide the *DUM* until 1855, Waller brought to the magazine a combination of middle-class values, mid-Victorian smugness, and late-collegiate wit that showed political or social vision of but the narrowest kind.

Many of the *DUM*'s contributors for this period project a style depressingly similar to that of the magazine's editor. With most of Waller's editorials evoking the hothouse air of an English or Irish country garden, Percy Boyd takes this oppressively playful leisure on the road through his accounts of German student life or his European travelogues such as "A Scamper in the Long Vacation" by "Geoffrey Briefless, Barrister-at-Law." (28 [Nov.–Dec. 1846]).[3] Even the short fiction that claims to offer matter for serious thought seems mired in banality. "Grace Kennedy," by the Irish writer Samuel George Cotton, portrays a young girl adopted into a peasant family whose Catholic mother brutalizes her. The girl is eventually restored to her rightful place, her sterling character in no danger from her newfound riches, just as her manner of speech has avoided contamination by the coarse brogue of her foster family. The mother, meanwhile, is packed off to prison, and good riddance to her (36 [Sept.–Nov. 1850]).

Similar values emerge from five short stories by Dinah Maria Mulock, later Mrs. Craik. Beginning with "The Rosicrucian—A Tale of Cologne" (29 [Feb. 1847]), Mulock did most of her work for the *DUM* before the success of her first novel in 1849. In the story "Philip Armytage; or, The Blind Girl's Love," for instance, she accomplishes the remarkable feat of having her heroine Stella go blind twice during the narration, once from a disease (which is curable), later from a stroke of lightning (which is not). The title character is so inspired by his love for Stella, however, that they manage to triumph over all of their hardships until she finally dies in childbirth. Philip lives on, longing for Stella and waiting for death as a welcome relief from the unlikely events with which Mulock has surrounded him (29 [June 1847]).

At the same time, we oversimplify the *DUM* if we see in it only a trend here toward didacticism, triviality, and the ideological identity capsulized by Foster's shorthand terms. Amidst the frequent examples of political insensitivity and aesthetic banality during Waller's tenure can also be found two powerful social critiques of the Famine by Isaac Butt, while the literary offerings also include William Carleton's novel *The Black Prophet* and several tales by Joseph Sheridan Le Fanu. Primarily through such writers as these, the magazine during Waller's tenure continued to advance its original goals and to assert its role, maintained from its founding in 1833 to its conclusion in 1877, as Ireland's premier literary-political journal. It is true that the magazine sought consciously to serve as the voice of Ireland's Protestant, Unionist, Tory minority and further to define the social vision that would help to advance the interests of this minority. At the same time, that vision contained unpredictable impulses and frequently shifting uncertainties. The full range of the *DUM* for this period thus demonstrates a complexity and ambiguity that resists easy categorization. Especially through its literary offerings, the magazine provides us with some powerful metaphors with which to understand the conflicts and tensions evoked by Ireland's Famine.

William Carleton, *The Black Prophet*

Waller's earliest coup as editor, and one of the most significant works ever to appear in the *DUM*, running from May to December of 1846 through eight installments, was *The Black Prophet—A Tale of Irish Famine*. Carleton himself, "in his later years," regarded this novel as "his best work,"[4] and by the end of the century it would appear on W. B. Yeats's list of "The Best Thirty Irish Books."[5] At the time of the novel's writing, Carleton was enjoying a period in his life that his biographer David O'Donoghue describes as "the most fertile" and energetic of his career.[6] Not only was his novelistic output especially prolific during this decade, it also, Vivian Mercier writes, "offers brilliant insights into the politics of its time,"[7] while Robert Lee Wolff claims that *The Black Prophet* in particular "attains an impressiveness as a social document unmatched by any other fictional treatment of the Irish Famine."[8]

If such comments establish both the literary and the political creden-
tials of the novel, however, they simultaneously raise questions of genre
and purpose: Are we to read *The Black Prophet* primarily as a social commentary on the specific historical phenomenon known as the Great Famine, or as a literary portrayal of universal human suffering and passion?

From the vantage point of twentieth-century readers, at least, one cannot answer this simply by claiming that those two strands of the novel
unite into one harmonious whole. As Wolff himself acknowledges of
Carleton's dialogue generally, the humor in many of his works "can be
tiresome: the reiterated 'Ha! ha! ha!' of Carleton's peasants is almost a
sure sign that they are not going to say something funny."[9] More to the
point of the above question, it can also be tiresome that the novel's social
commentary keeps interrupting the story even as its aesthetic conventions keep diffusing the political impact. When Carleton published *The
Black Prophet* in book form in 1847, he dedicated it to Prime Minister Lord
John Russell and further added a preface blaming the government for its
failure to respond to the misery of the Famine and also hoping that the
novel itself might help to change British minds. Even without benefit of
preface, however, the polemical character of the work is heavily apparent
in the serialized version. It is this combination of the polemical and the
fictional that lends to the novel both its emotional force and its aesthetic
flaws.

SETTING HIS NOVEL during the famine in 1817, Carleton could draw upon
his own memories of such events in Ireland's history; in a lengthy foot-
note, he further credits another source, D. J. Corrigan's 1846 pamphlet
"On Famine and Fever as Cause and Effect in Ireland" (28 [Sept. 1846]:
353–54). *The Black Prophet* thus seeks to re-create for its readers the experience of famine, to bring the abstract statistics, disconnected anecdotes,
and dry government reports to life. Its narrative line drags us through
one cabin after another, all "untidy and dirty" through neglect, showing
little more than "the marks and tokens of gradual decline" (27 [May 1846]:
611). The natural landscape also appears invariably "deplorable," a "dreary
and depressing" atmosphere in which grain lies beaten flat and rotting
under the nearly constant rain. During the short periods between down-
pours, a "brooding stillness" oppresses the land, with the half-light casting
a "spectral hue" over everything. Even as such weather adds to the human misery below, however, the clouds simultaneously seem to shape

themselves to accord with the events that they overshadow: "Hearses, coffins, long funeral processions, and all the dark emblems of mortality were reflected, as it were, on the sky, from the terrible works of pestilence and famine, which were going forward on the earth beneath them" (28 [Sept. 1846]: 335).

Such a generalized backdrop further sets the stage for the narrator's long commentaries. At the exact midpoint of the novel, and heading off the September installment, a chapter entitled "National Calamity" presents a panoramic and bitterly ironic overview. "Day after day, vessels laden with Irish provisions, drawn from a population perishing with actual hunger, as well as with the pestilence which it occasioned, were passing out of our ports, whilst, singular as it may seem, other vessels came in freighted with our own provisions, sent back through the charity of England to our relief" (ibid., 337). As with the description of clouds and hearses linked within a mutually reinforcing pattern of gloom, a grim symmetry also unifies this passage, further reflected in other ironies that Carleton's narrator highlights: despite the famine, one may also find, "studded over the country, a vast number of strong farmers, with bursting granaries and immense haggards," who keep these supplies until prices have been driven to their highest (ibid., 336).

The main example of such avarice feeding upon human desperation is a stereotyped miser named Darby Skinadre. A kind of evil genius of the famine, Skinadre convinces many people that their own religious and spiritual failures have led them into hardship: ". . . we have brought all these scourges on us by our sins and our transgressions; thim that sins . . . must suffer" (27 [June 1846]: 744). Since Skinadre uses religion to obscure his own profiteering, the novel thus exposes as hypocrisy the theory that the famine has been sent by God as a deserved punishment.

Within the novel's broad sweep, however, people like Skinadre, hoarding grain so that it may then be sold at exorbitant rates, account for but a fraction of the horror. In seeking to explain such misery, Carleton ranges widely, focusing, for instance, on the Irish land system with its complex layer of middlemen, "one of the worst and most cruel systems that ever cursed either the country or the people" (ibid., 754–55). The landlords themselves are not really to blame, the narrator argues, because they have no control over a system of subletting that keeps dividing the land into increasingly smaller and less viable holdings. Caught in such complex and long-established cycles, the estate owners are just as helpless as the peasants. The narrator suggests that the English legislature might have intervened more aggressively in an attempt to change the behavior of the Irish people, through a better system of public health, for instance. Some government measures, such as the public-works projects, do make a temporary difference in the novel; but since no one attends to the spiritual improvement of the populace, wandering agitators easily stir up more social chaos. The reliance on the potato, too, has clearly left the peasantry vulnerable: "The climate of Ireland is so unsettled, its soil so various in quality, and the potato so liable to injury from excess of either drought or moisture . . ." that there is always some degree of famine or "potato cholera" somewhere in the country (28 [Sept. 1846]: 350). Over and over in the face of attempted solutions or explanations, the novel runs up against insurmountable Irish complexities. The very landscape resists the imposition of external remedies, and the question of responsibility for the famine dissipates within the vagaries of Irish weather.

In portraying the peasantry, Carleton frequently uses a romanticized style, praising their willingness to share even in a time of famine: "In this respect there is not in the world any people so generous and kind to their fellow-creatures as the Irish, or whose sympathies are so deep and tender, especially in periods of sickness, want, or death" (28 [July 1846]: 92). The pride of some victims keeps them from begging, even to prevent their own death from starvation. Others resist the temptation to strike out at the rich, or they observe their religious duty and attend to those even worse off, despite the danger of contracting typhus or cholera. At other times, however, the novel describes social conditions of a quite different order. The pressures of famine lead to frequent outbreaks of "the insanity of desolation" in which violence rules; "wanton and irrational outrages" cause people "to forget all the decencies and restraints of ordinary life" (28 [Sept. 1846]: 351).

Such seeming contradictions draw their terrible logic from a world turned upside down by hunger and fever, in which the narrator can calmly weigh the merits of death by typhus versus death by cholera. "Alas! little do our English neighbours know or dream of the horrors which attend a year of severe famine in this unhappy country," the narrator adds, as if to remind us that any expectation of consistency is hopelessly inappropriate for such times (ibid., 354). The novel thus deals, not with potential chaos, but with degrees of chaos. Many of the characters are only barely able to control their constant impulse to lash out, and passions frequently burst forth into violence that typically leaves someone wracked with guilt. One young woman becomes pregnant and seeks to marry the father of her child but is instead rejected and disgraced by her outraged parents. When the woman and her new baby subsequently die of famine fever, her parents alternate between famine-induced delusions and clear-sighted remorse over their own intolerance.

Along with Darby Skinadre, the novel's most memorable individual character is the Black Prophet, Donnel Dhu M'Gowan, to whom even his own wife says, "you're a hardened and a bad man . . . hard, an' dark, an' widout one spark o' common feelin' . . ." (ibid., 334). The Prophet's brooding, sinister appearance is reinforced by the famine itself, by the tendency of his predictions to promise disaster, and also by the ongoing atmosphere of mystery regarding an unsolved murder in the past. Now the pressure of famine threatens, from the earliest stages of the novel, to force the truth into light, even as that same pressure seems to render individual guilt negligible. The crime occurred over twenty years ago. With death now a commonplace and with survival often possible only at the expense of someone else's life, what purpose is served in seeking to establish the murderer's identity and guilt? In such times, one seems to meet murderers at every turn.

Even with the famine and the various tragic resolutions, the novel still ends in a largely positive manner, primarily by clarifying some mistaken identities. The corpse turns out to have been that of someone other than the presumed murder victim, and the man who all along has believed himself to be the murderer is innocent, with none other than the Black Prophet himself finally exposed as the real culprit. Such acts happen, the novel suggests, because of hasty passions, and people are thus advised to curb their emotions and to guard against moments of rage. The women characters, Mave Sullivan in particular, embody the novel's highest values through their bravery, quiet stoicism, capacity for sacrifice, and loyalty to those they love. Besides seeing justice finally served, then, the novel also asserts the overriding virtue of love, as when the Prophet's wild, beautiful, heroic daughter Sarah remains true to him to the moment of his execution.

Despite the compelling nature of such women characters, the ultimate triumph of justice still feels artificially imposed. First, it relies upon the enlightened intercession of an estate owner who has occupied only the fringes of the novel until at last he emerges to exert the needed power.

Then, the novel's conclusion ignores the ongoing human misery occasioned by famine conditions that would continue to revisit Ireland's peasantry. While someone like the Prophet may be more fascinating, our main feelings of sympathy extend beyond individual characters, and the society as a whole remains as vulnerable as ever to famine. Most important, though—even if more trivial within an objective scheme of things—is the novel's violation of our own sense of fair play. The Prophet has behaved like a murder suspect since our first encounter with him. Yet the novel itself not only acknowledges this, it also provides plenty of evidence to prove that he could not have been the murderer. Paradoxically, then, he is at once too obvious to be a good suspect and also not obvious enough since the novel seems to account for any suspicions about his guilt. When he turns out actually to have been the murderer all along, then, we feel that the novel has failed to play fair with us as readers. As with the uneasy symmetry between vice and virtue, clouds and hearses, incoming and outgoing ships, or as with the discordant combination of the historical with the fictional, the polemic with the aesthetic, the social commentary with the literary portrayal, the novel's resolution feels frustratingly incomplete and fragmented. Individual vignettes may portray the effects of the famine with great power, but any causes or explanations for that famine, any answers to the questions that it raises, are rendered finally futile.

Isaac Butt and the Famine in the Land

With the Famine now wearing on through its second winter, and itself prompted by the same sense of desperation that had unsettled Carleton's novel, the DUM in January 1847 drastically modified its previous editorial tone and position: "We are, indeed, involved in the greatest National Calamity" (29 [Jan. 1847]: 141). The magazine criticized England for its refusal to help out more fully during this crisis, and it defended the landlords who had been forced to assume so much responsibility for famine relief. Then, in April 1847, Isaac Butt published one of the longest essays ever to appear in the DUM, reiterating many of the positions that The Black Prophet had stated in its expository passages but carrying those sociological and economic analyses much further. Entitled "The Famine in the Land," it was followed in May by a companion piece, "Measures for Ireland," in which Butt reviewed many of his points from the previous month. The first of these pieces, especially, reprinted that same year as *A Voice for Ireland,* stands as one of the most profound analyses of the Famine written during the period.

Butt began by describing the Famine as "a calamity, the like of which the world has never seen. Four millions of people, the majority of whom were always upon the verge of utter destitution, have been suddenly deprived of the sole article of their ordinary food" (29 [April 1847]: 501). Like Carleton, he was also bitterly aware of the ironies of the situation:

> [I]n a country that is called civilized, under the protection of the mightiest monarchy upon earth, and almost within a day's communication of the capital of the greatest and richest empire in the world, thousands of our fellow-creatures are each day dying of starvation, and the wasted corpses of many left unburied in their miserable hovels, to be devoured by the hungry swine; or to escape this profanation, only to diffuse among the living the malaria of pestilence and death. (Ibid., 501–2)

The answer, Butt argued, should be a massive relief effort financed by the British government, to include enough imported food to replace the blighted potatoes and enough payments to individuals to purchase that food.

The difficulty in obtaining such relief arose in part out of the abstract principles of laissez-faire economics. England did not adhere to a pure laissez-faire line in its response to the Famine, as shown in R. D. C. Black's classic study *Economic Thought and the Irish Question.*[10] Still, the tendency within British economic policy was to highlight the limits and abuses of Famine relief and to let independent market forces establish their own balance as far as possible, even if this required considerable human sacrifice. Painfully aware of concrete effects lurking within the theoretical abstractions, Butt's essay raised the possibility that the Irish people were being allowed to starve "by a deliberate compact to the gains of English merchants . . ." (ibid., 507) since the net result seemed to be only higher food prices and greater profits for the middlemen.

BUTT ALSO CRITICIZED the Tory party in general for having long denied the existence of any genuine famine, although he praised the early efforts of Sir Robert Peel, who had then wisely imported Indian corn during the winter of 1845–46 to prevent widespread starvation. While Peel's efforts had been too limited, he still seemed to be the only major official able to understand the nature of the crisis. In July 1846, however, Lord John Russell's Whig government returned to power determined to minimize government intervention in Ireland and instead to leave relief assistance to private enterprise, a position that Butt attacked as foolhardy, irresponsible, and cruelly self-serving. He felt that Ireland's landed gentry and tenant-farmers had so far acquitted themselves well in responding to the crisis, yet they were slowly being driven into bankruptcy because they were forced to finance too much of the relief effort for the poor by themselves. While England's main legislative gesture toward relief had merely been to provide for public-works projects, even these were woefully inadequate. Butt pointed out the extensive work on roads that led nowhere at a time when other projects, such as the Irish railway system, could well have profited from such government assistance. In addition, the pointlessness of the relief efforts encouraged negligence and indolence when the peasantry might be learning better work habits, respect for law and order, and some useful alternatives to the old barter economy.

Butt urged Irish landlords to take a more active role in promoting further government action and also in assisting their tenants to emigrate to alleviate the distress. In developing a general concept of Irish federalism, though, he also raised the vague threat that British heartlessness would swiftly increase support for repeal of the Union between Great Britain and Ireland, since "Britain is now branded as the only civilized nation which would permit her subjects to perish of famine, without making a national effort to supply them with food" (ibid., 508). The events of the Famine, and the response of British hypocrisy, left Butt further removed from his earlier political conservatism than ever before. "Civilization" had been the cultural goal for Ireland that the *DUM* had been striving for since its outset, yet in the case of Union with England, civilization had failed Ireland totally.

As the Famine wore on, the issue of respect for authority became increasingly complex for the *DUM*, and Butt was not the only conservative Irish Protestant to challenge England. In April 1848, when the Protestant Repeal Association was founded, Samuel Ferguson joined up, a year later publishing a long poem in the *DUM*, "Inheritor and Economist," that criticized English doctrines of free trade (33 [May 1849]).[11] On the issue of repeal, a June 1849 article cited a letter of Isaac Butt to the Earl of Roden. Butt foresaw the possibility that repeal might come as a way for England to divest itself of its problematic Irish connection. Ireland should thus prepare for such an eventuality, not because it was desirable, but because it might happen. The magazine approved of Butt's sentiments, for it had itself already endorsed this position in earlier articles. In October 1847, for instance, the *DUM* observed that "when Repeal of the Legislative Union has been brought to pass, Ireland shall have, within her own limits, among her own sons, the materials of which a legislature can be constructed" (30 [Oct. 1847]: 496). Another piece, in January 1848, had contemplated repeal in a similar fashion. Absent from all of these discussions and forecasts were the *DUM*'s pre-Famine notes of hysteria that had arisen at the prospect of repeal. British compassion for Ireland might well be dead, but the magazine was not about to waste further time in bemoaning this loss.

A Wavering Vision of a National Literature

The years of the Famine thus led the *DUM* into new areas of national consciousness. An 1846 essay, "Native Art and National Advancement," gave particular support to Irish artists (28 [Sept. 1846]), and in 1849, "Ireland's Industry and Ireland's Benefactors" urged the country to support domestic manufacturing and production (33 [Jan. 1849]). English attitudes were satirized in "English Notions of Irish Improvement" (35 [Apr. 1850]), and in a review of the work *Paddiana; or, Sketches of Irish Life, Present and Past*, the magazine complained: "The whole of the English press, without distinction of party, seems animated by the one common object of vilifying and holding up to odium every thing in our unhappy country" (31 [June 1848]: 715). In the *DUM* for February 1847, the poet James Clarence Mangan introduced a new series, "Anthologia Hibernica":

> the great and general impulse given to the Irish mind of late has exercised its legitimate influence over us. Slender as our talents are, we have become exceedingly desirous to dedicate them henceforward exclusively to the service of our country. For that country—and we now express ourselves merely in reference to its literature—we see a new era approaching. (29 [Feb. 1847]: 239)

The sentiments here serve admirably to define the *DUM*'s broader concerns with a national literature. Reviewing Henry R. Montgomery's collection of translations from Irish poetry, the magazine was equally hopeful for the future: "The mind of Ireland is becoming educated; a taste for the cultivation of her literature and history is daily on the increase; people are no longer quite absorbed in the stormy pursuits of politics" (30 [Aug. 1847]: 128). Another review complained that ancient Irish literature was too often subjected to a mocking or bantering treatment in translation, making it "almost unfit for the serious purposes of a lofty and ambitious native literature" (31 [Mar. 1848]: 305).

The magazine also saw fit to print the work of Jane Francesca Elgee, already better known as "Speranza" of the militantly nationalist *Nation*. The year after one of her more fiery contributions to *The Nation* had led to its suppression for July 29, 1848, the *DUM* published two of her poems (33 [Jan. and Apr. 1849]), with Joseph Sheridan Le Fanu's poem "Shamus O'Brien" soon to follow (36 [July 1850]). With its ballad style, its defiant speech from the dock, and its complete sympathy with one of the rebels of '98 who escapes from the gallows with the help of a Catholic priest, Le Fanu's poem marks how far the *DUM* was willing to go in the direction of national literature.

More than in previous times, too, the magazine scrutinized the fortunes of the Irish publishing industry. An 1847 review of a work by James Thomas O'Brien, bishop of Ossory, criticized him for having it published in London rather than Dublin (29 [June 1847]). Later that same year, the *DUM* jabbed at the *Dublin Review* as "a periodical affecting nationality, though it is printed and published in England . . ." (30 [Nov. 1847]: 616). A review of Waller's 1854 volume *Poems,* by contrast, praised him for directing his career and work toward a specifically Irish reading public. As the *DUM* rightfully noted, this was a courageous decision for a literary writer (43 [Jan. 1854]).

As with every previous departure from the magazine's conservative and pro-Unionist ideological origins, however, the *DUM*'s writers again wavered, in this case on the issue of just how national they hoped to become. Mangan's idealistic series would run through only three installments (29–30 [Feb.–July 1847]), with his most typical contributions to the magazine going into yet another series, "Lays of Many Lands" (30–33 [Sept. 1847–Jan. 1849], 8 installments). A review of Daniel O'Connell's life deplored "the present state of social disorganization in Ireland," going on to urge that *"All agitation* for a Repeal of the Union should be made highly penal" (32 [Sept. 1848]: 343, 353). Even more revealing of the *DUM*'s ambiguous and unsettled attitudes is the direction that Carleton's own writing was now to take. His short story "O'Sullivan's Love," published in the

DUM just a few months after the serial version of *The Black Prophet* had concluded, continued the novel's theme of love's ability to triumph over all (29 [Mar.–Apr. 1847]). Just as in the novel, however, this claim is strained in the short story, where harmony is restored only because of some timely graverobbers. As Ireland faced its second year of the Famine, the growing weight of human tragedy made any literary expressions of optimism increasingly difficult to sustain. For the summer of 1847, observers estimated that only one fifth of the usual acreage of potatoes had been planted, and it was clear that *The Black Prophet* had taught Lord John Russell nothing.

In August 1847, then, the *DUM* began "An Irish Election in the Time of the Forties," a two-part sketch in which Carleton portrayed a world of bleak and savage hopelessness. The sketch is set during the 1820s, at a time before the forty-shilling-freeholders (or "forties") lost the franchise through Emancipation in 1829. While this class still had the vote, the narrator states, Irish elections lacked all dignity and, in fact, revealed an awful truth about human nature:

> No man can know until such an occasion as this occurs, the melancholy and humiliating materials of which the mass of society is composed throughout all its grades. It is indeed a painful and a mournful thing to think of it, and to reflect that every day in the week you are surrounded by falsehood, dishonesty, perjury, fraud, venality, and corruption, in their worst forms, and that, although you see them not, unless in the more diminished and less obscurable escapes of ordinary social trial, yet that they are before you, and behind you, and on each side, lying latent and ready to leap into active life whenever the adequate temptation shall present itself. (30 [Aug. 1847]: 179)

Within such a futile vision of humanity, the results of such an election are naturally quite pointless. The narrator scorns any possibility of "a domestic parliament" functioning in Ireland until such time as "a sound and truthful education" becomes available (ibid., 190).

In the latter part of 1846 and early months of 1847, through such measures as the Labour Rate Act of 1846, the British government kept on distancing itself from Ireland's plight. By August 1847, the same month in which Carleton's sketch began in the *DUM*, even the English-sponsored soup kitchens in Ireland had started closing their doors. While the times clearly demanded expressions of rage, Carleton had lost all sense of where to direct his efforts, now lashing out, with indiscriminate paranoia, at the

Irish. The values proposed in his sketch similarly missed the mark, since the kind of education that Carleton advocated had so far done little to enlighten mid-nineteenth-century England.

J. S. Le Fanu and the Metaphors of History

It is in the short stories of Joseph Sheridan Le Fanu, however, that we find the most efficient expression during this period of the *DUM's* wavering ambivalence on such issues as repeal, nationality, and the Union. Le Fanu's metaphors further serve, moreover, to illuminate other problems that the magazine wrestled with during these years: the discordant tensions and uncertainties that unsettled its vision of Ireland; the bitterness, pain, and anger within Butt's essay; the frustrating resolution at the end of Carleton's novel; the inescapable sense of human futility before the spread of the Famine.

The best of Le Fanu's stories here is perhaps "The Fatal Bride" (31 [Jan. 1848]), narrated by an outside observer to the events he describes, involved mainly because he has stumbled into a complex world of compounded guilt and secrecy. His friend Jennings was formerly married to a terrible woman, who then left him. Like Jane Eyre's Rochester, Jennings now prefers to regard that contract as dissolved and to hide it in his past, especially since he now wishes to marry a Miss Chadleigh. While one of Miss Chadleigh's two brothers knew of the first marriage, his death will keep that secret safe, even from the intended bride. Nonetheless, since Miss Chadleigh's father now forbids this union, she and Jennings must marry in secret, an arrangement that successfully fools everyone while she continues to live at home.

Predictably, the secrets blow up in ambiguous ways, what would normally be good news having disastrous overtones. Miss Chadleigh becomes pregnant, yet this will expose the current marriage. Her brother turns out to be alive after all and on his way back to England, yet this will expose the previous marriage. Before he arrives, she gives birth, an event that precipitates a duel between her other brother and her husband. Or perhaps he isn't her husband. Jennings first explains that he possesses papers showing how the marriage to Miss Chadleigh, through a legal technicality, never actually became final. In his dying moments, however, he claims that these papers are forgeries. Amidst all the bewildering differences between the two Chadleigh brothers and the two Jennings marriages, a reader may well feel that the legal status of the Jennings-Chadleigh marriage remains hopelessly clouded, none of which prevents the son of that union from growing up to become a Member of Parliament and heir to the wealthy Chadleigh estate in—naturally—Ireland.

What conclusions are we then to draw? Most explicitly, "The Fatal Bride" counsels prudence, a virtue for which Jennings himself, thoroughly ambivalent about his various marriages, is the strongest advocate. The narrator shares in this ambivalence insofar as he has also felt a romantic and totally irrational impulse to fight on Miss Chadleigh's behalf, even while stressing that his own status as a bachelor is important to his self-identity. Yet he avoids Jennings's personal entanglements more through chance than through design, and prudence rises to the didactic surface more through guilty hindsight than through persuasive wisdom. Beneath that surface, more powerful forces lend "The Fatal Bride" its main literary energy: guilt-ridden doubts about identity, sexuality, and social legitimacy.

Le Fanu's narrative frame further expands this combination into an elaborate historical metaphor. In the late 1840s, at the time when we learn of these events, the narrator is seventy-five. Around 1790, Miss Chadleigh's mother ran off and left her family; around 1805, the above story took place. The narrator does not need to remind us that the Act of Union between Great Britain and Ireland occurred between those two earlier events, a political marriage built upon guilt and shaken ever since by questions of legitimacy and legality. The product of that marriage may indeed now occupy a place of prestige on the floor of Parliament, but only because we suppress the facts of his heritage. Mired in the complexities of the past, those facts can perhaps never be fully understood, and prudence offers little help in planning other family events. Le Fanu's metaphor does, however, allow us to foresee that such marriages inevitably contain ruin.

Le Fanu's story "The Watcher," published just two months before "The Fatal Bride," portrays the same themes but more simply and directly (30 [Nov. 1847]). Set in Dublin in 1794, the story concerns a man named Barton whose guilt is also built upon sexual indiscretion. When he plans to marry, his shadow self emerges to terrorize and eventually kill him. In "Some Account of the Latter Days of the Hon. Richard Marston, of Dunoran" (31 [Apr.–June 1848]), Marston participates in the same sexual guilt that preys on other Le Fanu characters, much of it generated by marriages of the same questionable nature. He abandons his wife to marry the family governess, only to learn that she is already married and that her previous husband, posing as her brother and living in the same house, is trying to seduce Marston's daughter. Like "The Watcher" and "The Fatal Bride," then, "Marston" also contains an act of sexual indiscretion that occurs in the 1790s, just in time for the Act of Union.

Written during Le Fanu's own guilty involvement with the nationalist Young Ireland movement, all three of these tales explore the various and shameful consequences of that Union. While prudence would lead him to sever his dangerous political alliances before they could destroy him publicly, these private experiences still emerged as literary metaphor. In such a form, they may further remind us of similar patterns within *The Black Prophet*. In Carleton's novel, too, a crime occurs shortly before the Union, a murder spawned by sexual jealousy and spawning in its turn another generation of repressed guilt and suspicion. If a character like Mave Sullivan is an impossibly virtuous heroine, others may be all too realistic, particularly those who fascinate us with their impulse or capacity to destroy. In a letter to Carleton shortly after the publication of *The Black Prophet,* and seeking to patch up a quarrel with his friend, Charles Gavan Duffy wrote: "In a gust of passion you are one of the most unjust of men, and shut your eyes to everything but your wrath. . . . you were as merciless as Skinadre. . . ."[12] According to Stephen Dedalus' theory in *Ulysses,* Shakespeare "drew Shylock out of his own long pocket."[13] The creators of "The Fatal Bride" or *The Black Prophet* could both likewise look within themselves for the tortured villains they portrayed.

If the Union was once a shameful political marriage within such a vision, the Famine has become the most monstrous of its offspring. Out of the whole range of responses to the Famine within the *DUM* for these years, amidst all the uncertainties and ambivalences and contradictions, we will find no expression of a response more powerful than the literary work of Carleton and Le Fanu, providing us as they do with such compelling metaphors for the Famine.

Le Fanu's Barton believes that "there is a God—a dreadful God—and that retribution follows guilt." In the grip of a system that is "malignant" and "implacable," he suffers "the torments of the damned" (30 [Nov. 1847]: 534). Another Le Fanu character, the Honorable Richard Marston, meets up with the same God, "a malignant, or, at best, a reckless one, if you will. Why, look around you; see disease—madness—hunger—hatred" (31 [June 1848]: 730). Carleton too had himself become a kind of Black

Prophet, witnessing the Famine with the same bewildered guilt and rage that burdened Le Fanu.[14] In such a time, amidst such shattering events, with England unwilling to acknowledge the Famine as one of its offspring and with Ireland unable to care for it, one could comfortably take one's stand nowhere.

Notes

1. *DUM* 5 (Jan. 1835): 2. All subsequent citations to the magazine will be given parenthetically in text, giving volume number and date.

2. R. F. Foster, *Modern Ireland 1600–1972* (New York: Viking Penguin, 1988), 305–6. Histories of the *DUM* itself are limited, the most readily accessible being the introduction to that section on the magazine in *The Wellesley Index to Victorian Periodicals 1824–1900*, ed. Walter Houghton, vol. 4 (Toronto: University of Toronto Press, 1987), 193–213. This introduction is written by Executive Editor Jean H. Slingerland, from notes compiled by General Editor Walter Houghton before his death in 1983. For an influential early survey of the *DUM*, see Michael Sadleir, "Dublin University Magazine, Its History, Contents and Bibliography," *Bibliographical Society of Ireland Publications* 5, no. 4 (1938): 59–85, as well as "Dublin University Magazine," an anonymous lead article from the *Irish Book Lover* 10 (April–May 1919): 75–79. While short and sketchy, this article also provides a great deal of the information that later turns up in Sadleir's article and in the *Wellesley Index* introduction. Other valuable overviews, surveying the *DUM* up until 1852 in both cases, include John P. McBride, "The *Dublin University Magazine:* Cultural Nationality and Tory Ideology in an Irish Literary and Political Journal, 1833–1852," diss. Trinity College, Dublin (1987), and Joe Spence, "Nationality and Irish Toryism: The Case of *The Dublin University Magazine,* 1833–1852," *Journal of Newspaper and Periodical History* 4, no. 3 (Autumn 1988): 2–17.

3. Boyd's title anticipates other popular Victorian travelogues such as Edward Whymper's *Scrambles Amongst the Alps* (1871) and Leslie Stephen's *The Playground of Europe* (1871).

4. David O'Donoghue, *The Life of William Carleton: Being His Autobiography and Letters; and an Account of His Life and Writings, from the Point at which the Autobiography Breaks Off,* vol. 2 (London: Downey, 1896), 86.

5. This list appeared in the Dublin *Daily Express* for Feb. 27, 1895, while a similar list, also including *The Black Prophet,* appeared in *The Bookman* in Oct. 1895. One convenient source for both lists is Phillip L. Marcus, *Yeats and the Beginning of the Irish Renaissance,* 2nd ed. (Syracuse: Syracuse University Press, 1987), 285–87.

6. O'Donoghue, *The Life of William Carleton,* 2:72.

7. Vivian Mercier, *Modern Irish Literature: Sources and Founders,* ed. Eilis Dillon (Oxford: Clarendon, 1994), 59.

8. Robert Lee Wolff, *William Carleton, Irish Peasant Novelist* (New York: Garland, 1980), 110.

9. Ibid., 7.

10. R. D. Collison Black, *Economic Thought and the Irish Question* (Cambridge: Cambridge University Press, 1960).

11. Christopher Morash, *Writing the Irish Famine* (Oxford: Clarendon Press, 1995): 80–84, discusses this poem as one that links the fate of the Irish landed gentry with the fate of Ireland itself.

12. O'Donoghue, *The Life of William Carleton*, 2:77.

13. James Joyce, *Ulysses*, ed. Hans W. Gabler (1922; New York: Vintage, 1986), 168.

14. Morash, *Writing the Irish Famine*, describes the Famine as a "terminal crisis in Carleton's aesthetic" (178), "a crisis of authenticity" (179) that would cripple his subsequent output as a writer because the experience of the Famine victims, as Carleton came to understand it, "lies beyond the bounds of representation" (178).

4

JILLIAN STRANG AND JOYCE TOOMRE

Alexis Soyer and the Irish Famine

"Splendid Promises and Abortive Measures"

Introduction

THE NATURE, extent, and effectiveness of relief programs during the
Great Famine is an important but vexed historical problem.[1] While it
is certain that neither government nor traditional philanthropic initiatives
were adequate to deal with the crisis and that a large percentage of the
Irish poor died from starvation or famine-related disease, profound regional differences and lack of coordinated relief measures make general-
izations difficult. An assortment of expedients ranged from food distributed by Poor Law Unions, Quaker soup kitchens, and donations of food
from the United States to food distributed by individual landowners.[2]
Among these relief efforts the soup kitchen in Dublin, funded by the British government and presided over by Alexis Soyer, received a great deal
of attention in both the British and Irish press. A microstudy of the way
Soyer's initiative was conceived and implemented, and an estimate of its
effectiveness as a model, illustrates some major issues of mid-nineteenth-
century famine relief: on a philosophical level, the contrast between
laissez-faire government and philanthropic energy; in practice, the popularity of soup kitchens as a relief vehicle, the state of nutritional knowledge, and available sources of food and funding.

In February 1847, at the height of the Famine, Alexis Soyer (1809–1858),
London's most renowned chef, offered his services to the British government.[3] He would personally go to Ireland and set up efficient, economical
soup kitchens that would save the Irish from starvation. Soyer's initiative,
and the alacrity with which the government accepted his proposal, illus-

trates the dependence of Victorian governments on individual philanthropy. Soyer relished his heroic role as fervently as the Treasury welcomed an inexpensive solution to the Irish crisis. That the government should have relied on the expertise of a chef, however distinguished, nevertheless indicates the low priority accorded famine relief by Whitehall, as well as an uncritical acceptance of Soyer's plan. British popular sentiment, as measured by newspaper accounts and correspondence, was itself ambivalent about the Famine. Genuine desire to alleviate human suffering mingled with an anti-Irish bias that contributed to general frustration and lack of practical alternatives. London newspapers continued to applaud Soyer and to offer optimistic admiration even when the miracle he promised failed to occur. The Irish press, on the other hand, became increasingly Anglophobic in its scathing assessment of Soyer's soup kitchen.[4] The bungled relief effort added fresh fuel to the fire of Irish grievances and emphasized the ineffectualness of good intentions without adequate funding. Soyer's soup kitchen is a cautionary tale that underlines the limits of gastronomy.

Alexis Soyer

As *maître de cuisine* of the Reform Club, Soyer was an affable and eccentric chef with a strong sense of showmanship and a flair for publicity. Soyer loved to dazzle, and to do the seeming impossible.[5] He attracted a loyal following of devoted admirers, while the press reported his elaborate banquets for state occasions, like those for Queen Victoria's coronation and for the visit to London of the Turkish pasha.

Soyer attributed his success to his organizational abilities and efficiency in the kitchen. High society flocked to the Reform Club to watch the chef at work and to marvel at the efficiency of his newly designed kitchens. A perfectionist in all he did, Soyer was both practical and artistic. An enthusiastic inventor, all his life he devised and promoted a stream of gadgets and such labor-saving kitchen equipment as a gas cooking range, a boiling-stewing pan, a tendon separator, and portable boilers for the military. Like Rumford earlier,[6] Soyer reduced direct expenses and labor costs through technology, streamlining, and economizing on fuel. He had designed the Reform Club's new kitchens with these goals in mind, and over the years constantly tried to refine his system.

Soyer elaborated some of these goals in his immensely successful new cookery book, *The Gastronomic Regenerator*, published in 1846. While intended for use in the kitchens of the wealthy, the book assumed the existence of ample staff, facilities, and costly ingredients. At the same time it stressed the need for economical and efficient management, albeit on a grand scale. Reviewers quickly noted the new principles of cost-efficient scientific management,[7] a theme Soyer later emphasized in his own analysis of the Irish crisis.[8]

Some of the women who toured the kitchens of the Reform Club requested Soyer to give them lessons in making soup for the poor. In conjunction with visits to various London soup kitchens, the lessons led Soyer to think about ways to organize a methodical and large-scale delivery system. Soyer was appalled by what he saw on these visits; his professional pride was stung by the gross inefficiency and mismanagement of such well-meaning charitable organizations. Much of the soup offered to the poor in London was undercooked or burned: it was hardly palatable, barely even edible. Soyer knew that he could markedly improve the lot of the poor simply by showing others how best to use available ingredients; he was determined that nothing should be spoiled or wasted through either ignorance or ineptitude.

Like many in England, Soyer was profoundly moved by the accounts of Irish starvation and destitution; unlike them he felt uniquely qualified to offer practical help. Soyer had mixed, but compelling, motives for volunteering to go to Dublin and set up soup kitchens. Neither the immensity of the task nor fear of famine fever deterred him. On the contrary, the sense of challenge and danger appealed to him and may be connected to the pattern of overwork he developed after his wife's sudden death in 1842. Without doubt he recognized an opportunity for self-advancement, but altruism was an important factor, too. Together with his ambition and professional pride Soyer was didactic; he felt impelled to share his expertise through his cookbooks, lessons, and demonstrations. Moreover, he confidently expected his mission to succeed. Economy, efficient organization, and expert use of raw materials—his strong points—were all needed in Ireland.

The Famine

In the winter of 1847, famine gripped Ireland. Although the upper classes had sufficient food and Ireland continued to export wheat to England during these years, the poor were starving to death due to the failure in 1845 and 1846 of the potato crop, which formed their staple diet. The food shortage was exacerbated by absentee landlords who continued to export foodstuffs (particularly wheat and cattle) from their Irish estates throughout the Famine. To avert total collapse of the country, immediate relief was urgently required for unprecedented numbers of people. Eventually, about one million out of a total population of eight million died of starvation and related causes.[9] In an effort to meet the crisis in 1846, Sir Robert Peel had appointed a relief commission, established a public works program, and early in November 1845 had ordered supplies of Indian corn (maize) to be bought in America. Together with only a partial loss of the 1845 potato crop, Peel's actions were sufficient to avert a catastrophe that season.

In late 1846, the new Whig government under Lord John Russell faced a more severe crisis and eventually yielded to the increasingly strong demand for food relief. In Parliament on January 25, 1847, Russell introduced the Soup Kitchen Act, which, after acrimonious debate, became law on February 26. The plan was simultaneously to phase out the ineffectual public works program by March 20 and phase in the soup kitchens, funded by a loan to be repaid out of Irish rates (taxes), which were to remain operative until October 1. It was hoped that these measures would break the catastrophic cycle of dependence on public works and assure the survival of the population until new crops were ready for harvesting in the fall.

The questions of what was to be prepared, how, and by whom were addressed, not in Parliament, but in the press. The newspapers were full of articles about the Irish, together with readers' solutions for the crisis. Some were ludicrous, others small-minded, still others impractical. In 1845 the duke of Norfolk had advocated that the Irish, like the Indians, should subsist on curry powder mixed with water;[10] "S" suggested that horses be deprived of their corn and oats and that the grain thus saved be diverted to the Irish;[11] and "A Club House Secretary" suggested collecting the "victuals left unconsumed" in the London clubs for the use of the poor and needy.[12] In a similar vein, a later correspondent noted that Soyer's soup could be improved if a cart lined with clean linen went door to door to collect leftover soup bones from the tables of the wealthy and from the local butcher shops for the soup of the poor.[13] The English had no monopoly on preposterous suggestions; the Irish also experimented with some outlandish substitutes for the potato. *The Freeman's Journal* reported an exhibition of famine food, where "a dozen different kinds of bread were submitted for examination, consisting of rye, barley, Indian meal, parsnip, yam (sweet potato), beetroot, artichoke, carrot, Iceland moss, and hay." All but the last two were deemed acceptable and these, according to the reporter, were "black, and fit only to be used as human food when terrors, similar to those described by Josephus of the last siege of Jerusalem, shall fall upon us." [14]

Soyer's Solution

In contrast, Soyer's sample recipes and plans for a model kitchen seemed genuinely enlightened. When he wrote to *The Times* offering several recipes and announcing new methods of mass-producing soup for the poor, he quickly became the popular focus for British relief efforts. [15] (See the Appendix for the text of Soyer's first, and most controversial, recipe, and a parody of that recipe which appeared soon thereafter in *Punch*.) Claiming he could provide nourishing soup at three pence a gallon, he envisioned a central kitchen in Dublin with auxiliary mobile units for outlying areas. By modern nutritional standards, of course, Soyer's soup, consisting of two gallons of water, four ounces of pearl barley, with vegetables and seasoning, was grossly inadequate. [16] The more insidious issue, however, was that the easy appeal of Soyer's soup kitchens diverted attention from the need to address the underlying causes of the Famine. Nevertheless, soup was the accepted medium of relief as the Quakers had shown so effectively, and was requested by the Irish themselves. Soyer was one of the first to contribute soup recipes to the press, but he was followed by many others, including Francatelli, [17] who was briefly Queen Victoria's chef.

The novelty of Soyer's kitchen plans with separate work stations devoted to different preparations captivated the English public. Many Victorians were fascinated by gadgetry and, as positivists living in an age of mechanical inventiveness, they believed that science and technology could produce limitless improvements in everyday life. Soyer's plans for a model kitchen minimized waste and disorder. While charitable soup kitchens were numerous, other groups had neglected these problems. Only Soyer drew up complete specifications for an efficient kitchen to meet the needs of the Irish famine.

Soyer had political connections through the Reform Club—twelve of the sixteen members of the Whig cabinet, including Lord John Russell the prime minister, were members of the Reform Club in 1846, as was John Delane, editor of *The Times*—and Soyer's offer of assistance was quickly accepted by the government even before the bill was passed into law.[18] The press reported that Soyer's plans were "examined both by the authorities of the Board of Works and at the Admiralty, and have, after mature consideration, been deemed quite capable of answering the object sought," a claim the rapidity of the government decision hardly justified.[19] Only about ten weeks (January 25–April 5) elapsed from the time the bill was introduced to the gala opening of the government soup kitchen in Dublin. Soyer throve under the pressure of this feverish activity: it was no mean feat for him to develop recipes, draw up plans for the model kitchen, order supplies, superintend the construction of facilities, and train the staff for the opening on April 5. Nevertheless, decisions were made and plans adopted much too precipitately in this crisis-ridden atmosphere. Whereas Soyer can be faulted for being carried away by his own enthusiasms, the government, which had failed to develop plans beforehand to meet the quickening emergency, now succumbed to the need for hasty action without adequately considering the merits of Soyer's plan.

On the whole, the initial editorial reaction of the English press to Soyer's mission was favorable. Although London newspapers focused on the political and financial aspects of the Irish crisis, they also reflected public concern for the plight of the starving and, in this connection, extensively covered Soyer's activities in Ireland. Ireland was, however, only one of the many topics of the day, and editorial emphasis was more often on the Famine's impact on British politics than on the plight of the Irish peasant.

Editorials in *The Times* between January 1 and March 31, 1847, for example, inveighed against Irish landlords, Irish ingratitude, and Russell's program and were particularly opposed to spending the money of English taxpayers for relief of the Irish. While in no way minimizing the catastrophic nature of the distress, the paper opposed "the begging box remedy hit upon for Ireland,"[20] complained that all Ireland would be on the civil list,[21] and grumbled, "What has England done to deserve the perpetual blister of thankless obligations and exacting obloquy?"[22]

The Irish, as might be expected, were more dubious about the Temporary Relief Act. *The Pilot*, a nationalist paper, distrusted English motives; *The World* was critical of the Whig ministry, "who have proved themselves quite incapable to deal with the present crisis";[23] while *The Nation*, which referred to the English ministers as "cold-blooded and stupid,"[24] also had little faith in the new measures. *The Freeman's Journal* greeted the act with enthusiasm, however, and considered the legislation enlightened since it allowed the Irish peasant relief from the public works scheme. He could thus till the fields and plant crops for the next harvest. In an editorial accompanying the text of the act, the paper stated, "we confess the developments of their scheme are fast drawing us to the persuasion that the present executive are now earnestly bent upon devising and carrying out the most effective measures of relief."[25] All in all, the editorial concluded, "it really furnishes strong evidence that the government are about to deal with the calamity in a bold and comprehensive manner," and "in the hands of a good executive it may be made a most effective measure."

Soyer therefore arrived in Dublin on a wave of favorable publicity and began setting up his model kitchen. Despite the widespread influence of the late-eighteenth-century reformers Rumford and Colquhoun, Victorian soup kitchens were often little more than emergency establishments set up wherever a boiler could be obtained or donated. *The Illustrated London News*, for example, reprinted from *The Southern Reporter* (Cork) an approving account of a soup kitchen at Cork that dispensed hominy or sold meat soup to the "famishing and clamorous crowd who beset the gates" of the old potato market each day.[26] To avoid chaos the first eight hundred were admitted and penned in groups of a hundred, each under the supervision of police. The food was cooked in a second-floor room, handed down to assistants standing on tables below, ladled into tins, and, on a signal, given to the first hundred to be let out of the first pen by the guard. They picked up their portion of hominy, crossed the yard, and ate it in a shed. Once fed they were let out at another gate, and when the entire eight hundred had been fed, a further five or six hundred were admitted, and the process began again. In all, 1,300 were fed per day, at the rate of 270 per hour—meaning that some people were penned up for nearly three hours before receiving a portion of soup.

The Quaker soup store in Cork appears to have been organized more humanely, but was too small to cope with the number of needy. The Quaker Soup House provided 150 to 180 gallons of soup daily, but claimed to have the capacity of expanding its daily production tenfold. Mostly, however, the Quakers concentrated on establishing soup kitchens in the outlying rural districts, where lack of transport rather than lack of facilities hindered relief efforts.[27]

By contrast, Soyer's kitchen was larger and more streamlined than any other charitable kitchen then in operation. Encompassing an area of forty-eight by forty feet, it had steam boilers on wheels and an oven to bake one hundredweight of bread at a time. There were bain-maries for heating water, separate cutting tables for vegetables and meat, and safes, hung seven feet above the ground, for the storage of meat, vegetables, grain, and condiments. Tables were at the outer boundary of the kitchen.

> [They were] . . . eighteen inches wide, in which a hole is cut, and therein is spaced a quart iron, white-enamelled basin, with a metal spoon attached thereto by a neat chain: there are one hundred of these, . . . Outside the tent is a zig-zag passage, capable of containing one hundred persons in a small space in the open air; at the entrance is a check-clerk, and an indicator or machine which numbers every person that passes; and on the other side is a bread and biscuit room, where those who have partaken of the soup and are departing, receive on passing a quarter of a pound of bread or savory biscuit. When the soup or food is ready, notice is given by ringing the bell, and the one hundred persons are admitted, and take their places at the table—the basins being previously filled, grace is said—the bell is again rung for them to begin, and a sufficient time is allowed them to eat their quart of food. During the time they are emptying their basins, the outside passage is again filling: as soon as they have done, and are going out at the other side, the basin and spoons are cleaned again and filled: the bell rings, and a fresh number are admitted: this continuing every successive six minutes, feeding one thousand persons per hour; . . . [28]

Orderly and civilized, Soyer's kitchen with its zigzag passages, which conserved space and reduced crowding, was a vast improvement over the policed pens used in Cork.[29] The steam-cooking conserved fuel and ensured the correct preparation of the ingredients. Thus, it was not only economical but avoided two abuses that bedeviled earlier distribution schemes, deliberate adulteration and waste through unfamiliarity with grains such as maize. Much as these improvements were needed, however, they did not go far enough. A glance at Soyer's Recipe #1, cited in the Appendix of this essay, shows that no improvement in cooking methods could compensate for the lack of basic ingredients, for the caloric deficiency and lack of protein, in his soup.

Conflicting Assessments circa 1847

Soyer's initially warm reception did not last long; within a month the tide had changed. As the administration moved to close down the public works without providing any significant amount of food relief for the poor, a public outcry arose against the government and targeted Soyer as the most visible symbol of its "splendid promises and abortive measures." In an editorial of March 16, *The Freeman's Journal* declared:

> We value at its proper worth the science and economy of M. Soyer. If he succeeds he will be a grand deliverer. But with all due respect to his gastronomic profundity, we do not think that a man can work on his pint of soup and Woolwich biscuit . . . we have strong apprehension that the end may not be satisfactory.[30]

From the very beginning, the two aspects of Soyer's scheme—recipe development and plans for a model kitchen—were received very differently. Whereas no one seriously questioned his kitchen plans, his recipes immediately evoked a stream of protests. One correspondent, "Medicus," who was opposed to a liquid diet in general and Soyer's soup in particular, wrote to *The Times* in an attempt to save the government from "becoming the dupe of another reckless experiment."[31] Another objected to the paucity of meat in Soyer's recipes and charged that his soup ought "to be called 'poor soup' [rather] than soup for the poor,"[32] while a third pointed out that "the kitchen of the Reform Club was not exactly the best school for the study . . . of the theory and practice of treating starvation."[33] The most pointed letter of criticism appeared in the *Morning Chronicle*. An indignant subscriber wrote that he was astonished that none of the London papers had "exposed the humbug of Mr. Soyer's soups." "I am sure, sir," he continued, "there is not a medical man in London but would tell you that such 'relief' to the poor would not keep body and soul together."[34]

These protests by individuals, although important in retrospect, largely went unheeded at the time. The science of nutrition was then in its infancy, and with no authoritative nutritional standards for guidance, political expediency ruled against really generous and substantial rations for the Irish. As the debates in Parliament showed, bitterness against the Irish landlords buttressed resistance to providing any form of outdoor relief whatsoever. Typical protests echoed the fear of many Victorians that if the poor were helped they would cease to struggle to provide for themselves.[35]

Nutritional standards were at best variable during this period, and were especially lax during the Irish crisis, when even the term "soup" itself became quite elastic. According to the relief commissioners, the general term "soup" was understood "to include any food cooked in a boiler and distributed in a liquid state, thick or thin, and whether composed of fish, vegetables, grain or meal."[36] As Henry Labouchere, chief secretary for Ireland, reported in the House of Commons, "a ration was to consist either of 1 1/2 lbs of bread or 1 lb of biscuit, or 1 lb of meal or flour, or any other grain, or one quart of soup thickened with a portion of meal, according to any known receipts, and one quarter ration of bread, or biscuit, or meal, in addition." "These quantities," stated Sir Charles Trevelyan, "had been 'declared by the best medical authorities to be sufficient to maintain health and strength'." All complaints regarding the nutritional insufficiency of these rations received the same official reply: "the ration issued had been approved by the Board of Health."[37] In other words, Soyer's soups may have been poor, but they were consistent both with government regulations and with the mood of *The Times*. Practically speaking, Soyer had few choices: with public opinion against a more generous allowance, he made the best use he could of the meager alternatives available.

There is no denying, however, that the Irish were treated badly. Even a brief comparison with the prison diets of the period shows that as far as diet was concerned, the Irish fared worse than refractory prisoners on reduced rations.[38] In response to his critics, Soyer had answered that the meat in his soup was for taste, not nutrition, and that "the poor do not want fattening—they want feeding." And indeed, if restricted only to Soyer's soups, they would want a good deal more feeding. With immediate starvation as the alternative, this "prisoner-of-war" diet was welcome, but it was nevertheless meretriciously misleading, paving the way as it did for the later onset of such famine-related diseases as typhus, "famine fever," dysentery, and scurvy.[39]

But at the time, the battle was waged more on political than on scientific grounds. The scientific "facts" only became significant when the quality of Soyer's soup turned into a political issue. While the English papers reported that Soyer was getting on "swimmingly,"[40] the Irish press documented the growing dissatisfaction with Soyer and his soup. The Archbishop of Tuam, who had characterized the government efforts as "splendid promises and abortive measures," also sarcastically referred to Russell's "Pythagorean cooks," who were trying to "embue with the elixir of life a worthless mass of roots and warm water."[41] *The Freeman's Journal* continued the attack, saying that ". . . while we freely admit that a gallon of water can be made palatable and soup-like with four pennyworth of ingredients, artistically combined, we have no faith in the magic that professes to convert a quart of water with the addition of one pennyworth of ingredients . . . [into] a ration sufficient . . . for the sustenance of a healthy man." Three weeks later on April 12, 1847, *The Pilot* repeated the same charge that "this gastronome is inventing soups much more artistic than nutritious" and called for a chemical analysis of his "elaborations and decoctions."

The opening of Soyer's kitchen, so long awaited, brought further storms of ridicule and sarcasm.[42] The quality of the soup, the humiliating and degrading way it was served, and the fact that the gala opening had the effect of making the poor an exhibit for the gentry were all emphasized in the press. On that grand occasion, the lord lieutenant and his family and other Dublin notables came to taste the soup and pay tribute to Soyer and to watch as the poor filed in for their share. The *Morning Chronicle* was one of the few English papers to review the opening.

> Soups of various kinds were then served, and the company having discussed the merits of each decoction as it had been presented, the signal bell to retire was tolled, and the great people gave way to an equal number of paupers, in order that they might regale themselves upon M. Soyer's soup. The contrast was sudden and bold. A moment before and a great number of lovely faces smiled their approval of everything they saw, and a moment after decrepit age, upon whose faces it would be hard to say whether time or hunger had made the most havoc, were ranged at the same time. Ladies Emily and Kathleen Ponsonby, Mrs. Williams, the Misses Brady, Mr. Gerald Ponsonby, Mr. C. Connellan, the Lord Chancellor, the Dean of the Chapel Royal and several others remained inside the square formed by the range of tables whilst the poor people were enjoying their meal, and the pleasure which those benevolent personages derived from seeing the poor people give every token of their approval of the "steam-engine soup," was visible upon every countenance, the ladies seeming to take the deepest interest in the subject.[43]

The Irish press interpreted the event very differently. With heavy sarcasm *The Nation* reported that "those genteel persons did actually file through the 'labyrinth' (yet unpolluted by contact with rags) into the penetralia of the soup kitchen and handled the chained spoons (yet untainted by lip of beggar), and even, then and there, vouchsafed to sip the dysentery juice itself wherewith Ireland is to be drenched during the ensuing summer and pronounced it good."[44] *The Freeman's Journal* minced no words in its condemnation: "Of all the impudent and insulting humbugs that ever were perpetrated against a suffering people, we hold the exhibition of yesterday, at the Royal Barracks, to have been the most outrageous." After reviewing the event in scathing terms, the paper concluded:

> Seriously, however, we ask, was it humane, was it kind, was it decent, to make such a public parade of wretchedness—wretchedness that naturally shrinks from all recognition? Was it done in order that the crowd, and the ceremony, and the splendour—the "ladies and gentlemen," tasting and approving of the soup, might remove from it in the eyes of the poor, the stigma of unwholesomeness and innutriciousness [sic], indelible, and, as we believe, most truly fixed on this Frenchman's decoctions by Doctor M'Keon? If it was necessary that the great and the titled of the land should afford a cook a triumph, somewhat resembling the ovation of a conqueror, could it not have been done without outraging every feeling of rectitude, every principle of humanity?[45]

But Soyer himself seemed impervious to Irish outrage. He alluded to the difficulties briefly at the Farewell Banquet given in his honor, but otherwise did not mention them again. And the issue was never taken up in the English press; indeed there is very little coverage of Soyer and his activities after April 1. He just dropped from sight, as if soup kitchens were no longer newsworthy. Conceivably, Soyer had become an embarrassment to the government since the chancellor of the exchequer, Sir Charles Wood, later reported on the success of the Soup Kitchen Act in Parliament, but did not at all refer to Soyer.[46]

Soyer did have his defenders, but they were few in number. Essentially, their arguments hinged on Soyer's providing a better product than that to which the poor were accustomed. "A Housekeeper" wrote to confirm that "the Irish and Scotch peasants habitually live on meal and vegetables," and that Soyer's soup #1 "is very like that which in my early days formed the usual supper in an Irish farmer's kitchen."[47] "An Admirer of Disinterested Benevolence in a Foreigner" reiterated the same theme, saying that "M. Soyer never proposed his soup as the sole food, but as furnishing a cheap, a comforting, and a wholesome meal." According to the writer, "the grievance of this country in general, and on the lower orders in particular is, that so much food is not only wasted, but made unwholesome by bad cooking."[48] Only The World attempted to defend Soyer in Ireland:

> A vast deal of abuse and ridicule has been poured upon the devoted head of M. Soyer, for his benevolent efforts to supply, upon the most eco-

nomical terms, a wholesome soup to the lower orders, as well as to introduce among them a better culinary system than they had hitherto enjoyed.

For attempting so much, even had he failed, the maître d'hotel of the
Reform Club, would have deserved the thanks of the community, but
when he eminently succeeded in his task, as it appears he has done from
the evidence of competent judges, to treat him with apparent ingratitude,
is a stain upon *The National* character. M. Soyer did not pretend to revive
the miracle of "the loaves and fishes" . . . he only promised that by his plan
a great saving could be made, and a larger number of persons supplied
with a nutritious diet. He did not undertake that his pauper soup should
tickle the palate of an alderman, but he pledged himself that it should
be better than the class for whom it was intended were in the habit of
consuming.

The Doctors led by Sir Henry March, and the press, with *The Freeman's
Journal* and the *Packet*, hunting down humbug together, have endeavoured
to sacrifice at the shrine of their indignation, the ill-fated M. Soyer . . .

Mr. Gresham and some other gentlemen assembled to pay a tribute of
respect to M. Soyer, and they have been sneered at by persons who cannot
bear that useful public services should be recognized and rewarded.[49]

Conclusion

The World expressed a minority opinion in Ireland, and reflected the tone
of the London papers. For Soyer's reputation in London remained high.
Irish criticism did not cross the Irish Sea, while English objections evapo-
rated more quickly than the soup itself. The British chose to celebrate
Soyer's success, not to scrutinize facts.

Soyer's personal involvement was a compassionate attempt to alleviate
suffering. He achieved part of his mission, namely, to make flavorful soup
for the Irish at trifling expense. In this he provided a workable plan far
superior to those of his contemporaries, and devised a streamlined
kitchen capable of producing soup on an immense scale. At the same
time Soyer failed to recognize that tasty soup was no substitute for the
substantial aid demanded by the Irish crisis. Limited by the existing state
of nutritional knowledge, he was oblivious to the difference between a
food supplement and the provision of total sustenance. Enthusiasm for
the mechanics of his scheme blinded him to its shortcomings. His Dublin experience, nevertheless, both enhanced Soyer's standing as an expert
and reinforced his commitment to institutional management. After his
return from Ireland, Soyer increasingly shifted his attention to catering—

notably in a military context. Soyer did not save the Irish, though he acquired that reputation among contemporaries—a reputation that instigated his later intervention in the Crimean War, when he successfully reorganized the provisioning of the entire British army.

Alexis Soyer's intervention in the Irish famine well illustrates the heroic entrepreneurial style that found favor in mid-Victorian England. His failure to save the Irish is, however, more significant than the mere failure of a model soup kitchen. The episode underlines the pitfalls of dependence on private charity to deliver large-scale relief. Without benefit of adequate funding or distribution systems and based on unscientific nutritional theories, Soyer's solution was palliative at best. Soyer refused to admit, and the government neglected to investigate, charges that the food was not nutritious. By omitting to report the well-founded storm of abuse in the Irish press that greeted the gala opening of the Dublin kitchen, the London papers gave the false impression that Soyer's mission was an unqualified success. Appearance was all.

The obtaining philosophy of government that left social welfare to the private sector led to an uncritical acceptance of Soyer's plan. In a crisis of such magnitude, reliance on gastronomy had political consequences: the further embitterment of Anglo-Irish relations.

Appendix

The Receipt for Soup No. 1

I first put one ounce of dripping into a saucepan (capable of holding two gallons of water), with a quarter of a pound of leg of beef without bone, cut into square pieces about half an inch and two middling-sized onions, peeled and sliced. I then set the saucepan over a coal fire, and stirred the contents round for a few minutes with a wooden (or iron) spoon until fried lightly brown. I had then ready washed the peeling of two turnips, fifteen green leaves or tops of celery, and the green part of two leeks (the whole of which, I must observe, are always thrown away). Having cut the above vegetables into small pieces, I threw them into the saucepan with the other ingredients, stirring them occasionally over the fire for another ten minutes: then added half a pound of common flour (any farinacious substance would do), and half a pound of pearl barley, mixing all well together; I then added two gallons of water, seasoned with three ounces of salt, and a quarter of an ounce of brown sugar, stirred occasionally until boiling, and allowed it to simmer very gently for three hours: at the end of which time I found the barley perfectly tender. The above soup has been tasted by numerous noblemen, members of Parliament, and several ladies who have lately visited my kitchen department, and who have considered it very good and nourishing. The cost, at full price, was as follows:

Quarter pound of a leg of beef at 4d. [pence] per lb	1d.
Two ounces of dripping fat at 4d. per lb	0 1/2d.
Two onions and other vegetables	1d.
Half-a-pound of flour, seconds, at 1 1/2d. per lb	0 3/4d.
Half-a-pound of pearl barley at 3d. per lb	1 1/2d.
Three ounces salt, with half-an-ounce brown sugar	0 1/4d.
Fuel	1d.
Two gallons of water	0.
Total:	6d.

This soup will keep several days, when made as above described.

The above expenses make it come to 3/4d. per quart in London; but, as almost everything can be had at much less cost in the country, the price of this soup will be still more reduced. In that case a little additional meat might be used, and by giving away a small portion of bread or biscuit, better support would be given to the poor at a trifling cost, and no one, it is to be hoped, hereafter would hear of the dreadful calamity of starvation.[50] A month later, *Punch* published the following parody:

Economical Grog
on the Plan of Monsieur Soyer's Economical Soups

Take a pint of boiling water, and put into it a thin slice of lemon. Add to this a few grains of nutmeg, and three lumps of white sugar. Pour out into wine-glasses, stir up with silver spoon, and drink warm. The cost is as follows:

Water	0d.
Firing	1/4.
Three lumps of sugar	1/2.
Nutmeg	1/4.
Slice of lemon	1/4.
Total:	1 1/4d.

The above quantity will suffice for at least a dozen people. The flavour is something quite novel, and, besides having the recommendation of excessive cheapness, is found to be very refreshing, and, providing it is taken in moderation, exceedingly healthy. It is just the thing to take before singing a convivial song, or after proposing a friend's health. A person may take six tumblers of it with the greatest comfort, without feeling any of those boisterous effects or nervous headaches the following morning, which result from drinking grog made of gin, whisky, rum, or brandy. It is strongly recommended for the use of families.[51]

Notes

1. The subtitle of this chapter is taken from an open letter of the archbishop of Tuam to Lord John Russell, in which he inveighed against Russell's government and charged that "every act of this ministerial drama" had been marked by "splendid promises and abortive measures." *The Freeman's Journal,* Mar. 20, 1847, 3abc.

2. R. M. Foster, *Modern Ireland 1600–1972* (London: Penguin, 1989, 330–31) emphasizes both regional variations in the severity of the Famine and the varying role of landlords. Although some Irish landlords, like their Scottish counterparts, slaughtered cattle on their estates to distribute as food to the starving, Foster concludes that they were the exception.

3. The only biography of Soyer is the very flattering *Portrait of a Chef: The Life of Alexis Soyer* (Cambridge: Cambridge University Press, 1938; rpt. Oxford: Oxford University Press Paperback, 1980) by Helen Morris. A particularly glaring example of Morris's bias is that she only mentions that ballads praising Soyer were sold in the London streets, but overlooks the ballads ridiculing Soyer printed in the Irish newspapers. Her citation (79) of the following laudatory "Ode to Soyer" is typical.

> . . . Amidst the din of party strife,
> Illustrious chef! you bare the knife
> To save—not to extinguish—life . . .
> For place or pension many fight,
> You only war with appetite . . .
>
> Yet, Soyer, great as was thy fame,
> New glories now adorn thy name;
>
> For though the rich thy art did claim
> Thou's heard'st the poor man's cry . . .

4. Cecil Woodham-Smith, *The Great Hunger* (New York: Harper & Row, 1962; reprint, Signet, 1964, 173–74), considers Soyer's mission to Dublin a failure.

5. *Memoirs of Alexis Soyer,* comp. and ed. F. Volant and J. R. Warren (London: W. Kent & Co., 1859), 177–78.

6. Late in the eighteenth century, Benjamin Thompson, Count von Rumford (1753–1814), become the leading advocate of soup as an economical, nutritious, and palatable food for the poor. Rumford's ideas became widely known in England after he published two essays in 1796 giving a detailed account of the financing, administration, and dietary requirements of his workhouses in Munich, and a prescription for mass feeding. See "Of the Fundamental Principles on which General Establishments for the Relief of the Poor May be Formed in All Countries," and "Of Food: and Particularly of Feeding the Poor," in *The Collected Works of Count Rumford,* vol. 5: *Public Institutions,* ed. Sanborn C. Brown (Cam-

bridge, Mass.: The Belknap Press of Harvard University Press, 1970), 99–165 and 165–262.

7. The book ran to four editions in its first year, its popularity helped by very favorable reviews, such as that published in *Illustrated London News* on July 3, 1847, 5.

8. *Charitable Cookery, or the Poor Man's Regenerator* (London: Simpkin, Marshall & Co., 1847), 9–10.

9. For a full discussion of the number of deaths from famine and how to account for varying estimates, see Joel Mokyr, *Why Ireland Starved: A Quantitative and Analytical History of the Irish Economy, 1800–1850* (London: Allen & Unwin, 1983, revd. 1985), especially pp. 262–68, including Table 9.1 on p. 266.

10. Woodham-Smith, *The Great Hunger*, 43.

11. *The Times*, Feb. 11, 1847, 7c; *Punch* picked up this item and mercilessly ridiculed S's suggestion in the issue of Jan.–June 1847, 54, 95.

12. *The Times*, Feb. 15, 1847, 6a. The "Secretary" claimed to write on behalf of a committee drawn from representatives of twenty London clubs including the Reform Club, but there is no indication that Soyer himself knew about or supported these ideas.

13. *The Sun*, Mar. 11, 1847, 31.

14. *The Freeman's Journal*, Feb. 19, 1847, 3e.

15. Soyer reputedly published four letters in *The Times*, on Feb. 10, 18, and 25 and Mar. 3, 1847. Although references to the first letter are common, we have found a copy of this elusive document only in *The Sun*, Feb. 12, 1847, 3b.

16. Patrick Colquhoun (1745–1820), a metropolitan police magistrate and noted social reformer, helped to establish a soup kitchen in Spitalfields in 1797, reputed the first of its kind in London. Later that same year, he published two important pamphlets on soup kitchens: *An Account of a Meat and Soup Charity, Established in the Metropolis, in the year 1797, with Observations Relative to the Situation of the Poor . . . by a Magistrate,* and *Useful Suggestions Favourable to the Comfort of the Labouring People, and Of Decent Housekeepers,* 2nd edition, January 1800.

17. *The Times*, Mar. 11, 1847, 6d.

18. George Woodbridge, *The Reform Club: 1836–1978* (New York: Privately printed for Members of the Reform Club in association with Clearwater Publishing, 1978), 34. Notice of Soyer's appointment also appeared in *The Sun*, Feb. 20, 1847, 4d.

19. This notice, which first appeared in *The Observer* on Feb. 21, 1847, 4e, was reprinted in several newspapers including the *Morning Chronicle* of Feb. 22, 1847, 3b, and even *The Freeman's Journal* of Feb. 23, 1847, 2e.

20. *The Times*, Jan. 9, 1847, 4c.

21. Ibid., Feb. 3, 1847, 6b.

22. Ibid., Feb. 10, 1847, 5f.

23. *The World*, Jan. 30, 1847.

24. *The Nation*, Jan. 23, 1847, 248.

25. *The Freeman's Journal*, Feb. 1, 1847, 2f.

26. *Illustrated London News*, Mar. 13, 1847, 176.

27. Ibid., Jan. 16, 1847, 44. At one point Soyer also planned to supply soup to the rural areas of Ireland, but that part of his plan never seems to have been implemented, even on a trial basis.

28. Soyer, *Charitable Cooking*, 39–43.

29. Although Soyer himself was temperamentally fond of zigzag things (for instance, he always had his clothes cut on the bias), it is well to remember that Colquhoun had recommended the use of a maze for crowd control in his pamphlet of 1797 (Colquhoun, *Useful Suggestions*, 12–13). The Reform Club owns a copy of this pamphlet, but it is not known when it was acquired or whether Soyer ever saw it.

30. *The Freeman's Journal*, Mar. 16, 1847, 2cd.

31. *The Times*, Feb. 24, 1846, 7d.

32. *The Freeman's Journal*, Feb. 25, 1847, 2e.

33. *The Times*, Mar. 3, 1847, 6a.

34. *Morning Chronicle*, Feb. 27, 1847, 7e.

35. Lord Radnor, for instance, lodged a formal protest against the Destitute Persons (Ireland) Bill, including the following two (of six) objections: "2. Because it is dangerous for a Government to take any step which is calculated to instil into the minds of the people the belief that they need not rely on their own exertions for their well-being, and a hope that if they omit to take proper care of themselves, it will relieve their necessities, and gratuitously support them" and "3. Because the Irish people are of a temperament peculiarly likely to be so misled." (*Hansard's Parliamentary Debates*, 3d ser., vol. 89, cols. 1352–53).

36. Woodham-Smith, *The Great Hunger*, 294–95.

37. Ibid. Charles Edward Trevelyan (1807–1886), assistant secretary of the Treasury, was responsible for relief policy during the Famine.

38. Refractory prisoners at Parkhurst, a new model prison for juveniles opened in 1847, had gruel for breakfast, bread and potatoes for dinner, and potliquor for supper. And by Irish peasant standards, the regular prisoners' diet was positively luxurious. Breakfast was: cocoa made with 1/4 pint milk and 3/4 oz. molasses; 6 oz. bread; dinner: 1 pint soup made with 3 oz. beef, 3 oz. potatoes, 2 oz. barley or rice, 1 oz. onion or leek; 1 lb. potatoes; 6 oz. bread; supper: 1 pint gruel made with 2 1/2 oz. oatmeal; 6 oz. bread. Four days a week soup at dinner was replaced by 4 oz. cooked meat without bones. (*Illustrated London News*, Mar. 13, 1847, 166.)

39. Crawford, citing the nutritionist W. R. Aykroyd, points out that the watery soup may have contributed to edema. See E. Margaret Crawford, "Subsistence Crises and Famines in Ireland: A Nutritionist's Views," in Crawford, *Famine: The Irish Experience 900–1900: Subsistence Crises and Famines in Ireland* (Edinburgh: John Donald, 1989), 200. According to an analysis carried out for the authors by Joseph Carlin, regional nutritionist of New England, Administration on Aging, U.S. Department of Health and Human Services, a quart of Soyer's soup contained 360 calories and 14 grams of protein, or about 25 percent of the protein and 10–15 percent of the calories required by adults. The portion of bread adds another 450–800 calories. Current U.S. standards indicate that a male between

the ages of twenty-three and fifty (154 lbs and 5'10" tall) and doing light work needs 2,700 Kcal (2,300–3,100 Kcal range). Women in the same age group (102 lbs and 5'4" tall) need 2,000 Kcal (1600–2400 Kcal range). Most modern nutrition intervention programs try to deliver 750–800 Kcal and 50 grams of protein, plus one third of the RDA (reference: 1980 U.S. recommended dietary allowance) for vitamins and minerals at each meal.

40. *The Observer*, Mar. 22, 1847, 6c.

41. *The Freeman's Journal*, Mar. 20, 1847, 3abc.

42. One telling example is this Irish excerpt from the play "The Soup Kitchen," where three cooks chant over a cauldron like the three witches from *Macbeth*.

All 3 cooks:	Double double, toil and trouble;
	Fire burn, and boiler bubble.
3rd cook:	Scale of codfish, spiders' tongues,
	Tomtits' gizzards, head and lungs
	Of a famished French fed frog,
	Root of phaytee digged in bog;
	Of D'Israeli's heart a slice,
	Roebuck's gall, a grain of rice,
	Celery heads paired [*sic*] to the tips,
	Brougham's nose, and Soyer's lips,
	Sweetened by the Ponsonbys's
	Fastidious taste—it sure must please
	Such rude, ill-mannered folk as these—
	And thereto a spring of 'shamrogue'
	For the ingredients of our humbogue.

(The *Scene from the "Soup Boiler"* originally appeared in *The Nation* and was reprinted in *The Freeman's Journal*, Apr. 5, 1847, 2f.)

43. *Morning Chronicle*, Apr. 7, 1847, 3c.

44. *The Nation*, Apr. 10, 1847, 424.

45. *The Freeman's Journal*, Apr. 7, 1847, 2d.

46. *Hansard*, vol. 92, cols. 1349–50 (May 31, 1847).

47. *The Times*, Feb. 27, 1847, 6f.

48. *Morning Chronicle*, Mar. 1, 1847, 3d.

49. *The World*, Apr. 17, 1847, 4. The stance of this newspaper is unclear. While it clearly criticized Russell and the Whig government, it was one of the few Irish papers to openly defend Soyer's efforts. On the other hand, the Irish government (i.e., Britain) subsidized the paper from 1848 to 1850 and promised to provide intelligence from the Foreign Office. See A. Aspinall, *Politics and the Press, 1780–1850* (London: Homes & Val Thal, 1949), 192.

50. *The Freeman's Journal*, Feb. 20, 1847, 4d; rpt. from *The Times*, Feb. 18, 1847, 5f.

51. *Punch*, Mar. 27, 1847, 127.

5

DAVID S. JONES

The Transfer of Land and the Emergence of the Graziers during the Famine Period

Introduction

DURING THE nineteenth century, ranch farming became a major sector of the Irish agricultural economy. Its practitioners, commonly called graziers, ranchers, or simply grazing farmers, occupied extensive tracts of grassland on which they reared large numbers of dry cattle and sheep. This was undertaken purely as a commercial activity. The holdings of graziers often were above two hundred acres; in some cases the acreage exceeded four figures. There were two types of graziers: those who specialized in rearing young store cattle, developing the muscle and bone structure of the animal during the middle stage of growth; and those who later fattened the cattle, adding flesh weight prior to slaughter or export. Many of the cattle reared on the store ranches, located in Connaught and north Munster, were subsequently sold to fattening graziers, mainly found in north Leinster.

Ranching had been established in Ireland from early in the eighteenth century, but steadily expanded in the first part of the nineteenth century. By the eve of the Famine the graziers were already numerous and economically powerful in the grazing counties of the east (especially Meath, Westmeath, and Kildare). However, it was the famine which presented significant opportunities for the development of ranch farming in the western counties, especially in north Munster and Connaught.

This essay will consider how and why the graziers in the west of Ireland became the beneficiaries of the famine, focusing on the opportunities and incentives that arose during the famine period to acquire land on competitive terms and convert it to commercial pasture. The essay will also examine the social origins of such graziers and the attributes they possessed that enabled ranch farming to expand during the famine period.

The Relinquishment of Land during the Famine

During the period of the Famine there occurred, in the words of the preface to the 1850 agricultural returns, an "immense alteration in the numbers and wealth of different classes of farmers."[1] Through the exigencies caused by repeated failure of the potato crop, on which they depended for their income and subsistence, many small and medium tenants left or were forced to leave their holdings, especially in western counties, "with great quantities of land given up to the landlords."[2] The land was then consolidated and relet in enlarged units. The result was a significant decline in the numbers and acreages of both small and medium holdings.[3] This decline is reflected in Table 1. By 1861 the total of holdings under one acre was only a small fraction of the number on the eve of the Famine. In addition, the number and total acreages of holdings of 1–4 acres fell by about 60 percent, and the number and total acreages within the 5–49 acres category fell by about 30 percent in the same period. While holdings under one acre continued to decline sharply during the 1850s, nearly all the decrease for the 1–4 and 5–49 acre categories occurred between 1845 and 1851, with only a slight decline thereafter for holdings under thirty acres (see Table 2).

The decline in small and medium holdings during the Famine years was in part due to voluntary relinquishment. In great desperation, starving, often disease-ridden and impoverished tenant occupiers in Munster and Connaught were forced to abandon the land and seek relief in the workhouse, from food handouts at the corn storage depots, or on public works schemes where a small daily wage could be earned.[4] Further compelling such tenants to abandon their holdings was the stipulation under the so-called Gregory clause that relief could not be given to those occupying more than a quarter acre of ground.[5] In Westport, one of the worst affected unions, the temporary poor law inspector, Captain Primrose,

TABLE 1. Numbers of Holdings and Total Acreages for Different Classes of Holding in 1845, 1851, and 1861

Size of holding (acres)	below 1	1–4	5–49	50–99	100–199	200–499	500+
1845							
No. of holdings (est.)+	197,591	208,502	564,193	46,457	16,335	5,476	954
Total acreage (est)*	98,796	729,757	11,283,860	3,461,047	2,515,590	1,960,408	1,282,176
1851							
No. of holdings	69,947	88,083	403,258	49,940	19,753	7,847	1,457
Total acreage (est)*	42,878	308,291	7,971,265	3,665,596	2,962,950	2,676,611	1,821,250
1861							
No. of holdings	41,561	85,469	397,631	53,933	21,531	8,329	1,591
Total acreage	25,470	298,131	7,976,778	3,959,865	3,229,864	2,841,442	1,988,374

+Note on the calculation of the numbers of land holdings in 1845: The 1845 return enumerated land occupiers, not land holdings. The numbers of holdings in 1845 were estimated by using the ratio of the numbers of holdings to occupiers within each acreage class in the 1861 agricultural returns.

*Note on acreage calculations: The acreage in each of the different classes of land holdings in 1845 and 1851, which were not enumerated, was estimated by multiplying the number in each class by the average size of holdings in that class as given in the 1853 agricultural returns. Acreages for 1861 were given in the agricultural returns of that year.

Source: *Report from Her Majesty's Commissioners of Inquiry into the State of Law and Practice in Respect to the Occupation of Land in Ireland*, pt. 4: Appendix, 280–83 [672], H.C. 1845, 22, 1; *Census of Ireland for the year 1851*, pt. 2: *Returns of Agricultural Produce*, iii [1589], H.C. 1852–53, 93, 1; *Agricultural Statistics of Ireland for the Year 1861*, xii [3156], H.C. 1863, 69, 547.

TABLE 2. The Estimated Percentage Changes in Total Acreages within the Different Classes of Holding, 1845–51 and 1851–61.

Acres	under 1	1–4	5–49	50–99	100–199	200–499	500+
1845–51	−56.6	−57.8	−29.3	5.9	17.8	36.5	42
1851–61	−40.6	3.3	0.1	8	9	6.2	9.2

reported in January 1849 that "small farmers who held from 3 to 4 acres have nearly all been obliged to give up their holdings and seek relief."[6] Others were even less fortunate, perishing on their holdings through starvation and disease.

Other tenants gave up their land in order to emigrate. Many were paupers, who, like those who had sought poor relief, fled the land to escape starvation and extreme privation. They were often financially assisted by landlords eager to remodel their estates, or by relatives who had already emigrated and had sent back remittances. However, by no means were all the emigrants in this category; a significant proportion were farmers of capital with medium-sized holdings. One proprietor in county Limerick, Aubrey de Vere, informed the House of Commons select committee on the Irish Poor Laws in 1849 (chaired by Sir John Young) that "farmers, occupying considerable tracts of ground, have relinquished their farms and abandoned the country."[7] Their reason for emigrating was not so much extreme poverty and starvation, but rather their fear at the prospect of losing their capital and becoming themselves impoverished if they remained on the land.

This fear partly stemmed from the steep increases in the poor rates, payment of which was shared in roughly equal proportions with the landlord. These increases were a response to the burgeoning numbers who were receiving relief, and were most acutely felt in the western unions where the rate struck sometimes exceeded 5s/£ in the Famine.[8] What made matters worse was the sharp fall, across the board, in the price of commercial crops after 1846. Wheat, for example, fell from 16s per hundredweight in 1846 to 7s 6d in 1852, and oats from 11s 8d to 4s 10d.[9] Moreover, cereal output and farm income were adversely affected by poor cereal harvests in 1848 and 1850.

Land also fell vacant as a result of eviction. During the period of the Famine, numerous tenants and cottiers were turned out of their holdings and plots under eviction orders, and in many cases their houses were leveled. In some areas of the west, entire townlands were left without habitation. Such wholesale evictions were popularly termed "the clearances."[10]

The extent of the dispossessions is difficult to quantify during the early part of the Famine. The main source of data is the ejectment figures furnished by the courts, which show that the number of ejectments served on tenant households increased substantially during the Famine from

19,704 in 1846 to 69,899 in 1848.[11] However, many of the ejectments obtained by landlords did not result in an eviction, since tenants, once they were served, often paid up their rent and were allowed to stay.[12] The publication of eviction figures by the constabulary office from 1849 revealed the true scale of the clearances. In 1849, 13,384 families (72,065 persons) were turned out of their holdings and not readmitted; in 1850, the figure rose to 14,546 families (73,871 persons). In 1851 the number of actual evictions was 8,815 families (43,449 persons), dropping further in the following year to 6,550 (32,160 persons). Thereafter, the rate of eviction substantially declined.[13] It should be noted that even when an eviction was executed, tenants could be readmitted. In each year, between one fifth and one third of those formally evicted were readmitted, usually those who were solvent. Examples of land agents who cleared the land and then readmitted those "who were capable of holding the land" were Marcus Keane in county Clare and Joseph Kincaid in Sligo and Mayo.[14]

The eviction figures may have underestimated the extent of dispossession on two counts. First, it is not clear how far evictions that did not involve a formal legal or ejectment process, mainly of subtenants who had no formal tenancy title, were included in the eviction figures. Arthur Kennedy, the temporary Poor Law inspector for the Kilrush Union, recorded many such evictions in that union in 1848 and 1849.[15]

Second, many evictions occurred under the guise of voluntary surrender. Tenants were prevailed upon by their landlords to give up possession, under the threat of eviction but with the inducement of a small cash handout and the waiver of rent arrears. Although not strictly speaking evicted, they often had little choice but to leave when faced with a landlord who had made up his mind to take the land and was prepared to offer financial incentives to induce them to leave. This option was favored by landlords and agents because it involved the minimum of fuss and expense. They were spared the necessity to engage in the bothersome litigation of the ejectment process and were able to avoid court and solicitor's fees, which could easily exceed any handout to the outgoing tenant. With voluntary surrender, confrontations with resistant occupiers were less likely, and unwelcome publicity was avoided. For the tenants facing destitution and starvation, even the offer of a few shillings could not be refused. In the Kilrush Union, for example, the vice-guardians reported in October 1848 that tenants were giving up land, having been allowed "a small sum" and promised "a discharge from all claims of rent on the house being thrown down and possession given up." In his return of evic-tions for the same union, Arthur Kennedy included the names of tenants on the property of Nicholas Westby in the Moyarta Electoral District who "compromised with the Agent and gave up their holdings with their own free will." [16]

Despite being so numerous, evictions were probably not as extensive a source of land as voluntary surrender. The eviction returns from the Kilrush Union from July 1848 to June 1849, furnished by Arthur Kennedy, listed 1,694 holdings (including about 200 cabins without any land at-tached) from which tenants were dispossessed. Nearly all were under 5 acres, with the average size between 2.5 and 3 acres. The amount of land that became vacant in the Kilrush Union as a result almost certainly did not exceed 5,000 acres.[17] The Kilrush Union was by no means untypical of other areas in the west that experienced clearances. In contrast, those who voluntarily surrendered their land and headed for the emigrant ship included a significant number who, as indicated above, were occupiers of moderately sized holdings (between 20 and 50 acres and with a Poor Law valuation above £10). Two or three of these holdings could be worth more in terms of acreage and valuation than the land forfeited by fifty small-holders. Thus, in determining the supply of land to the rental market, the size of holdings was as crucial as the number.

The immediate causes of the mass evictions in the western counties were twofold. First, tenants were turned out because of nonpayment of rent. On the smallholding estates in the west during the Famine, rents were not paid at all or paid partially and irregularly, even though tenants were constantly importuned by land agents. The reason for the nonpay-ment was not only the failure of the potato crop, a surplus of which pro-vided a small cash return, but also the sharp downturn in cereal prices during the Famine years and the poor grain harvests in 1848 and 1850. Furthermore, in certain unions in the west, tenants with holdings valued at £4 and above were impaired in paying their rent by steeply increasing poor rates, which siphoned off some of their much-needed cash. Cottiers who were supposed to pay rent on labor days (the work rent) were often prevented from paying because of the lack of agricultural work, or the inability to work due to disease and lack of sustenance.

A second reason for the mass evictions was the exemption from the poor rate granted under the Poor Law legislation to tenants with hold-ings below £4. For these holdings, the landlords were required to pay the full poor rate. Most affected by this, of course, were landlords in the western areas, whose tenants were preponderantly smallholders with farms under £4 valuation, and who were also subject to sharp increases in the poor rate poundage during the late 1840s. As a measure of the extent of their liability, in twenty Poor Law unions in counties Clare, Galway, Leitrim, Mayo, and Roscommon (excluding Clifden and Tuam in Galway), there were 129,012 holdings under £4 valuation in 1849 (totaling 860,995 acres and accounting for 30 percent of ratable land area) on which the landlords paid the full rate. This can be compared to 112,945 holdings of £4 and above. In several of these Poor Law unions, landlords paid the full rate on over 40 percent of the tenanted acreage. In contrast, in many eastern unions, landlords were fully ratable on less than 2 percent of total tenanted acreage.[18] The rate burden of western landlords was felt all the more acutely if the land on which they paid the full rate yielded little or no rent in return as a result of defaulting by the tenants. It became evident to them that to stop the decline in their economic position due to the increasing rate liability and falling rental returns, it was necessary to remove tenants with holdings under £4 valuation and relet the land in enlarged units.

The Reletting of Land to Graziers

The farms left vacant were then consolidated and, wherever possible, relet "to the best advantage" as extensive holdings to "a better and more industrious class of men."[19] Many of these were cattle and sheep graziers who, according to Henry Brett, wished to take advantage of the availability of a "great quantity of grasslands" in the west, especially through land distribution schemes.[20]

Two observers who separately visited the west of Ireland shortly after the Famine, James Caird, a Scottish agriculturalist and himself a grazier, and the physician and traveler Sir John Forbes, frequently adverted to the availability of large grazing farms, usually in excess of four hundred acres, from which, in many cases, the previous small occupiers had only recently been turned off. Indeed, Caird referred to graziers as now "the only class of large farmers in Ireland, occupying under a landlord, and really possessed of capital."[21] Many years after the Famine, writers and commentators such as Henry Coulter, Innes Shand, Hugh Sutherland, the French author Louis Paul-Dubois, Sir Ernest Barker, and the German writer Bernard Becker also visited the west of Ireland and from their conversations with local people recounted vivid stories of how the land was cleared during the Famine to make way for graziers. The same was true of various witnesses to two royal commissions several decades after the famine, the Richmond commission on agriculture of 1881 and the royal commission on congestion of 1906–1909.

The extent to which land was consolidated and rearranged in extensive farms is evident from Table 1. It is estimated that between 1845 and 1861 the total extent of land comprising holdings of 200–499 acres increased by nearly one million acres, a rise of 45 percent.[22] For holdings of 500 acres and above, the increase between 1845 and 1861 was estimated to be 700,000 acres, a rise of 55 percent. By contrast, as already indicated, the acreage and numbers of holdings under 50 acres declined sharply during this period. As shown in Table 1, most of the increase in the acreage of holdings of 200 acres and above occurred during the latter half of the 1840s. It should be noted that the vast majority of holdings in this category were grazing farms, which could be adduced from the very high percentages of usable land on such holdings devoted to pasture (87.2 percent for holdings of 200–499 acres, and 96.1 percent for holdings of 500 acres and above in 1853).[23]

The scale of the transfer of land from small occupiers to large graziers during the Famine period can also be ascertained from a comparison of the townland population and house figures in 1841 and 1851 contained in the county census books with the townland entries of ratable occupiers in the Griffith primary valuation books for three western poor law unions, Athlone, Tulla, and Belmullet. In this comparison it was possible to identify townlands in which small tenants had been displaced by extensive landholders. In Tulla Union, the land area of those townlands that had been cleared of smallholders and had passed into the hands of graziers was 7,652 acres (39 out of 262 townlands), which was 9 percent of the total land area of the union (14 percent of the total valuation of the union). In almost every case, one or two graziers took the entire townland. The land in question had a higher than average valuation at 10s per acre and was obviously much sought after as reasonable quality store pasture. In Belmullet, the area of the townlands that were totally depopulated and occupied by graziers was 24,018 acres (15 out of 176 townlands), comprising 14 percent of the total area. In Athlone, however, only 2,625 acres (11 out of 220 townlands), covering 3 percent of the land area, was so affected.[24]

A substantial amount of land let to graziers during the Famine period was rough mountain and moorland pasture of a very low valuation, usually well below 2s 6d per acre, commonly referred to as "wasteland" (the term "waste" had another meaning, referred to below, denoting vacant farms on cultivatable land). In many of the Poor Law unions of the west, especially in Connemara and along the Atlantic seaboard, there were vast stretches of rough mountain and moorland pasture. Such land could provide grazing for young cattle and sheep, although at very low stocking densities. Landlords increasingly saw an opportunity to exploit their reserves of rough pasture as a commercial resource by creating vast hill ranches, or by "adding mountain tracts to farms."[25] One example was the vast hill ranch of 70,000 acres which was let to the Scottish grazier Captain Houstoun in Westport in the 1850s, referred to below. Such land, together with bogland, was denoted officially as "uncultivated land" which was enumerated at just over 5,200,000 acres in 1851. However, the accuracy in enumerating "wasteland" acreage was seriously affected by the lack of clear and consistent guidelines for enumerators, and their frequent failure to differentiate "wasteland," such as rough pasture, from fertile land on the same holding.[26]

The letting of hill pastures to graziers was made possible either by the exodus of small tenants from their holdings through eviction or surrender, or by the abrogation of customary grazing rights. In upland and moorland areas, tenants often enjoyed grazing rights on such land, conferring upon them "the valuable privilege . . . of turning out cattle during the summer months, on the neighboring mountains, moors and wastelands." The sale of the cattle was one of the main sources of cash income for the small tenants. "It paid their rent, clothed them, and supplied them with milk to drink with their potatoes."[27] Grazing rights on rough hill pastures were nearly always held in common. The cattle and sheep of all the tenants within a townland were allowed to range freely over the same stretch of rough pasture, described as the "run of the mountain," and "each [tenant] had a common right to the whole."[28] A significant number of tenants who surrendered or were evicted from their holdings during the second half of the 1840s and the early 1850s also left behind large tracts of rough mountain and moorland pasture, which could then be relet to graziers. In some cases, though, landlords did not evict small tenants from their residential plots, but simply abrogated their rights to the common grazing, so that the land could be relet to a grazier. It was observed in the prefatory remarks to the agricultural return of 1853 that a number of holdings of five hundred acres and above had been created out of existing large holdings by the "addition of tracts of land hitherto returned as untenanted 'bog and waste' . . . encroaching upon the present system of grazing in common."[29]

One area where graziers displaced small tenants on rough upland and moorland pastures was Belmullet, referred to earlier. Most of the 14 percent of the land that was transferred from small tenants to graziers in this union between 1841 and 1855 consisted of lowly valued hill and moorland pastures. This was testimony to the increased willingness of landlords to regard such pastures as a commercial resource, which could be profitably exploited through ranching. Although landlords readily sought extensive grazier tenants for their vacant grasslands, the reletting of such land during the Famine years was not without difficulty. With rising rate liabilities and the temporary fall in agricultural returns from 1849 to 1853, demand for land lessened. During their tours of Ireland in 1849 and 1852, both Caird and Forbes noticed the number of grass farms still lying vacant. At Ballina, Forbes observed that "one proprietor has dispossessed all the cottagers except about five or six, over a tract of 1,500 acres; but like Lord Lucan, he has not yet obtained tenants for the large farms thus created."[30] In the hearings of both the House of Commons and House of Lords select committees on the Poor Law in 1849, it was repeatedly mentioned that much land in the west, formerly tenanted, was now lying "waste" (i.e., unoccupied).[31] In 1849, the land agent, Joseph Kincaid, found "it extremely difficult to get men with capital to undertake fifty, or an hundred or two hundred acre farms," even when he offered such farms at "much below their former rents."[32]

However, as cattle grazing became more profitable from 1853 and the fear of rate liabilities began to subside after the Famine, it is likely that landlords were able to let the vacant holdings that had been in their possession. Of the sixty-one townlands referred to above, in the unions of Athlone, Belmullet, and Tulla, where the tenant population had been displaced, only in eleven townlands was all or most of the land still unlet in 1855. In some cases, the retention of this land by the landlord may have been by choice rather than necessity.

Even when land was relet, landlords were often unable to secure the same rent per acre as paid by the previous smallholders, again the consequence of falling returns and rising rate liabilities. Indeed, in the words of Henry Brett, speaking to the House of Lords committee on the Poor

Law in 1849, "where [big tenants] are obtained, it is at a great reduction of rent." Another witness to the committee, Caesar Otway, a Poor Law inspector and writer, mentioned the unwillingness of graziers from Scotland to take grassland at the previous rents. As a result, in the words of Bernard Becker, the landlord "let his property to the hated foreigner for less than the natives had paid ... He let land by thousands of acres to Englishmen and Scotchmen at a pound an acre, whereas he had received twenty-five and thirty shillings from the starving peasants of Connaught."[33]

Why Land Was Relet to and Taken by Graziers

For the landlords, there were significant and obvious advantages in replacing small tenants with ranchers, which clearly outweighed any delay in letting the land or any shortfall in the rental value of the land. As already indicated, it relieved them of full poor rate liability. It also simplified estate management and guaranteed more regular rent payment. Landlords frequently had serious difficulties during the Famine years in collecting rents from a populous but severely destitute smallholding tenantry scattered in large numbers over an extensive area. The task required the tenants to be constantly harangued and importuned, and, not surprisingly, many were able to escape payment or were allowed to accumulate arrears. However, as the writer Hugh Sutherland put it, recalling the clearances of the Famine years, letting "the same land to half a dozen big graziers ... rid him (the landlord) of a lot of trouble and saved him the annoyance of constant agitation about excessive rents."[34] Moreover, he was guaranteed punctual and regular payments of the full rent. A rancher earning good profits was much less likely to evade paying rent than an indigent smallholder. This point was made by Bernard Becker on his visit to Ireland in 1880. He noted that during the Famine period, "great landowners in county Mayo had found it so difficult to get rent out of their tenants that they determined to let their land to large farmers only at such a price as they could get, but with the certainty that the rent whatever it was, would be well and duly paid, and there would be an end to the matter."[35]

The contrast was exemplified on the estate of Sir James Fitzgerald Mahon at Castlegar, county Galway. In 1849, he collected from his 307 smallholding tenants, by no means the most impoverished in the west of

Ireland, a total rent of £1,150, but was still saddled with outstanding arrears of £736. To make matters worse, in the same year, a further £300 of arrears had to be permanently written off. On the other hand, the yearly rents from his 13 large grazing tenants, amounting to over £2,000, were paid up promptly by the gale days, with hardly any outstanding arrears.[36]

To underpin the advantages in reletting to graziers, the newly created grass holdings were usually relet under medium-term leases (e.g., twenty-one years, thirty-one years, or three lives). Such leases allowed the estate owners greater control over their properties through the covenants inserted into the lease contracts, the most important being those that prohibited subdivision and subletting. The insistence on such covenants testified to the determination of landlords not to return to the social conditions and system of agriculture prior to the Famine.[37]

For their part, graziers and others with capital were induced to take the new ranch holdings by the prospect of good returns. Most graziers purchased their replacement stock, and so their gross margins (gross income minus variable expenditure, which largely consisted of cattle and sheep purchases) and net profits (gross income minus variable and fixed expenditure) were determined by the difference in price between the cattle when they were bought in and when they were sold nine to eighteen months later. That depended crucially upon price margins between stock of different ages in the market. An analysis of the price series in the *Irish Farmers' Gazette* and *Thom's Directory* shows that such price margins held up well during the main years of the Famine, 1845–49, but then narrowed substantially. The normal price margins for store graziers were about £4 per head until 1849, and then fell to about £2. The price margins for fattening graziers reached a healthy £7 per head during the Famine, but then dropped to £3–£5 per head. In both cases, price margins recovered strongly from 1853 to exceed even those of the Famine years.[38]

This trend was confirmed from the accounts of two graziers, Arthur Henry of Lodge Park, county Kildare, and William Filgate of Ardee, county Louth. Henry's ledger accounts show that his gross margins for a herd of 50 to 70 cattle during the famine period remained quite healthy, exceeding £300 (over 70 percent of variable expenditure). From 1849 they declined sharply, plummeting to a mere £134 (20 percent of variable expenditure) in 1851–52, but recovered strongly thereafter, exceeding £700 in 1853–54. On the grazing farm of William Filgate, gross margins from 1845 to 1850 were moderately good, in most years exceeding £150 (above

50 percent of variable expenditure). Also, from 1845 to 1849, Filgate expanded his cattle herd (consisting of both store and fat cattle) from 27 to 82, and his sheep numbers from 69 to 370. However, in 1850, he reduced his cattle herd to 42 and his sheep flock to 190, possibly a response to the unfavorable price trends that began in 1849. Unfortunately, Filgate's accounts end in the early part of 1851, so it is impossible to know how he fared during the downturn of 1849–53.[39]

It would appear, therefore, that ranch farming remained economically attractive during the main years of the Famine itself, which would have sustained the demand for both fattening and store pasture. However, from 1849 to 1853, profits were seriously squeezed, and some graziers may have found it difficult to make ends meet. In fact, Joseph Kincaid referred to the squeeze on ranch profits in 1849 since "store cattle purchased at very high prices in May last by graziers, sold . . . very low in October and November."[40] This explains the temporary dampening of demand for pasture referred to above. But as returns improved from 1853, that demand was revitalized. Underpinning the confidence of graziers was the burgeoning cross-channel trade in both stores and partly finished cattle, due to the demand from British fatteners and meat wholesalers.

Social Origins and Attributes of the New Graziers

Prominent in taking the newly created grass farms were local townspeople who had accumulated capital from retailing and services: shopkeepers, publicans, solicitors, auctioneers, and land agents. They sought a profitable outlet for their capital, and also the additional status that came from being an extensive landholder. They therefore availed themselves of the opportunity to acquire grassland. Shopkeepers were especially prominent in taking pasture, having built themselves up by providing retail services and credit to the local farming population. Ranch farming was an ideal parergon for shopkeepers and the like, given the small amount of supervision and labor it required. Only occasionally were they obliged to be absent from their place of business in order to attend to the cattle and sheep. This they could readily afford, since for many, outside market and fair days, business was often slack, allowing them sufficient time to visit the ranch.[41]

Among those who acquired land in the west during the Famine were existing graziers. Some lived in the locality and "if a poor man's land happens to join theirs . . . may often intrigue with the bailiffs and that class of man generally succeeded in getting the poor man out and absorbing his land."[42] Others from farther afield—from Leinster, the north of England, and Scotland—were lured by the availability of cheap land and the prospect of good returns. In 1849, Joseph Kincaid referred to the visit of "several deputations from England and Scotland to see unoccupied lands in counties Roscommon, Galway and Sligo. They were perfectly satisfied that there was a fair prospect of a return and they could get the land at a fair rent."[43] Landlords leasing extensive hill farms, in particular, were keen to attract the graziers from the north of England and Scotland in view of their experience and knowledge of upland grazing, as well as the capital they could invest in such enterprises.[44] When visiting the Tiernaur district of county Mayo nearly thirty years later, Bernard Becker was able to recount that in the Famine period the greater part of the local population was "swept away and the country reduced to a desert in order that it might be let in blocks of several square miles each to Englishmen and Scotchmen, who employ the land for grazing purposes only." In consequence, there now existed "perhaps a score or two of people where once a thousand lived—after a fashion."[45] One of the most extensive of the immigrant graziers was Captain Houstoun from East Lothian, who came to Ireland in 1857 and acquired a huge stretch of rough moorland pasture, over seventy thousand acres, in the Erriff Valley of Mayo between Westport and Leenane. The smallholding tenantry had been dispossessed by Lord Sligo, and the land was let to Houstoun on a ninety-nine-year lease at 4 1/2d per acre.[46]

Some of the new graziers had previously been rentier middlemen. Unlike other groups, they were attracted to cattle grazing more out of necessity than out of choice. The exigencies of the Great Famine and the general impoverishment of the peasant class led to a marked decline in their rents, as a result of which, in the words of Henry Brett in 1849, they "are now reduced to a very low condition."[47] This was all the more true if the landlord refused to grant an abatement of the head rent. To avoid financial ruin and dispossession, certain middlemen took the preemptive step of ejecting their subtenants. If they had not already lost too much capital, they may have recovered their fortunes by switching to grazing and stocking their land.[48]

Not all of the vacant farms that had been subsequently consolidated and enlarged into extensive holdings were relet. Certain landlords retained some of the vacant holdings in their immediate possession if they were unable to find suitable tenants or let the land at an acceptable rent. In other cases, landlords retained possession because of a desire to directly engage in ranching themselves. Whether by necessity or choice, landlords, as one prominent Poor Law guardian observed in 1849, "are getting more into grazing." Landlords, thereby, became graziers in their own right.[49]

The retailers, land agents, middlemen, and landlords in the west, as well as existing graziers (especially from the eastern counties and northern England and Scotland), provided the necessary money capital upon which the expansion of ranching in the west depended. Although the initial cost of establishing a ranch enterprise was not prohibitive (far less than for a tillage enterprise), a certain amount of capital was required at the outset to purchase a herd of cattle or a flock of sheep and a sufficient quantity of hay and other feed for wintering if so required, and also to pay the first installment of rent. The commercial elements referred to above were of sufficient means and liquidity to afford this initial expenditure.

In addition to being a source of capital, such elements provided the necessary entrepreneurship and commercial acumen, which were essential to creating and managing ranch enterprises. Part of the business acumen of the grazier was a willingness to take risks coupled with an ability to play the market to the best advantage. This included knowing when to buy and sell stock, at what age and in what quantity, and also knowing what fairs offered the best prices. Also part of the business acumen of the grazier were skills in keeping rudimentary accounts required when dealing with large numbers of cattle and sheep. In possessing such qualities, graziers were aptly described later in the century by the land valuer, Thomas Roberts, as "men with fairly good business ideas" and "fit to go it alone."[50]

Furthermore, when establishing a new ranch enterprise, it was equally important to possess a basic competence in pasture and stock management, and also an aptitude in judging the quality of cattle and sheep (from their appearance and conformation) in the sale ring. Such competence and judgment may have been initially lacking among shopkeepers and others with little previous experience of ranching, but would have been possessed by existing graziers, especially from the eastern counties, Scotland, and England.

Conclusion

Through the increased availability of land that could be converted to pasture and relet on competitive terms, the Famine created a major opportunity for the development of commercial ranching in the west of Ireland. As a result of the exigencies of the Famine, numerous small and medium farms had been left vacant through voluntary surrender or eviction, many of which were then consolidated and leased to graziers. The availability of a large quantity of land was essential for the development of ranching in view of its land-extensive nature, characterized by open pasture feeding, low stocking ratios, and low output per acre. Ranch businesses therefore required large tracts of pasture in order to yield a sufficient return.

While the growth of ranching was made possible by a land market created by the Famine, it also depended upon the conjunction of other conditions that happened to prevail during the Famine period. The most important of these were the availability of money capital and entrepreneurship, a pool of expertise in stock raising, and the prospects of profitable returns as a result of good price margins between cattle of different ages. Equally necessary was an expanding supply of young cattle that could be purchased by graziers to stock the new pastures. This was made possible in the 1840s by a reduction in the slaughter of calves. With the conjunction of these conditions, the Famine represented an important step in the development of commercial agriculture in the west of Ireland. This aspect of the Famine contrasted with the other more familiar aspect, namely, the human catastrophe of widespread starvation, suffering, destitution, and emigration.

Notes

1. *Returns of Agricultural Produce in Ireland in the Year 1850*, ix [1404], H.C. 1851, I, 1.

2. See agricultural report from the temporary Poor Law inspector for the Tuam Union, Jan. 23, 1849, in *Fourteenth Report from the Select Committee on Poor Laws (Ireland)*, appendix, 281, H.C. 1849 (577), 15, Pt. 2, 177 (chaired by Sir John Young; hereafter cited as *Young Comm., 14th Report*). See similar reports from vice-guardians and temporary Poor Law inspectors in other unions, ibid., 248–49, 260, 263, 283.

3. *Second Report from the Select Committee of the House of Lords Appointed to In-*

quire into the Operations of the Irish Poor Law . . . , 318–19, H.C. 1849 (228), 16, 301 (hereafter cited as H.L. Poor Law Comm., 2nd Report).

4. H.L. Poor Law Comm., 2nd Report, 37; 4th Report, 786, H.C. 1849 (365), 16, 543; Young Comm., 2nd Report, 9, H.C. 1849 (93), 15, Pt. I, 5.

5. Kerby Miller, Emigrants and Exiles: Ireland and the Irish Exodus to North America (New York: Oxford University Press, 1985), 287; James Donnelly, "The Administration of Relief, 1847–51," in A New History of Ireland, V: Ireland under the Union, 1: 1801–71, ed. W. E. Vaughan (Oxford: Clarendon Press, 1989), 323–26.

6. Agricultural report for the Westport Union, Jan. 22, 1849, in Young Comm., 14th Report, appendix, 283.

7. Young Comm., 7th Report, 75, H.C. 1849 (237), 15, Pt. 1, 415. For a similar observation, see Young Comm., 9th Report, 86, H.C. 1849 (301), 15, Pt. 1, 647; 13th Report, 10, H.C. 1849 (416), 15, Pt. 2, 173. See also H.L. Poor Law Comm., 1st Report, 95, 210, H.C. 1849 (192), 16, 1; 2nd Report, 308; 4th Report, 887; 5th Report, 950, H.C. 1849 (507), 16, 927; Miller, Emigrants, 294–96.

8. Return of the Gross Amount of Sums Levied under the Head of Poor Rates . . . in Scotland and Ireland, from 1840 to 1851 . . . , 3, H.C. 1852 (319), 45, 51; A Return for Each Union in Ireland of the Dates and Amount of the Last Rate Struck previous to the to the 1st day of March 1849, 1–18, H.C. 1849 (608), 47, 745; H.L. Poor Law Comm., 2nd Report, 37; Young Comm., 2nd Report, 9; 9th Report, 83.

9. Figures taken from "Prices of Irish Agricultural Produce—1830 to 1879," Irish Farmers' Gazette, Nov. 1, 1879. See also James Donnelly, "Production, Prices, and Exports, 1846–51," in Vaughan, A New History of Ireland 5, 1, 289.

10. For discussion of the clearances, see James Donnelly, "Landlords and Tenants," in Vaughan, A New History of Ireland 5, 1, 336–43.

11. Returns . . . of the Number of Ejectments . . . and of the Number of Civil Bill Ejectments . . . , 7 H.C. 1849 (315), 49, 235.

12. See Report from the Select Committee on the Kilrush Union . . . , 69, 91–92, 151, H.C. 1850 (613), 9, 529 (chaired by George Scrope; hereafter cited as Scrope Comm. Report); H.L. Poor Law Comm., 2nd Report, 311; 5th Report, 915; J. C. Wylie, Irish Land Law (London: Professional Books, 1975), 761–63, 766–71. See also Donnelly, "Landlords," 343–45.

13. Return by Provinces and Counties . . . of Cases of Eviction which Have Come to the Knowledge of the Constabulary in Each of the Years from 1849 to 1880 Inclusive, 3–23, H.C. 1881 (185), 57, 725.

14. Scrope Comm. Report, 91–92; H.L. Poor Law Comm., 2nd Report, 331.

15. Reports and Returns relating to Evictions in the Kilrush Union, 10–53 passim [1089], H.C. 1849, 49, 315 (hereafter cited as Eviction Reports and Returns, Kilrush).

16. Reports and Returns of Evictions, Kilrush, 30, 51; for references to landlords financially assisting small tenants to emigrate, see Miller, Emigrants, 296, 303–4, 312, 356; Donnelly, "Landlords," 337–39.

17. Calculated from Eviction Reports and Returns, Kilrush, 8–57.

18. Figures calculated from a return in H.L. Poor Law Comm., 6th Report, appendix, 145, H.C. 1849 (507–11), 16, 1019.

19. From testimony of Arthur Kennedy in Scrope Comm. Report, 89. For a simi-

lar observation, see *H.L. Poor Law Comm., 5th Report*, 915. See also Donnelly, "Landlords," 343–45.

20. *H.L. Poor Law Comm., 2nd Report*, 496.

21. John Forbes, *Memorandums Made in Ireland in the Autumn of 1852* (London: Smith Elder, 1853), vol. 1, 153–54; vol. 2, 35, 389; James Caird, *The Plantation Scheme; or, the West of Ireland as a Field for Investment* (Edinburgh: Blackwood, 1850), 3, 6, 16–23, 33–34, 44–45, 61–63, 84–85.

22. In 1845, the Poor Law commissioners furnished a return of the number of land occupiers in different acreage classes from under one acre to five thousand or more acres (statute acres) for all Poor Law unions. This was the first comprehensive return to discriminate acreage classes above thirty acres, and to enumerate land occupiers, as opposed to land holdings. The full citation is given in the Source for Table 1.

23. *Returns of Agricultural Produce in Ireland in the Year 1853*, vi [1865], H.C. 1854–55, 47, 1.

24. Figures calculated from *Census of Ireland for the Year 1851*, pt. i: *Area, Population and Number of Houses . . .* , vol. 2 *Province of Munster*, pp. 3–11, 34–42 [1552], H.C. 1852–53, 91, 383; vol. 4 *Province of Connaught*, 143–46, 179–86 [1542, 1555], H.C. 1852–53, 92, 339; Primary valuation books: Poor Law union of Athlone (1855); union of Tulla (1855); union of Belmullet (1855).

25. *Returns of Agricultural Produce in Ireland, 1853*, vi.

26. *Census of Ireland for the Year 1851*, pt. 2: *Returns of Agricultural Produce*, 6, 28 [1589], H.C. 1852–53, 93, 1.

27. G. J. Shaw-Lefevre (1st Baron Eversley), *Agrarian Tenures: A Survey of the Laws and Customs relating to the Holding of Land in England, Ireland and Scotland, and of Reforms therein during Recent Years* (London: Cassell & Co., 1893), 95; Bernard Becker, *Disturbed Ireland: Being the Letters Written during the Winters of 1880–81* (London: Macmillan Press 1881), 93.

28. Becker, *Disturbed Ireland*, 91.

29. *Returns of Agricultural Produce, 1853*, vi.

30. Forbes, *Memorandums*, vol. 2, 35. See also Caird, *Plantation Scheme*, 21, 34, 44–45, 84–85.

31. The meaning of "waste" here is to be distinguished from its other meaning (i.e., rough mountain pasture and bogland).

32. *H.L. Poor Law Comm., 2nd Report*, 317. For a similar view, see evidence of Henry Brett, ibid., 484.

33. *H.L. Poor Law Comm., 2nd Report*, 484; *4th Report*, 896; Becker, *Disturbed Ireland*, 38.

34. Hugh Sutherland, *Ireland Yesterday and Today* (Philadelphia: The North American, 1909), 67–68. For the difficulties in collecting rents in the famine period, see Donnelly, "Landlords," 334–36.

35. Becker, *Disturbed Ireland*, 38–39.

36. Rental of part of the estate of Sir James Fitzgerald Ross Mahon, situated in the County of Galway, 1850 (N.L.I., Mahon papers, MS 8553).

37. D. S. Jones, *Graziers, Land Reform and Political Conflict in Ireland* (Washington, D.C.: Catholic University of America Press, 1995), 172–75.

38. Calculated from "Prices of Irish Agricultural Produce—1830 to 1879," *Irish Farmers' Gazette*, Nov. 1, 1879; *Thom's Irish Almanac and Official Directory . . . 1849*, 487; *1853*, 501; *1858*, 551.

39. Calculated from Stock register and account book, Arthur Henry, Lodge Park, co. Kildare, 1840–57 (N.L.I., MS 23573); Farm account of the Lateboys farm of William Filgate, co. Louth, 1845–51 (N.L.I., Filgate Papers, MS 11945).

40. *H.L. Poor Law Comm., 2nd Report*, 316. See also *H.L. Comm., 4th Report*, 731; Donnelly, "Production, Prices, and Exports," 291–93.

41. Jones, *Graziers*, 82, 140–41, 150.

42. From evidence of Mathew Harris, *Report from the Select Committee on the Irish Land Act, 1870 . . .* , pt. 1, 271, H.C. 1877 (328), 12, 1.

43. *H.L. Poor Law Comm., 2nd Report*, 321, 487, 497.

44. Henry Coulter, *West of Ireland: its Existing Condition and Prospects* (Dublin: Hodges and Smith, 1862), 207, 244–45, 280–81; Becker, *Disturbed Ireland*, 37–40; A. Innes Shand, *Letters from the West of Ireland, 1884* (Edinburgh: Blackwood, 1885), 111–14; Ernest Barker, *Ireland in the Last Fifty Years, 1866–1916* (Oxford: Clarendon Press, 1917), 44.

45. Becker, *Disturbed Ireland*, 37.

46. Shand, *Letters*, 111–12; Becker, *Disturbed Ireland*, 73; Matilda Houstoun, *Twenty Years in the Wild West, or Life in Connaught* (London: John Murray, 1879), 36, 229, 232.

47. *H.L. Poor Law Comm., 2nd Report*, 504.

48. The fate of middlemen in the 1840s was discussed by Donnelly, "Landlords," 333–35. See also W. E. Vaughan, *Landlords and Tenants in Ireland, 1848–1904* (Dublin: Studies in Irish Economic and Social History, 1985), 1.

49. For references to landlords during the Famine who used the land after eviction to graze their own stock, see Caird, *Plantation Scheme*, 19, 23; Shand, *Letters*, 113; Becker, *Disturbed Ireland*, 36–39; George Pellew, *In Castle and Cabin, or Talks in Ireland in 1887* (New York and London: G. P. Putnam & Sons, 1888), 97.

50. *Report from the select committee on land acts (Ireland), together with the proceedings of the committee, minutes of evidence, appendix, and index*, 386 H.C. 1894 (310), 13, 1.

6

GEARÓID Ó HALLMHURÁIN

The Great Famine

A Catalyst in Irish Traditional Music Making

THE 150TH ANNIVERSARY of the Great Irish Famine has yielded an unprecedented wealth of publications from academic communities on
both sides of the North Atlantic. While many of these have rekindled the
polemics of revisionism and nationalism, others have sought to expose
the complex nuances of the tragedy through an examination of nontradi-
tional historiographical sources. Recent work on the folkloric and literary
evidence has thrown considerable light on the catastrophe from the *gemeinschaft* perspective of the Famine victims.[1] Similarly, regional surveys
by historical geographers, economists, and historical anthropologists
have emphasized the spatially selective impact of the Famine—which
found its primary victims among the *clachan* communities in the west of
Ireland.[2] Pitted within a cross-disciplinary perspective, the present study
will explore the impact of the Great Famine on Irish traditional music
makers, their folk repertoires, and above all their relationship with an
audience that was changed irrevocably by starvation, death, and diaspora.

Different perhaps from the official chronicles of the period, the *gemeinschaft* insight of the music maker offers a unique picture of Irish society
undergoing one of the most brutal mass fatalities in modern European
history. Although meager in content, the immediate song evidence in
Irish for the period 1845–1852 focuses ostensibly on the interwoven themes
of mortality, destitution, and emigration from the inside perspective of
the victims. Later on, the canon of emigration ballads, particularly those
which were popularized in urban America in the decades after the Famine, reveals a poignant sorrow in the wake of tragedy, together with a
retrospective politicization of the calamity in the immigrant mindset. Traditional music makers were particularly affected by the Famine cataclysm

and the subsequent diaspora of which they were part.[3] Thousands died with the immediate onslaught of starvation and disease, while others followed their audiences into exile in the New World. Those who were fortunate enough to survive and chose to remain in Ireland had to adapt to a new economic and cultural ethos which for the most part was radically different from the pre-Famine intimacy of the *clachan*—a nucleated cluster of farmhouses with communal holdings—and the townland, which sustained an indigenous corps of folk poets, dancing masters, and traveling musicians. Folkloric evidence is explicit in its treatment of pipers, fiddlers, and dancing masters ending their days in the workhouse, while contemporary collectors of traditional music reflect sadly on the silence that had been inflicted on the land of song by the Famine tragedy.[4] A century and a half after the Great Famine, the topography of traditional music making in the west of Ireland still bears the cultural scars of rural depopulation, while its dialectic landscape still mirrors the changes in land use that were imposed by the profit economics of post-Famine farming.[5] Any evaluation of the Famine as a watershed in Irish traditional music must contrast the pre-Famine environment of the music maker with that of his post-Famine successor. While focusing on the musician as an artistic figure in rural Ireland, it is critical to consider the extent to which this anonymous artist—who was both a performer and a folk composer—not only mirrors the Famine in his repertoire, but also tailors his craft to meet the exigencies of a new political and moral order in the wake of the tragedy.

Traditional Music and Song before the Famine

Contemporary chroniclers in the decades prior to the Famine left an eclectic set of records of Irish social life. Census commissioners and geographers, land valuators and colonial novelists, each in their own way drew attention to the enduring realities of poverty, social disaffection, and land hunger.[6] Travelers from England and mainland Europe also contributed to this mosaic of commentary and observation. Although collectors of traditional music, like Edward Bunting, George Petrie, and William Forde (the latter who collected for Patrick Weston Joyce), traveled extensively among rural communities in the years prior to the Famine, their focus was primarily musicological. Their published collections contain a variety of dance tunes, traditional airs, songs, and harp compositions, albeit in western art classical format. With the exception of Petrie and Joyce, the collectors were not concerned enough to tender a critical appraisal of the cultural environments of the traditional performers from whom they transcribed.[7] While the peasant collections of Bunting were being appropriated by Romantic nationalists like Thomas Moore and anglicized for a drawing-room populace, other less myopic observers were turning their attention to the hereditary keepers of music in rural Ireland. Mr. and Mrs. Samuel Carter Hall, who traveled throughout Ireland in the second quarter of the nineteenth century, have left a perceptive account of the dilemmas facing some uilleann pipers in the wake of Father Theobald Matthew's temperance crusade in the 1830s. Recounting their meeting with Rory Oge, a piper in Killaloe, county Clare, they recall:

> We followed the music, and after walking through a gathering crowd . . . we made our way into a tent, and were there introduced, not to the bard of the brave Brien, but to his successor, the village piper, and, perhaps one of the last of his *original* race—for the class is rapidly "going out;" faction-fights have altogether ceased, and dances are now-a-days, few and far between. The piper finds it a hard matter to live by his music. But his worse "enemies" are the "brass-bands" of the Temperance Societies; they are now becoming so numerous as to be found nearly in every town, and at the time of which we write, had attained sufficient popularity to make the old pipers, and their adherents, tremble for the results.[8]

In extolling the graces of the Temperance Society's brass bands, however, the authors add their own evangelical epilogue to their critique. They favor the building of humble assembly rooms to house temperance society meetings and recommend the circulation of instructive books to educate the victims of whiskey. Above all, they hope that the brass bands will increase:

> for the wonderful change that has been wrought in the habits of the people has unquestionably driven the piper and the fiddler out of fashion: and any mode of giving amusement extensively should be carefully encouraged. Indeed, it is absolutely necessary that some healthful excitement should be introduced to replace the unhealthy excitement formerly induced by whiskey.[9]

In contrast to these detailed if chiding observations of the Halls, Capo de Feuillide's interpretation of the role of the traditional musician is somewhat more discriminating. A journalist and literary critic writing at the height of the Romantic Movement in France, de Feuillide traveled throughout Ireland in 1837. His two-volume *l'Irlande*, pitched ostensibly within a prevailing climate of Romantic scholarship, was published in France in 1839. Echoing the sociopolitical tenets of his contemporary, Gustave de Beaumont, de Feuillide devotes considerable attention to the musical and literary traditions of the west of Ireland.[10] An implicit negligence and indifference toward the Irish language as a vehicle of music making characterized much of the Romantic nationalist movement in pre-Famine Ireland. This is particularly underlined in de Feuillide's work. Mindful of the complex cultural tensions between Irish-speaking rural communities and the colonial exterior, de Feuillide is critical of Thomas Moore's usurpation of songs in the Irish language. He posits that *"quant au peuple, il ne sait pas ce que c'est que Thomas Moore."*[11] He laments the passing of the harp, which has ceded its place to the piano in the drawing rooms of the ascendancy and, in the thatched houses of *le peuple,* to the uilleann pipes. Spending much of his time with Irish-speaking fishing communities in Connemara, de Feuillide noted the words of songs that he had dictated to him by his hosts. Reflecting on his experiences, he excuses himself humbly for not being able to transcribe their melodies.[12] Yet he describes in sensitive detail the nocturnal ambiance of the *ragairne*—house session—when community elders gathered around the turf fire to share their songs and dances.[13]

If, as Capo de Feuillide suggests, *"dans la langue du pays, poète et musicien sont synonymes, le mot barde, à lui seul, signifie l'un et l'autre,"* the sociological insight proffered by the Cork poet Mícheál Óg Ó Longáin throws significant light on the living conditions and social outlook of some traditional musicians in pre-Famine Munster.[14] In the bleak despondency of his poem *"Fuacht na Scailpe-Se,"* written in 1823 and translated from Gaelic here, he portrays an abysmal world of misery and hopelessness:

Fuacht na scailpe-se, deatach is gaoth gheimhridh,
cruas na leapa-sa 's easpa brait lae 's oíche,
muarchuid teacsanna, deachmhaithe 's glaoch cíosa,
tug buartha cathach mé, easpaitheach éagaointeach.[15]

The coldness of this sod hut, smoke and winter wind,
the hardness of this bed and the lack of a mantle day and night,
an abundance of taxes, tithes and rent calls;
filled me with sad lamentation, wanting and mournful.

While the physical hardships of Ó Longáin's environment correspond with similar portrayals by the Halls, Gustave de Beaumont, Capo de Feuillide, and others during the following decades, not all traditional performers shared his fate. In 1839, collector George Petrie, whose commentaries were heavily influenced by the Romantic Movement, reminds us that uilleann piper Patrick Conelly, one of his principal sources of music in Galway, lived in tolerably comfortable circumstances. According to Petrie, Conelly had a high opinion of his musical talents, and a strong feeling of decent pride. He played only for strong farmers and gentry, and would not lower his dignity by playing in a tap room. Blind from infancy, yet mindful of his superior status, Conelly would perform for commoners only on rare occasions.[16] But what of the communal entertainment of these commoners from whom Conelly dissociated in the late 1830s? It is clear that by now the new fashion of set dancing had become a vibrant pastime among these lower social orders.

Folkloric evidence suggests that quadrilles were introduced into Irish rural communities by soldiers returning from the Napoleonic wars. Evolving into traditional set dancing, these reached their apogee in the years between the end of hostilities and the onset of the Great Famine. Their popularity was such that even the Knight of Glin in West Limerick gave orders that dancing masters within his domain should teach this new dance form as it was danced in France and Portugal.[17] Various adaptations of quadrille figures developed during the 1830s and 1840s. The most prominent of these were the "Lancers," the "Plain Set," and the "Caledonian," the latter of which was believed to have been introduced into county Clare by Scottish sappers who came to work there for the ordnance survey commission. Other supposedly urban adaptations of the quadrille were the "Orange and Green," the "Paris Set," and the "Televara." Rivaling established solo dances, these new dance forms were propagated by dancing masters who were to be found among all social classes on the eve of the Famine. Writing in *The Limerick Reporter* and *Tipperary Vindicator* on November 8, 1867, historian and journalist Maurice Lenihan (1800–1895) recalled some of the dancing masters who were popular in his youth:

> In my youth the elder Garbois was the leading man in the South of Ireland as a teacher. Some used to say that he gallicised his name to appear fashionable, and that his real apostrophe was the old Irish one of Garvey. . . . He never appeared at school-hours except in full dress. His hair, which he wore in dark profusion, was oiled and curled and parted in the style of the Prince Regent. . . . The old dancing master . . . occupies a middle place between the fashionable Terpsichorean professor of the present day and

the village "hop merchant," who practiced the heel and toe step, and the cut and shuffle, à la Donnybrook, while preparing young boys and girls for the Sunday dance, at "cakes" or fairs, and who had been admirably described by William Carleton as performing on an unhinged door, or "welting the flure" in the village alehouse.[18]

Occasions of music making in rural Ireland prior to the Famine followed the cyclical calendar of the agricultural year. *Imbolg* (the feast of St. Brigit), *Bealtaine* (Mayday), *Lughnasa* (festival of the god Lugh in late July or early August), and *Samhain* (Halloween) marked the main coordinates of this cycle. Communal sowing, harvesting, and potato digging were planned in relation to climatic conditions on or around these feasts.[19] The completion of these time-honored rituals was usually celebrated with traditional music and dancing as the *meitheal*—cooperative workforce—of neighbors and extended kin congregated in *clachan* kitchens and at flagstone hearths. These celebrations often coincided with race meetings, fairs, and hurling matches. With the exception of patron days, orthodox Catholic festivals did not enjoy the same prominence as they did in post-Famine Ireland.[20] The custom of "hunting the wren" on St. Stephen's Day, which marked a high point in the musical calendar, was popular enough to merit a journal entry from Elizabeth Smith of Blessington, county Wicklow, in 1840.

> A regular reveille—The Wren—under our windows. What can have been the origin of this strange custom? Is it St. Stephen's day—the first martyr, who was stoned to death—and what has a little harmless bird to do with that? They hunt the poor little thing to death, then set it on a pole, fix a kind of bower around it and then carry it all over the country with musick and dancing and all of them dressed up with all the rags and ribbons and bits of coloured paper they can collect.[21]

On the eve of the Famine, patron days were celebrated with music and dancing as well as by various religious rituals and superstitions. In keeping with an internal matrix of townland traditions, values, and ritual associations, local saints were venerated at holy wells, at sacred trees and cairns, or at the site of an early Christian monastery. Although attracting musicians and dancers from their immediate hinterlands as well as traveling pipers and peddlers from afar, these quasi-religious festivities appear to have degenerated into excessive drinking and faction fighting in many areas. This led to their eventual suppression by the Catholic clergy in the decades after the Famine. Music collector Captain Francis O'Neill of

Chicago recalled that tents that sold refreshments at these pattern days had a resident piper to play for dancing when repentant customers had completed their "rounds" at the blessed well.[22]

Wakes and weddings were also occasions of music making. While the former were mainly the preserve of the mná caointe or professional keeners, the latter attracted a full complement of musicians, singers, and dancers—with pride of place going to the piper, whose presence was more important than "common" fiddlers and flute players. In his *Fairy Legends and Traditions of the South of Ireland* (1825–28), Thomas Crofton Croker notes that the best room at the wedding was reserved for the bride and bridegroom, the priest, the piper, and the more respectable guests like the local landlord and neighboring gentry. After the wedding, two collections were taken up, one for the priest and one for the piper.

There is little doubt that the piper enjoyed superior status among traditional musicians prior to the famine. His veneer of social prestige was based to some degree on archaic precedents established by the native harpers—whose demise at the end of the eighteenth century was counterpointed ironically by the rise in prominence of uilleann pipers. As the music collector Edward Bunting scurried to salvage the last of the native harp music in the 1790s, the uilleann or union pipes had reached their present state of development combining drones, chanter, and regulators to create what some commentators called the "Irish organ." Published music and instructional tutors for the pipes followed shortly afterward. In filling a musical void left by the harpers, the piper became the keeper of ancient airs, clan marches, and piping pieces often written as personal eulogies for his patrons. Beneath this quasi-aristocratic repertoire was a thriving mass of dance music played for set dancers by an anonymous corps of flute players, fiddlers, and whistle players. In the absence of instrumental music, sets were also danced to *portaireacht* or mouth music, which contained verses sung to the airs of common jigs, reels, and polkas. The latter practice survived in some isolated parts of the west of Ireland down to the present century.

Although many rural communities may have had their own resident musicians, itinerant dancing masters and pipers appear to have enjoyed considerable standing in western townlands. Both were carriers of news as well as social entertainment, and their arrival in a rural community generally prompted a *ragairne*—house dance—or *swaree*.[23] On the one hand, dancing masters stayed in a district long enough to teach a number of basic steps and figure dances and were given lodgings by one of their patrons in return for free tuition. The itinerant piper, on the other hand, tended to be a more mobile figure and was less bound to a settled clientele than his dancing cohort. Both followed regular circuits that were tailored to suit the cyclical work year of their audience. Walking distance was a critical factor in measuring the length of a circuit, and blind pipers often traveled in the company of a child upon whom they depended for guidance from place to place.

While the diversity of dance music and the status afforded to its performers attest to the popularity of solo and set dancing, the songs of the period offer a more penetrating index of social life in pre-Famine Ireland. Love songs constituted the most popular class of folk songs in Irish since the demise of the bardic schools in the seventeenth century. The collections made in the decades prior to the Famine confirm that love songs like *"Dónal Óg," "Úna Bhán,"* and *"Saileog Ruadh"* still enjoyed considerable popularity among Irish-speaking communities. All moods and emotions, "from the simple delight of the uncomplicated courtship to the numbed resignation following separation," are expressed in these songs.[24] Ironically, patriotic songs like *"Cáit Ní Dhuibhir," "Róisín Dubh,"* and *"An Druimín Donn Dílis"* were particularly scarce in Irish.[25] *Laoithe Fiannaíochta* (Fenian lays) was another genre of popular song to survive in Irish down until the Great Famine. Recounting the adventures of the mythological Fionn and the Fianna, the *laoithe* were filled with otherworldly creatures, enchanted ladies, invasions, and foreign expeditions.

Recalling his childhood in pre-Famine Clare, Eugene O'Curry proffers the following glance at the *laoithe* and their audience:

> I have heard my father sing these Ossianic poems, and remember distinctly the air and manner of their singing; and I have heard that there was a man named Anthony O'Brien, a schoolmaster, who spent much of his time in my father's house, and who was the best singer of Oisín's poems that his contemporaries had ever heard. He had a rich and powerful voice, and often, on a calm summer day, he used to go with a party into a boat on the river Shannon, at my native place, where the river is eight miles wide . . . On which occasions Anthony O'Brien was always prepared to sing his choicest pieces, among which were no greater favorites than Oisín's poems.[26]

The remaining store of songs in Irish was comprised of working songs, religious songs, the *caoineadh* or lament, humorous and satirical songs, as well as lullabies and children's recreational songs. Among the genres of Irish songs to perish during the Great Famine were songs of the supernatural. Fairy lore was an indigenous feature of Irish-speaking communities, whose songs acted as natural carriers of that tradition. The work of Petrie and O'Curry gives extensive coverage to songs of fairy abduction, changelings, and musical exchanges with the fairies. Both testify to the ardor of these beliefs among rural communities throughout the west of Ireland.[27]

The dispersal of English throughout most of the country during the eighteenth and early nineteenth centuries was precipitated by a major loss of traditional songs in Irish. Just as new dance forms replaced old ones, songs in English as well as bilingual macaronic songs had begun to replace songs in Irish in many parts of the west of Ireland by the 1840s. Both traditions, however, appear to have coexisted in some port hinterlands like Kilrush, Dungarvan, and Galway, where adjacent *Gaeltacht* communities prolonged the lifespan of Irish songs.[28]

Musicologist Breandán Breathnach has pointed out that folk songs in the English language fall broadly into two categories, namely, English and Lowland Scottish and Anglo-Irish songs, both of which genres enjoyed considerable popularity on the eve of the Famine. The first and older genre was brought to Ireland initially by English and Lowland Scottish settlers during the seventeenth-century plantations, and were reinforced by Irish navvies, tattie hookers, and bothy bands during the past two centuries.[29] On the one hand, many ballads were also dispersed through ballad sheets printed in England and circulated in Dublin and other towns along the east coast.[30] Songs that reached post-Famine audiences in this way include "Lord Baker," "Captain Wedderburn's Courtship," and "Barbara Allen." Anglo-Irish folk songs, on the other hand, were composed by Irish people whose mother tongue was English. One noticeable feature of these compositions in the decades prior to the Famine was a growing preoccupation with authorship. Unlike orally transmitted songs in Irish—in which authorship was an obscure concept—the Anglo-Irish ballad is frequently indexed according to its author and his agenda, hence its importance in the literary accomplishments of figures like Thomas Moore, whose Regency lyrics helped to gentrify Irish music in the early 1800s.[31] In contrast to the Irish-speaking folk composers from whom he culled traditional melodies, Moore claimed that his drawing-room songs, with their stage-Irish effusions of *mavourneens* and *acushlas*, were composed for "the pianofortes of the rich and educated." [32]

As with the older corpus of folk songs in Irish, love songs predominated in this newer genre, while every political movement from the rising of 1798 to the outbreak of the Great Famine had its own corps of balladeers. On the eve of the Famine, the writers of *The Nation*, which had been established by the Young Irelanders in 1842, set out to generate a new era in ballad compositions. *The Times* of London described their poems and ballads as being far more dangerous than the speeches of O'Connell. As well as attempting to rally popular support for rebellion, their songs helped to politicize the Famine catastrophe and, as such, enjoyed considerable patronage among middle-class nationalists on both sides of the North Atlantic throughout the latter half of the nineteenth century. [33]

Like composers of seditious songs, singers of seditious songs were considered equally guilty by the legal system in pre-Famine Ireland. Reminiscent of former edicts against pipers, rhymers, and harpers, court depositions for the period 1798–1841 contain an abundance of records of ballad sellers who plied their wares at street corners and marketplaces throughout the country. In his seminal work, *Narrative Singing in Ireland: Lays, Ballads, Come-All-Yes and Other Songs*, Hugh Shields provides the following account of ballad singer Denis Sheehan, who claimed that "the young persons of the country" had a strong preference for his more seditious ballads. On May 4, 1841, Sheehan was arrested

> for singing "The Brave Spalpeen Fanough". Over a period of sixteen months from January 1840, he says he ranged through the towns of Munster and the West Midlands: Thurles, Cashel, where he bought a pound's worth of ballads for four shillings, Tipperary, Limerick, where he spent four months, Ennis, Gort, Loughrea, Ballinasloe, Athlone, Roscommon, Boyle, Tuam, Galway, Ballinasloe, Birr, Nenagh, Limerick, where he spent another six months, Tralee, where he got married, Macroom, Cork, Bandon and Dunmanway, where he got arrested. [34]

While the English language was making strong inroads as a musical vernacular in urban areas, most communities in western townlands were still conducting their music making through the medium of Irish. In one count, there were approximately 62,205 townlands in pre-Famine Ireland, some consisting of one or two houses on one-acre plots. The average three-hundred-acre rural townland, however, contained fifteen to thirty families, most of whom were related and shared common surnames.[35] In appraising the cultural landscape of these townlands in the 1840s, historian Robert James Scally has pointed out:

> Regional differences in their size, their wealth, and building styles undoubtedly existed and distinguished the poorest from the more prosperous and from those that had been more or less transformed by the intrusion of commerce and goods radiating from the metropolis. Virtually all had felt the effects of these influences to some degree before the famine, especially those within the immediate orbit of the port and the market town. But even in these the persistence of traditional areas in material and mental life remained quite stubborn until hunger and emigration transformed them forever.[36]

On the eve of the Famine, social organization in the isolated uplands, blanket bogs, and shoreline settlements of the west of Ireland was influenced unambiguously by the rural *clachan*. The *clachan*—or *baile*—was a nucleated cluster of farmhouses within which holdings were organized communally, "frequently on a townland basis and often with considerable ties of kinship between the families involved." [37] Life within these communities was underpinned precariously by a potato diet, lazy bed cultivation, and a scattering of rundale plots which allowed land of varying quality to be shared by the community on an egalitarian basis. These rundale *clachan* housed nearly three-quarters of the population of Ireland prior to the Famine.[38] Historical geographer Kevin Whelan has pointed out:

> This type of settlement became practically universal on the poorer lands of the west of Ireland in the pre-famine period. They were an ingenious adaptation to the environmental conditions of the west of Ireland, where tiny patches of glacial drift were frequently embedded in extensive areas of bog or mountain. Collective use of the infield maximized utilization of the limited amount of arable land provided by those drift pockets. . . . Economic development, underpinned by the potato, rundale and clachan, and the lazy bed, engineered a massive shift in population density from east to west, from good land to poor land, and from port hinterlands and river valleys to bog and hill fringes. . . . The new areas of settlement were concentrated along the ragged Atlantic fringe, and on bog and hill edges. Rundale villages, powered by the potato, acted as a mobile pioneering fringe; the spade and the spud conquered the contours.[39]

Judging by the itineraries of the great collectors, and especially those of George Petrie and Eugene O'Curry in the period 1821–1857, it would appear that much of the traditional music collected in rural Ireland prior to the Famine was acquired from *clachan*-based informants. This is evident in the extensive corpus of dance music and song which Petrie published from informants on the Iorrus Peninsula in southwest Clare, Connemara, Mayo, the Iveragh Peninsula in Southwest Kerry and the blanket boglands of west Limerick. Petrie himself wrote:

> The music of Ireland has hitherto been the exclusive property of the peasantry—the descendants of the ancient inhabitants of the country. The upper classes are a different race—a race who possess no national music; or, if any, one essentially different from that of Ireland. They are insensitive to its beauty, for it breathed not their feelings; and they resigned it to those from whom they took everything else, because it was a jewel of whose worth they were ignorant. He, therefore, who would add to the stock of Irish melody must seek it, not in the halls of the great, but in the cabins of the poor.[40]

Of all the social classes in pre-Famine Ireland, few have received the same attention from music makers as the *spailpín*, or landless laborer. According to the Devon Commission, which was set up in November 1843, farm workers on the eve of the Famine could be divided into three categories: the unmarried farm servant living with his employer, the married laborer holding his own cabin and a small plot of land from a farmer at a fixed rent, and the *spailpín* holding nothing other than a cabin and obliged to hawk his labor wherever he found work. The latter survived largely on a system of conacre in the hope of growing enough crops to pay his rent and keep food on his table. Earning as little as eight pence to a shilling a day, the *spailpín*, the commissioners declared, belonged to the most "wretched of the many wretched classes in Ireland." To supplement the taking of conacre in times of crisis, the *spailpín* was obliged to become a temporary migrant worker.[41] This was particularly common among mountainy and bogland communities in the west of Ireland, from where the *spailpín* was dispatched to find work with "a strong farmer" along the riverine pastures of the Shannon and the fertile plains of Munster and Leinster. The scorned ritual of lining up to be "measured" at the "hiring fair" as hay making and potato digging beckoned from the nearby hinterland is well attested in the songs of the *spailpín*. Little had changed since the eighteenth-century Kerry poet described the contempt with which he was treated by the "big farmers" of Tipperary in the song *"An Spailpín Fánach"*:

Go deo deo arís ní raghad go Caiseal
Ag díol ná ag reic mo shláinte,
Ná ar mhargadh na saoirse ina shuí
  cois balla
I'm scaoinse ar leathtaoibh sráide—

Bodairí na tíre ag tíocht ar a gcapaill

Dá fhiafraí an bhfuilim hirálta.
O ! téanamh chun siúil, tá an
  cúrsa fada;
Seo ar siúl an spailpín fánach.[42]

I'll never again go to Cashel
Selling and bartering my health,
Nor at hiring fair sit down against
  a wall
Nor hang about the street—

The boors of the district coming
  on their horses
Asking if I'm hired.
O ! Start your walking, the journey
  is long
It's off with the wandering laborer.

One of the primary victims of the Great Famine, the *spailpín* is also re-membered in piping airs like *"Caoineadh an Spailpín"* (Lament for the Spailpín) and the song *"A Spailpín, A Rúin"* as well as in the Conamara song *"Peigín is Peadar,"* a versified form of a prose folk tale recounting the adventures of a *spailpín* who returns to his family after spending twenty-one years in service.[43]

If the *spailpín* received his share of posterity from the musician and songwriter, so too did his main staple, the potato. According to tradition, the potato was introduced to Ireland by the Tudor adventurer Sir Walter Raleigh. Originating in the Andean Highlands of South America, the po-tato created agronomic conditions in Ireland in which a landless cottier class could survive by tilling land with no capital other than a spade and a *ciseán* or basket of seed potatoes. In the half century before the Famine, this class proliferated at an unprecedented rate in Ireland despite its loca-tion at 20 degrees latitude farther north of the equator than any other class of its kind.[44] The life-giving importance of the potato did not escape the attention of the folk poet and music maker on the eve of the Famine. Corroborating the maxim *Dá mbeadh fataí is móin againn, bheadh ár saol ar ár dtóin againn* (If we had potatoes and turf, we would have life on our rear ends), the musician, singer, and dancer extolled the potato and the rituals associated with its cultivation. Writing in Dublin in 1880, Sir Wil-liam Wilde recalls his own memories of dancing in Roscommon, espe-cially the dance of the "planting stick"—*"Maide na bPlanndaí"*:

> There, the cake was generally fixed on the top of a churn-dish, which was
> set upright in the ground, and tied over with a clean cloth; and a fiddler
> and piper alternately lilted up their jigs, reels and planxties to the tunes
> of the *"Foxhunter's Jig,"* *"Miss McLeod's Reel,"* the *"Batha Buidhe"* or

"Drive the Geese to the Bog"; while between the more general dancing some one would step forward and to the tune of *"Madah-na-plandie,"* "the planting stick," imitate in pantomime dance the tilling, planting and digging of the potato.[45]

A solo dance, *"Maide na bPlanndai"* was danced to the air of the jig "Bryan O'Lynn." Similarly, other jigs like "The Gander in the Pratie Hole" and "The Frost Is All Over" underline the extent to which potato rituals were acknowledged in the repertoire of the traditional musician. Singers too paid their homage to the potato, as the following stanza declares:

Ba iad ár gcaraid iad ó am ár gcliabháin
Ach is é mo dhiobháil iad imeacht uainn
Ba mhaith an chuideacht iad is an t-údar rince
Bhíodh spóirt is siamsa againn in aice leo.[46]

They were our friends from the cradle
But their departure from us is my loss
They were good company, an excuse for dancing
We had fun and entertainment with them.

If poverty and the potato conspired to keep the bulk of the population on the precarious brink of subsistence, the successive potato blights of 1845–48 brought the world of the *spailpín* and the *clachan* to ruination. With the onslaught of famine, disease, and panic-stricken emigration, the music maker too went the way of his audience—to the mass grave, the workhouse, and the coffin ship. In the resulting diaspora, his trade would find its way to the sidewalks of Brooklyn, the music halls of vaudeville, and the lace-curtain parlors of Irish America. It would also find its way to the street corners of Camden Town, the cotton mills of Lancashire, or succumb sadly to vagrancy on the crime-infested waterfront in Liverpool, where the immigrant businesses had become as vicious as the recently abolished slave trade. For the traditional musician who was lucky enough to survive, the dour silence of post-Famine Ireland would eventually make new demands on his folk art and impose new priorities on his cultural habitat.

Traditional Music and Song after the Famine

The degree to which these traumatic events are recounted in the traditional music of the period is selective but by no means sparse. While the titles of dance tunes recall nothing of the catastrophe, a small corpus of songs in the Irish language bears poignant witness to the horrors of the tragedy in western rural areas. *Gaeltacht* songs like "Soup House Mhuigh-Iorrais" (from Connemara), *"An Droch-Shaoghal"* (from Uíbh Laoghaire, West Cork), and *"Amhrán na bPrátaí Dubha"* (from Ring, county Waterford) all voice the gruesome themes of hopelessness, disease, and deprivation from the internal perspective of suffering communities. Surprisingly few of these songs blame the political powers in Dublin or London explicitly for their misfortune. Neither do they chronicle the roles being played by the major political architects of the day—from Peel in the early years of the Famine to Trevelyan and Lord John Russell during the latter years. Any ire they exhibit is directed toward local landlords, bailiffs, proselytizers, corn dispensers, clerics, and Poor Law guardians. As well as indexing local fatalities, hunger, and emigration, the Irish songs also lament the lack of gaiety and courtship, music and matchmaking which clearly characterized the social life of rural communities before the Famine. A brief catalog of song themes and their related circumstances from south Connaught and west Munster will suffice to expose the wealth of local insights proffered by these folk scribes.

One of the last surviving Famine songs in the vernacular *sean nós* tradition of Connemara is "Johnny Seoighe," which was collected by Séamus Ennis from Colm Ó Caoidheáin of Glinsce, Carna, in 1945. Composed possibly by local scribe Tomás Shiúnach (or one of his contemporaries, Brídín Ní Mháille or Mícheál Mharcuis Mac Con Iomaire), the song is a personal request by the poet to Johnny Seoighe, who was responsible for dispensing corn to Famine victims in Carna. The singer has been refused entry to the local workhouse and appeals directly to Seoighe for "relief" for his wife and child. The song opens with the singer's optimistic appeal for charity. To strengthen his case, he eulogizes Seoighe and then implores God's blessing on his quest for food.

Is tú bláth na hóige is gile lóchrann	You are the flower of youth, the whitest lantern
A dhearc mo shúil ó rugadh mé	That my eyes have seen since I was born
Is as ucht Chríost tabhair dom relief	In the name of Christ, give me relief
Nó go gcaitear ithe Nollaig féin[47]	For one must eat even at Christmas

In the second stanza, the starving singer pleads his case further. The reference to his "wife and child out under the dew" reinforces the feeling of hunger and desperation, as well as an implicit sense of beholding to Seoighe, who now becomes a more respected "Mr. Joyce" in the remaining verses.

O lárnamháireach sea a fuair mé an páipéar	The following day I got the paper
Is nach mé bhí sásta is mé dhul chun siúil	And wasn't I happy starting my journey
Mar ní bhfuair mé freagra ar bith an lá sin	Because I had got no answer that day
Ach mo bhean is mo pháiste amuigh faoin drúcht	And my wife and my child out under the dew
Is a Mhister Joyce tá an workhouse lán	And Mr. Joyce, the workhouse is full
Is ní ghlacfar ann le haon fhear níos mó[48]	And they won't accept even one more man

Though the explicit message of the song appears to be clear and unambiguous, local folklore in Carna can read another more satirical message of deception and exploitation "between" the lines of "Johnny Seoighe." Oral history recalls that Seoighe (Mr. Joyce) tried to unseat Seán Mac Donncha from his position as a distributor of relief tickets in Carna. Mac Donncha was regarded as an honest man. Joyce, on the other hand, was an "outsider" with a reputation for corruption. In the ensuing dispute, Joyce convinced his lady friend, Peg Barry (daughter of a bailiff on the local Martin estate), to swear false testimony against Mac Donncha in Roundstone Courthouse. Such intrigue may well explain the reluctance of singers in the Carna area to sing the song in public.

While most of the Famine songs in Irish were composed by anonymous folk poets, "Na Fataí Bána" (The White Potatoes) was written by Peatsaí Ó Callanáin (1791–1865), a comfortable farmer with twenty acres of land near Craughwell in east Galway. Recalling the widespread suffering and hardship of his less well-off neighbors, Ó Callanáin's requiem recalls their traditional dependence on the potato. The first seven verses of his song eulogize the white potatoes and the sustenance they offered to young and old alike. It then focuses on the autumn blight of 1846, which he sees as an apocalyptic twist of fate, a heavenly sign that "the potatoes of the world" are rotting.

Nach é seo an scéal docharnach ag tíocht an Fhómhair	Isn't it a sad story now with the coming of autumn

An t-údar bróin dúinn agus briseadh croí	The cause of our sorrow and heartbreak
An bheatha a chleachtamar i dtús ár n-óige	The life that we led at the start of our youth
Bheith lofa dreoite gan mhaith gan bhrí	Rotten and empty without worth or meaning
Míle bliain agus ocht de chéadta	It's a thousand and eight hundred years
Dhá fhichead gan bhréig is sé ina cheann	Forty and six years no lie
Ó thuirling an Slánaitheoir i gcolainn daonna	Since our Savior descended in human form
Go dtáinig léanscrios ar fhataí an domhain[49]	Until the potatoes of the world rotted

Ó Callanáin states pessimistically that the poorhouse and the hospital are full. Bodies are now being buried on boards, and those who survive are eating *min bhuí* (yellow meal) twice daily. Complaint follows complaint throughout the closing stanzas. He is particularly critical of the poor wages given to those who work on the public work schemes, which are most ineffective in countering the hopelessness of the countryside. In the following two stanzas, he contrasts the flagrant indifference of the rich, whose tables are laden down with food and drink, with the helplessness of the hungry poor who no longer have the will to live.

Gan ór gan airgead, gan chreidiúint shaolta	Without gold or silver, without belief in life
Gan tnúth le tréan againn ach amháin le Dia	With no expectation of survival; longing for God
Ach muintir Shasana ag tabhairt páí lae dhúinn	But the people of England giving us a day's pay
Dhá bhonn ar éigin gan deoch gan bia	Barely two coins without drink nor food
Tá daoine uaisle i mbuaic an tsaoil seo	There are noble people at the pinnacle of life
Tá puins is, fíon acu dá n-ól ar chlár	Drinking punch and wine from their table
Tá feoil dá halpadh acu go méirleach craosach	Devouring meat with gluttonous spite
Gan trua ná daonnacht do fhear an chaill[50]	Without pity or charity for the man of need

A graphic folk recollection of the Famine on the Dingle Peninsula, *"Amhrán an Ghorta,"* is a penetrating appraisal of the tragedy in an area that suffered huge population depletion. According to local tradition, the song was composed by an anonymous female—possibly from Baile na nGall. Her song echoes Ó Callanáin's account of hunger and crop failure in south Connaught. As well as issuing a scathing attack on the local Poor Law guardians *"a bhí os cionn súip, is ná roinnfeadh é"* (who were in charge of the soup and did not distribute it), she laments the lack of gaiety, courtship, and music making which the hunger precipitated. Her observations were to prove astute and long-term.

Tá scamall éigin os cionn na hÉireann	There is some (dark) cloud over Ireland
Nár fhan dúil i gcéilíocht ag fear ná ag mnaoi;	Men and women desire no courtship;
Ní athníonn éinne des na daoine a chéile,	The people do not recognize each other,
Is tá an suan céanna ar gach uile ní.	And the same lull has befallen everything.
Ní miste spéirbhean bheith amuigh go déanach	An enchanted lady does not mind staying out late
Níor fhan aon tréine ins na fir a bhí,	With no strength left in the men that were,
Níl ceol in aon áit ná suim ina dhéanamh	There's no music anywhere nor a desire to make it
Is ní aithním glao cheart ag bean chun bídh[51]	And I hear no clear call to food from any woman

There is little doubt that the Great Famine marked a radical watershed in the history of Irish traditional music. In its wake, the Irish-speaking habitat of the musician was changed irrevocably. The former intimacy of the *clachan* and the townland was virtually erased, and in its place lay a materialistic world of profit economics and conservative social mores. In the resulting upheaval, archaic traditions like work songs and fairy laments, potato dances and *rogairne* gatherings, which were popular before the cataclysm, were gradually abandoned. Conversely, political ballads and emigrant songs, which were once peripheral, now became commonplace. In the west of Ireland, the accelerated transition from Irish to English as a song medium eroded further the *gemeinschaft* mindset of the *clachan*. Likewise, popular superstitions and folk beliefs associated with music, and especially songs in the Irish language, failed to translate into narrow-gauge English.

New songs in English were introduced from a broader *gesellschaft* exterior and they in turn interpreted the Famine in a manner that was different from the insights proffered by folk poets in Irish-speaking western communities. Some were nationalist ballads that viewed the famine as a callous act of British imperialism; others were songs of emigration that recalled the catastrophe in the midst of exile and loneliness. The nationalism of the Young Irelanders and the separatism of the Fenians both found their voices in the popular English ballads of the post-Famine period. In urban America, the songs of the Young Irelanders helped to retrospectively politicize the Famine in the immigrant mindset, while in Ireland the Fenian poets drew heavily on the emergent theme of Famine genocide to justify their separatist agenda. This retrospective politicization eventually found its way into local Famine songs which were written in English years after the events they describe. The Clare song "Lone Shanakyle" is a case in point. In focusing on the appalling reality of crowded workhouses, cartloads of uncoffined bodies, and quick-lime burials, the exiled Kilrush poet Thomas Madigan (1797–1881) laced his message of loneliness with a compelling series of nationalist metaphors. His song of exile is also a powerful political requiem to the 3,900 people who died in the workhouse in Kilrush in the years 1847–49, and who were buried in a mass grave in Shanakyle outside the town on the lower Shannon.

> Far, far from the isle of the holy and grand
> Where wild oxen fatten and brave men are banned
> All lonely and lone in a far distant land
> Do I wander and pine for poor Érin.
>
> Sad, sad is my fate in this weary exile,
> Dark, dark is the night cloud o'er lone Shanakyle
> Where the murdered sleep silently, pile upon pile
> In the coffinless graves of poor Érin.[52]

Regardless of Madigan's political intentions, his potent images of hunger and human suffering are well confirmed in the contemporary Poor Law reports of Captain Kennedy, who inspected the region between mid-November and late December 1847. Writing to the commissioners in Dublin on November 18, he said:

The admissions to the workhouse amounted to 200 in the past week. Such a tangled mess of poverty, filth and disease as the applicants presented, I have never seen. Numbers in all stages of fever and small pox mingled indiscriminately with the crowd and all clamoring for admissions. . . . Paper could not convey a description of the horrors and misery concentrated among two hundred persons.[53]

The Famine years were marked by a vigorous proselytism that was orchestrated by colonies of Protestant evangelists throughout the west of Ireland. The promise of soup and the hope of survival drove many a starving convert to abandon one form of Christianity for another. For "soupers" or "jumpers" who survived the Famine, the stigma of their conversion would haunt them and their families for generations. Few were given the benefit of their newfound convictions, at least by the folk scribes of the day. Writing on the social consequences of proselytism during the famine in county Mayo, Corduff points out that the satirist Michael McGrath in Erris

composed a number of songs condemning the Protestant religion, its founders, its apostate disciples who roamed the county making Catholic "perverts," and the "jumpers" of the time who deserted the Church. There is no doubt whatever, that these songs were sung out at festive gatherings and were in themselves a powerful influence in preserving the religious status quo in Erris.[54]

Other conversions to Protestantism were hastened by the zealousness of some clerics who regarded the catastrophe as a cue to purge the countryside of its incumbent sinners. The synods of Thurles and Maynooth (organized by the Catholic hierarchy in 1850 and 1875) unleashed a liturgical revolution which was to have a profound impact on post-Famine Ireland.[55] Henceforth, the role of the priest as social arbiter and moral policeman became sacrosanct—especially in rural areas where spontaneous communal entertainment had been the norm. Hunting the countryside for courting couples and purging fiddlers from crossroad dances, some priests conducted their own personal crusades against traditional musicians, who were seen as instigators of immoral pastimes in the post-Famine decades. Not all of these crusades, however, had the desired effect of quelling the enthusiasm of traditional performers. Tom Kennedy, the blind piper who gave the collector Canon James Goodman several hundred tunes in the 1850s, turned Protestant "and joined the souper colony at Ventry" on the Dingle Peninsula after being continually harassed by Fr. John Casey, parish priest of Feriter.[56] In referring to this episode, musicologist Breandán Breathnach posits that:

> A pathetic story current in folklore must relate to this incident. When Bishop Egan came to confirm children in the parish, an old infirm piper stationed himself on the road between the chapel and the priest's home, knowing that after the confirmation the bishop retired there for dinner. The lame piper stood in the road on the approach of the bishop and asked his permission to play at dances and gatherings, declaring that he had not the use of his limbs nor any other means but his pipes to earn the bit to put in his mouth. The boorish and unfeeling reply was "O, Father John must know what the position is and what suits."[57]

Father Casey's zeal for cleansing his parish of pipers is explicitly recounted in the diaries of Archdeacon John O'Sullivan, the former's colleague in Dingle. Describing a christening where Casey had to contend with a piper from an "outside parish," O'Sullivan says:

> The young people should have a dance and they had taken care before dinner to send to Dingle parish for a piper on the bounds of which one lived who would now and then make incursion into Casey's territory in spite of him. The piper, evidently in bodily fear of Casey, was induced to strike up, and jigs and reels and country dances were carried on with great vigor . . . the mirth and humor began to increase when Doctors Hickson and Fagan got up on a table to dance a jig on it, at which the shouting and cheering and laughing rose beyond all bounds so much so as completely to bother and confuse old Casey who was baptizing the child in the kitchen. He ran out in a fury with his stole on him and when he saw the two Doctors on the table, his whole parish again gathered about and beholding the profanation, his anger knew no bounds; he rushed over, laid hold of the innocent but unfortunate piper, kicked, cuffed and beat him unmercifully, broke his pipes and completely dispersed the whole assembly.[58]

While some musicians like piper Tom Kennedy found refuge inside coercive "souper" colonies, the Famine cleansed the countryside of thousands of others who were not as lucky or as morally supple. Workhouse records—especially in the midwestern counties of Galway and Clare—attest to the death of pipers within their dour precincts, while the field notes of collectors like George Petrie reference the passing of some of his primary musical informants.[59]

The Famine also spelled disaster for a thriving corps of instrument makers who served their needs. In the years prior to the Famine, flutes, fiddles, and uilleann pipes were often made by local blacksmiths, wheelwrights, and carpenters who turned their hand to instrument making to supplement their crafts. The Moloney Brothers, who ran a forge at Knockera, near Kilrush on the Iorrus peninsula in southwest Clare, catered for this dual marketplace in the 1830s. The saga of their "bankruptcy" is a classic case of such economic failure at townland level. Both were prosperous artisans in the pre-Famine era and folklore still recalls how they were beguiled by the duplicity of the Vandaleurs, the local landlords whose enthusiasm for mass evictions was in a class of its own. Writing about their fall from prosperity in the post-Famine years, Captain Francis O'Neill says:

> Thomas and Andrew Maloney . . . Made on the order of Mr. Vandaleur, a local landlord, what is claimed to be the most elaborate sets of bagpipes in existence. Thomas was a blacksmith and Andrew was a carpenter, but both were great performers on the Union pipes. . . . As the young man (Vandaleur) for whom the instrument was intended met with an injury, it remained on their hands, unsalable because of its expensiveness. The disastrous famine years ruined the Moloneys and they were obliged to part with their masterpiece for a trifling sum.[60]

Despite the failure of the Moloney business, one set of their pipes eventually found its way to New York in the 1860s with a Clare piper who made his career in vaudeville. In the interim between the initial coffin ship exodus and the American Civil War, thousands of Irish traditional musicians found their way across the North Atlantic. Some settled in the immediate vicinity of Quebec and contributed in turn to its musical traditions.[61] Others crossed the border into the United States. In this strange foreign nexus of crowded ghettos and rampant opportunism, their folk art found new outlets in a melting pot of urban entertainment and aggressive social mobility. The archaic music making of the *clachan* had now become a commodity in a brave new transatlantic world.

Mindful of the cultural cleansing effects of the Famine in Ireland, collector George Petrie reflected on the depressed state of his informants in the 1850s. His despair is matched by an urgency to collect what remained of the music of Gaelic Ireland.

> "The land of song" was no longer tuneful; or, if a human sound met the traveler's ear, it was only that of the feeble and despairing wail for the dead.

This awful unwonted silence, which, during the famine and subsequent years, almost everywhere prevailed, struck more fearfully upon their imaginations . . . and I confess that it was a consideration of the circumstances of which this fact gave so striking an indication, that . . . influenced me in coming to a determination to accept the proposal of the Irish-Music Society.[62]

Petrie's observations are corroborated by Séamus Dubh Ó Fiannachta, editor of the songs of Tomás Ruaidh Ó Súilleabháin (1785–1848), a Kerry poet and fiddler who lived through the worst excesses of the tragedy in Cahirciveen. Reflecting on the silence of the song tradition after the famine, Séamus Dubh laments that "the awful visitation of the Famine . . . rendering the land sad and songless, effected a distinct psychological change in the Irish character."[63] Similarly, the biographers of Father Dineen (one of the principal figures of the Irish language movement in the late nineteenth century), noting "that the people of *Sliabh Luachra* were not half as musical in the second half of the century as in the first, explained, *bhí an teaspach bainte díobh ag amhgar agus ag drochshaol"*—the spirit had been taken out of them by want and famine.[64]

One of the most blatant indicators of the silencing effects of the Famine on the song tradition is evidenced in the decline of work songs during the 1850s. With the radical shift in land use and the focused capitalization of Irish agriculture, tillage gave way to increased pasture, which was less labor intensive. Consequently, Irish songs associated with plowing, reaping, and sowing, as well as their related domestic chores, were deprived of the activities that sustained them. Writing about *"The Ploughman's Whistle"* in 1855, George Petrie pointed out that "such airs are now rarely or never to be heard" because of "the consequences of the calamities of recent years." His observation is corroborated by P. W. Joyce, who posited that the Famine period was a *terminus ante quem* for the use of popular work songs like *"Loinneóg Oireamh," "Aéire Cinn Bó Rúin," "Crónán na mBó," "An Sealbhán Seó,"* and others in a countryside that was once the preserve of widespread communal farming.[65]

In the west of Ireland, where the hemorrhage of emigration became the norm after the Famine, the topography of traditional music making was changed irrevocably. The widespread destruction of *clachan* communities deprived traveling pipers and dancing masters of their patrons. Similarly, the collective sense of time and space that characterized this domain was changed inexorably. The new anglicized place-names of post-Famine Ireland grafted ill-fitting spatial parameters onto an older world of townlands, rundale strips, and "walking" distances. The decline of the Irish language deprived the dance music of its former cultural geography as the *seanchas* and *dinnsheanchas*—folklore and place-name lore—associated with tunes failed to translate into utilitarian English.

In the bleak uplands along the Atlantic seaboard, where scattered remnants of the *clachan* mentality persisted, many traditional musicians continued to find listeners and dancers despite the moral policing of the clergy, the cultural indifference of their educational system, and the high art predilections of their urban neighbors. Occasions of music making in this archaic milieu still followed the cooperative work cycle of the *meitheal* and the ritual gatherings of the agricultural year. Inherent within this cultural calendar, however, was an ongoing *via dolorosa* of "American Wakes" where departing emigrants were fêted by neighbors and musicians. As long as these "wakes" persisted in rupturing the very fabric of Irish family life, the unquiet ghost of the Great Famine would continue to haunt the communal psyche of rural Ireland and impact the musical culture of its people at home and abroad.

Notes

1. See Cormac Ó Gráda, *An Drochshaol: Béaloideas agus Amhráin* (Baile Átha Cliath: Coiscéim, 1994); Cathal Póirtéir, "Folk Memory and the Famine," in *The Great Famine: The Thomas Davis Lecture Series*, ed. Cathal Póirtéir (Cork: Mercier Press, 1995); and Chris Morash, *The Hungry Voice: The Poetry of the Irish Famine* (Dublin: Irish Academic Press, 1989).

2. Robert James Scally, *The End of Hidden Ireland: Rebellion, Famine and Emigration* (New York: Oxford, 1995); Kevin Whelan, "Pre and Post-Famine Landscape Changes," in Póirtéir, *The Great Famine*; Cormac Ó Gráda, *Ireland before and after the Famine* (Manchester: Manchester University Press, 1993); and Joan Vincent, "A Political Orchestration of the Irish Famine: County Fermanagh, May 1847," in *Approaching the Past: Historical Anthropology through Irish Case Studies*, ed. Marilyn Silverman and P. H. Gulliver (New York: Columbia University Press, 1992).

3. Captain Francis O'Neill, *Irish Folk Music: A Fascinating Hobby* (Chicago: Regan, 1910), 274.

4. George Petrie, in Sir Charles Villiers Stanford, ed., *The Complete Petrie Collection of Irish Music* (London, 1902–5), vol. 1, xii.

5. Gearóid Ó hAllmhuráin, "The Concertina in the Traditional Music of Clare" (unpublished Ph.D. thesis, The Queen's University of Belfast, 1990).

6. T. W. Freeman, "Land and People, c. 1841," in *A New History of Ireland V:*

Ireland under the Union, 1:1801–70 ed. W. E. Vaughan (Oxford: Clarendon Press, 1989), 242–85. See also Thomas Flanagan, "Literature in English, 1801–91" in Vaughan, *A New History of Ireland V,* 482–522.

7. Breandán Breathnach, *Folkmusic and Dances of Ireland* (Dublin: Educational Company of Ireland, 1971), 108–24. See also Janet Harbison, "The Legacy of the Belfast Harpers' Festival," *Ulster Folklife* 35 (1989): 113–28.

8. Mr. and Mrs. S. C. Hall, *Ireland: Its Scenery, Character etc.* (London: Hall and Virtue, 1841–43), vol. 3, 421–27. The Halls' account is accompanied by an artist's impression of a rather plump and smiling Rory Oge sitting with his back to an enormous keg of whiskey.

9. Ibid., 422.

10. Capo de Feuillide, *l'Irlande,* 2 vols. (Paris, 1839). See also Marie-Hèléne Pauly, *Les Voyageurs Français en Irlande au Temps du Romantisme,* thèse pour le Doctorat d'Université (Université de Paris: Faculté des Lettres, 1939).

11. "As for the people, they know nothing of Thomas Moore." De Feuillide, *l'Irlande,* 356.

12. "*de n'être qu'un ignorant*" (for being such an ignorant man); de Feuillide, *l'Irlande,* 399.

13. The term *sean nós* is used today to describe traditional songs that are sung in the Irish language. It was first used during the early years of the Gaelic League's *Oireachtas.* Still prevalent among Irish-speaking *Gaeltacht* communities in the west of Ireland, these melodies are primarily modal in character and belong to a literary tradition of folk poetry that dates ostensibly from the seventeenth and eighteenth centuries.

14. "In the language of the country, the poet and the musician are synonymous, the word 'bard' signifies one and the other." De Feuillide, *l'Irlande,* 375.

15. Caoimhghin Ó Góilidhe, *Díolaim Filíochta* (Baile Átha Cliath: Folens, 1974), 191–92.

16. Conelly was immortalized by Petrie in the *Irish Penny Journal* in 1840. See Captain Francis O' Neill, *Irish Minstrels and Musicians* (Chicago: Regan, 1913), 212–15. See also Grace J. Calder, *George Petrie and "The Ancient Music of Ireland"* (Dublin: Dolmen, 1968).

17. Breandán Breathnach, *Dancing in Ireland* (Miltown Malbay: Dal gCais, 1983), 28.

18. Seán Donnelly, "Maurice Lenihan's account of some eighteenth and nineteenth century dancing masters," *Ceol na hÉireann: Irish Music* 1 (1993): 75–81. The reference to "cakes" in this extract recalls the custom of dancing for a cake. See also Seán Ó Dubhda, "The Cake Dance," *Béaloideas* 11 (1941): 126–42.

19. Many of the agricultural rituals originally associated with Bealtaine were shifted to St. John's Eve, which was celebrated on June 24, the longest day of the year. These included driving cattle through bonfires to protect them from disease and miscarriage. See Miller, *Emigrants,* 73.

20. Emmet Larkin, "The Devotional Revolution in Ireland, 1850–75," *American Historical Review* 77 (1972): 625–52.

21. David Thomson and Moyra McGusty, *The Irish Journals of Elizabeth Smith*

1840–1850 (Oxford: Clarendon Press, 1980), 25. This archaic custom still continues throughout the west of Ireland. It has been referenced among Irish communities in places as diverse as the outports of Newfoundland as well as among Irish communities in California and Australia.

22. O' Neill, *Irish Minstrels*, 153.

23. Still used in the rural vernacular of Clare, south Galway, and north Kerry, the term *swaree* (lit. *soirée*) is a remnant of the gallicized vocabulary of pre-Famine dancing masters.

24. Breathnach, *Folkmusic*, 23.

25. Ibid., 24. It is apparent, however, that many political songs in Irish were edited out of the collections (or were simply not considered worthy of collection) in the 1830s and 1840s. These included a number of supposedly Whiteboy ballads like *"Ó ' Bhean an Tighe nach suairc é sin,"* which Petrie collected from Tadhg Mac Mathúna on the Iorrus Peninsula. Its explicitly "seditious" radicalism proved "too much" for Petrie and, as such, was dismissed as having little "poetic merit."

26. Eugene O'Curry, *Of the manners and customs of the ancient Irish*, (3 vols. London and Dublin, 1873), vol. 3, 392. See also Breathnach, *Folkmusic*, 26. Although O'Curry speaks of the *laoi* being on the verge of extinction in the decades after the famine, two sung versions of *"Laoi na Mná Móire"* were recorded from Mícheál and Séamus Ó hIghne from Glencolmcille, co. Donegal, in the 1940s. Reminiscent of Latin plain chant, many *laoithe* were recorded from older singers in the Hebrides as late as the 1970s.

27. Among their more celebrated fairy songs collected in southwest Clare is *"A Bhean Úd Thíos."* It codifies the duties of a distraught husband who wants to rescue his wife from the fairies. See Hugh Shields, *Narrative Singing in Ireland: Lays, Ballads, Come-All-Yes and Other Songs* (Dublin: Irish Academic Press, 1993), 95.

28. Irish-speaking *Gaeltacht* communities are still vibrant near Dungarvan, co. Waterford (namely An Rinn) and Galway (Connemara). The Iorrus Peninsula to the west of Kilrush in southwest Clare is no longer regarded as a *Gaeltacht* area.

29. Irish tattie hookers (potato diggers) and bothy bands (groups of itinerant migrant workers) were commonplace in the rich tillage lands of Lowland Scotland during the past century and a half. Offering seasonal employment to landless laborers and marginal occupants of conacre holdings, this movement of workers attracted "recruits" mainly from the barren uplands of Ulster and north Connaught.

30. Breathnach, *Folkmusic*, 31.

31. Joep Leerssen, *Remembrance and Imagination: Patterns in the Historical and Literary Representation of Ireland in the Nineteenth Century*, Field Day Monographs 4 (South Bend, Ind.: University of Notre Dame Press, 1997), 174. See also Liam de Paor, "Tom Moore and Contemporary Ireland," *Leácht Chomórtha an Riadaigh 4* (Cork: Irish Traditional Music Society, University College, Cork, 1989), 11.

32. While his romantic paraphernalia of shamrocks and harps helped to formulate a mythology of Irish nationalism in the early nineteenth century, Moore's own performances were criticized by many of his contemporaries. William Hazlitt, for instance, regarded Moore's pseudo-tradition as an attempt to convert "the

wild harp of Érin into a musical snuff-box." See Frank Llewelyn Harrison, "Irish Traditional Music: Fossil or Resource," *Léacht Chomórtha an Riadaigh 3* (Cork: Irish Traditional Music Society, University College, Cork, 1988), 17; Leerssen, *Remembrance and Imagination,* 59; and de Paor, "Tom Moore and Contemporary Ireland," 7.

33. The chroniclers of *The Nation* were not without their scorn, however, for the "rude simplicity of the songs composed by peasants of little education for peasants of still less." As Breathnach (*Folkmusic,* 32–32) quite rightly affirmed, these "rural folk-songs proved more acceptable and enduring than the literary artifice of the Young Ireland writers" in the long term.

34. Shields, *Narrative Singing,* 139.

35. E. Estyn Evans, *Irish Heritage: The Landscape, the People and Their Work* (Dundalk: Dundalgan Press, 1949).

36. Robert James Scally, *The End of Hidden Ireland: Rebellion, Famine and Emigration* (New York: Oxford, 1995), 9–10.

37. Whelan, "Landscape Changes," 23–33. See also F. H. A. Aalen, *Man and the Landscape in Ireland* (London: Academic Press, 1978), 220–23.

38. Evans, *Irish Heritage,* 47–57.

39. Whelan, "Landscape Changes," 24.

40. Calder, *George Petrie,* 38–39.

41. John W. Boyle, "A Marginal Figure: The Irish Rural Laborer," in *Irish Peasants: Violence and Political Unrest 1780–1914,* ed. Samuel Clark and James S. Donnelly, Jr. (Madison: University of Wisconsin Press, 1983), 313–14. According to Connemara tradition, the word *spailpín* is derived from the Irish *speal* or 'scythe.'

42. Pádraig Ó Cannainn, ed., *Filíocht na nGael* (Dublin, 1958), 161. See also Boyle, "A Marginal Figure," 314.

43. Joe Heaney, *Irish Traditional Songs in Gaelic and English* (Cork: Ossian, 1989), notes by A. L. Lloyd.

44. Raymond Crotty, *Ireland in Crisis: A Case Study in Capitalist Colonial Underdevelopment,* (Dublin: 1986), 42. Crotty refers to these *clachan*-based cottiers and *spailpíns* as "a coolie class."

45. Sir William Wilde, *Memoir of Gabriel Beranger* (Dublin, 1880), 40. See also Breathnach, *Dancing,* 26.

46. Peatsaí Ó Callanáin, "Na Fataí Bána," cited in Ó Gráda, *An Drochshaol,* 50–53.

47. Ó Gráda, *An Drochshaol,* 54.

48. Ibid.

49. Ó Callanáin, cited in ibid., 50–51.

50. Ibid., 51.

51. Ó Gráda, *An Drochshaol,* 73.

52. Séamus Mac Mathúna, *Traditional Songs and Singers* (Baile Átha Cliath: Comhaltas Ceoltóirí Éireann, 1977), 22–23. This song was recorded from eighty-four-year-old Michey Flanagan of Inagh, co. Clare, in 1974. Sung to the air of an older song, *"An Páistín Fionn,"* it was probably written during the early 1860s in anticipation of the Fenian Rising, judging by its political agenda.

53. *British Parliamentary Papers: Famine Ireland*, vol. 2, 726. See also Michael MacMahon, "The Great Famine in Clare: Gleanings from the Parliamentary Papers," *Dal gCais* 5 (1979): 89–93.

54. Irish Folklore Collections, Department of Irish Folklore, University College, Dublin, 1245: 482–83. Cited in Breandán Ó Madagáin, "Functions of Irish Song in the Nineteenth Century," *Béaloideas* (1985): 167.

55. See Larkin, "Devotional Revolution," 625–52. See also his "Economic Growth, Capital Investment and the Roman Catholic Church in Nineteenth-Century Ireland," *American Historical Review* 72 (1967): 852–84.

56. Breathnach, *Dancing*, 40.

57. Brendán Breathnach, "Séamus Goodman (1828–96): Bailtheoir Ceoil," *Journal of the Kerry Archaeological and Historical Society* 6 (1973): 159–60.

58. Pádraig de Brún, "John Windale and Father Casey," *Journal of the Kerry Archaeological and Historical Society* 7 (1974): 83–84.

59. Recounting the life of piper John McDonough of Annaghdown, co. Galway, Captain Francis O' Neill suggests:

> To no class in the community did the terrible famine years prove more disastrous than to the pipers. Those who lived through plague and privation found but scanty patronage thereafter. "The pipers are gone out of fashion," as one of them ruefully expressed it, so poor John McDonough, the peerless piper, finding himself crushed between poverty and decrepitude, took sick on his way back to his native Galway and died neglected and ignored in the Gort workhouse.

See O' Neill, *Irish Minstrels*, 208–9.

60. O'Neill, *Irish Minstrels*, 157–58. This rare set of uilleann pipes with its unique trombone slide, five regulators, and twenty-four keys is housed today in the National Museum of Ireland. Its original cost was estimated at $500 in the early 1840s.

61. See Carmelle Bégin, "La musique traditionnelle pour violon: Jean Carignan" (thèse de Ph.D. musique, Université de Montréal, 1979). This thesis on the music of legendary Québecois fiddler Ti-Jean Carrignan indicates a correlation between his repertoire and an older core of Irish dance tunes. Robert Grace's seminal work, *The Irish in Québec: An Introduction to the Historiography* (Québec: Institut Québecois de Recherche sur la Culture, 1993) previews the research potential of this field.

62. George Petrie, in Sir Charles Villiers Stanford, ed., *The Complete Petrie Collection of Irish Music* (London, 1902–5), vol. 1, xii.

63. Séamus Dubh [O Fiannachta], *The Songs of Tomás Ruaidh O'Sullivan* (Dublin, 1914), 22. Cited in Ó Madagáin, "Functions of Irish Song," 197.

64. Proinsias Ó Conluain agus D. Ó Céilleachair, *An Duinníneach* (Dublin, 1958), 58.

65. The only documented example of an Irish language ploughing song is "*Loinneóg Oireamh*" (The Ploughman's Lilt). It was collected by George Petrie

from ploughman Tadhg McMahon in southwest Clare in the 1840s. It no longer survives in the vernacular tradition. *"Aéire Cinn Bó Rúin"* (The Herd of the Pet Cow) and *"An Sealbhán Seó"* (The Precious Treasure) were both weaving dialogues sung by women during *comhar* (cooperative) work sessions. The milking song *"Crónán na mBó"* was given to Petrie by Frank Keane, a Dublin law clerk who was born in Kilfearagh, co. Clare. Its use of vocables in the refrain suggests a magical incantation. The singing of charms to protect milk, young married women, mothers, and infants was a common feature of secular rituals and superstitions before the Famine. This folk tradition did not survive the liturgical revolution in post-Famine Catholicism. See Donal O'Sullivan, *Songs of the Irish* (Cork: The Mercier Press, 1981), 32–38; and Ó Madagáin, "Functions of Irish Song," 207–10.

7

MICHAEL QUIGLEY

Grosse Île

Canada's Famine Memorial

O N ST. PATRICK'S DAY, March 17, 1996, Sheila Copps, minister of Canadian heritage, announced Canada's recognition of Grosse Île as "the Irish Memorial." From now on, the National Historic Site will tell the story of the Irish tragedy in the quarantine station of 1847, of the mass graves of the Irish Famine victims, of the tall Celtic Cross, and of the only remaining hospital building from that time, a long wooden shed called the Lazaretto. Equally important, it will "pay homage to the welcome, generosity and devotion of the local population" who comforted the afflicted.[1]

Grosse Île is a place haunted by tragedy. Its landscape still bears the scars of the suffering of those for whom the island was not only their first footfall in the New World but also, for all too many, their last. Despite its name, Grosse Île is a small island, barely three miles long by a mile across, lying midstream in the St. Lawrence River about thirty miles downstream from Quebec City. Much of it is densely wooded with stands of oak, maple, pine, and birch; migrating ducks and geese rest on the beaches on its south shore. It is also a pretty place, a favorite picnic spot for officers in the Quebec garrison in the early nineteenth century. Robert Whyte, who arrived at Grosse Île in July 1847, called it "a fairy scene . . . the distant view of which was exceedingly beautiful," but, he added, "this scene of natural beauty was sadly deformed by the dismal display of human suffering that it presented."[2]

At the western end of the island is a broad meadow with a ridged surface, resembling nothing so much as the lazy beds, the old Irish ridge-and-trench manner of cultivation of the potato, whose remains can still be found in the west of Ireland. These ridges are manmade, for they mark the mass graves where the Irish famine victims of 1847 were buried, "stacked like cordwood," said one contemporary observer.[3]

In 1847, there were so many dead in the holds of the coffin ships that hundreds of bodies were simply dumped overboard into the river. Among those who survived the passage and landed on the island, thousands were desperately ill, driven half-insane by starvation and fever, and distraught with bereavement as they watched loved ones die before them. Hundreds wandered away from the reception sheds, dying along the shore and in the woods. The burial parties, overwhelmed by the magnitude of their task, often simply interred the bodies wherever they found them, without record or marker.

The Grosse Île Quarantine Station

Chosen because it is isolated in mid-river but still close to Quebec City, Grosse Île was first designated as a quarantine station by legislation published on March 26, 1832, and it would remain in use as a quarantine station for seaborne traffic until 1937. The initial need for a quarantine station was rooted in well-founded Canadian fears of the cholera epidemic which had swept westward across Europe from India since 1826. The Grosse Île quarantine station was created as "the centre of an outer defence to prevent the disease reaching Quebec City."[4] The medical officer, Dr. Griffin, and a party of soldiers took possession of the island on May 1, 1832, and began to set up hospital sheds, tents, and a bakery.

For the crucial years, 1832 and 1847, the wellspring of the tragedy at Grosse Île was in Ireland. It is instructive to recall that 1831 was a year of partial failure of the potato harvest in Ireland; hunger and physical debilitation proved a fertile breeding ground for cholera in Ireland, with the result that the bulk of the victims of the transatlantic cholera epidemic of 1832 were Irish.

In 1832, 51,000 immigrants, a larger than usual number, passed through the inspection facilities at Grosse Île. The best illustration of the rudimentary nature of the quarantine station, at the beginning, is the fact that when the cholera reached Quebec City, on June 8, 1832, aboard the brig *Carricks* from Dublin, the *Quebec Mercury* ascribed the cause to "some unknown disease." Indeed, before the end of June most ships simply sailed past Grosse Île to Quebec.[5]

The doctors and attendants on Grosse Île were overworked and underqualified to treat a disease many of them had never seen; the diagnosis, treatment, and epidemiology of cholera were all a mystery to them; the hospital facilities on the island, still incomplete, were overwhelmed; the numbers of sick from the ships arriving in the river kept mounting. By the end of the first week in June, when 15,000 people had been examined at Grosse Île, the Canadian authorities stopped trying to detain and inspect all vessels, only requiring full quarantine of the ships arriving from Irish and British ports. "At times," says C. A. Mitchell, "over thirty vessels were present in the anchorage. In a word, the capacity of the station was insufficient to deal with the vessels bearing infected immigrants." [6]

In 1832, the unavoidable failure to manage the quarantine station adequately resulted in some 7,000 deaths as the cholera epidemic swept down the St. Lawrence valley from Quebec to Montreal, Kingston, Toronto and Hamilton, Buffalo and Detroit. Traditionally, the number of those who died at Grosse Île is given as 3,000. As Marianna O'Gallagher writes, "By September 30, the newspapers reported the 'official burials' at Quebec City at 3,292. More than that had died at Grosse Île." [7] The Irish dead of 1832 on Grosse Île were buried in mass graves. It is reported that the original burying grounds were at low tide in Back Bay, from which the bay later, and down to the present, became known as Cholera Bay. [8]

The contrast with the following year, when the epidemic had passed, is remarkable: it is the difference between normal and extraordinary circumstances at the quarantine station. In 1833, only 27 deaths occurred among the 239 people, out of 22,000 immigrants, who were admitted to the island's hospital; again, in 1841–45 only 164 deaths were recorded at Grosse Île, out of a total of 140,539 people who landed at Quebec. [9] What happened in the summer of 1832 was a foretaste of the disaster that overwhelmed Grosse Île in 1847. The catastrophes of 1832 and 1847 were extraordinary, and for that very reason they stamped the Irish character irrevocably on the island's story.

The Catastrophe at Grosse Île

In 1846, after the first blast of blight, but before the full fury of the Famine swept Ireland, nearly 33,000 people, the majority of them Irish, entered Canada at Quebec City. Already the effects of the Famine in Ireland were evident in the report that twice as many people as usual were admitted to the hospital on Grosse Île. The Canadians were aware of the circumstances in Ireland; they did not know the full dimensions of the horror, but they knew a crisis was at hand.

In February 1847, before the year's first emigrant ships arriv   )r.
George Mellis Douglas, medical superintendent, warned the Legislative
Assembly that the approaching season would bring "a greater amount of
sickness and mortality" and that the closure of American ports would
"augment the number of poor and destitute who will flock to our shores."
Little had changed on the island since 1832: its establishment consisted of
a hospital shed, two chapels, a bakery, a barracks, and the doctor's house.
Douglas asked for £3,000 to expand the quarantine facilities to cope with
the expected increase in numbers; he was given £300 with which he managed to acquire fifty extra beds and extra straw for bedding. But even Dr.
Douglas was utterly unprepared for the reality.[10]

The first ship to arrive, the *Syria,* left Liverpool on March 24 carrying
241 passengers and anchored at Grosse Île on May 17. Nine people aboard
the *Syria* died on the voyage, and 84 fever victims were immediately admitted to hospital. The first person to die on Grosse Île in 1847 was Ellen
Keane, aged four years and three months, who was admitted to hospital
with fever on May 17 and died the same day. Six days later, 202 passengers
from the *Syria* were ill. The quarantine hospital on the island, built for
150 patients, could barely accommodate 200, and was already filled to its
capacity.[11] In the next few days, seven more emigrant ships arrived carrying 2,778 passengers; 175 passengers had died on board, 341 were ill.
Within a week, by May 24, another twenty-five ships had arrived; 260 of
the 5,600 passengers had died en route, and another 700 were ill. Already
"the catastrophe had taken place, and was beyond control."[12]

Dr. Douglas was astonished by the "unprecedented" "state of illness
and distress" on the coffin ships; he had "never contemplated the possibility of every vessel arriving with fever as they do now," all of them carrying
passengers "in the most wretched state of disease." On May 23, he reported between fifty and sixty deaths per day. He was resigned to the
prospect that many more would fall sick and require treatment but, he
told the authorities, "I have not a bed to lay them on or a place to put
them in." As a result, he was obliged to flout the quarantine law and
confine all passengers, healthy and sick alike, on board the ships at anchor
in the river.[13]

Before the end of May 1847, thirty-six coffin ships were at anchor in
the river. The hospital space on the island was entirely overwhelmed,
and the ships at anchor were all full of passengers, close to 12,500 altogether,
the healthy and the sick, the dying and the dead sharing grossly overcrowded quarters, packed as human ballast in the holds of vessels built

not as passenger ships but to carry Canadian lumber to England.[14] On May 29, Alexander Buchanan, chief emigration agent at Quebec, blamed the problem on the laxity of the British shipping regulations and the greed of the ship owners: "Much of the present disease and sickness is, I fear, attributed to the want of sufficient nourishing food."[15] This is a diplomatic understatement; all the eyewitnesses that summer agreed that conditions on the coffin ships, even the best of them, were unspeakably Hobbesian.[16]

British shipping regulations provided for the barest minimum as rations for emigrants; ship owners and captains seldom provided more. The crews were callous, brutal, capricious, and avaricious.[17] Profiteering ship's chandlers supplied moldy food and water that was unfit to drink, and many shipping agents in Ireland and Liverpool made a point of warning passengers to take aboard their own food supplies, an impossible demand on people who were already starving and destitute. The Irish who fled the Famine on the ships that reached Grosse Île tended to be the poorest emigrants: passage to Quebec was half the going rate to American ports, cheap enough for those who scraped together their last few shillings and a powerful attraction as well for landlords who offered the invidious choice of "assisted emigration" or eviction, such as the Mahons at Strokestown and Palmerston in Sligo. Steerage passengers, accommodated between decks in hastily constructed, rudimentary bunks, were allotted less space than British regulations had defined as adequate for the transport of slaves from Africa (ten square feet per person, as opposed to fourteen square feet required by American law).[18]

One of the most interesting witnesses of Grosse Île in 1847 was Stephen De Vere, who was anything but an ordinary emigrant. Scion of a noted Anglo-Irish family from county Limerick, landlord, magistrate, and social reformer, he took passage on an emigrant ship in order to provide a first-hand account to the Colonial Office. His account of conditions on the ship, which he was assured was "more comfortable than many," is a funeral dirge. "Hundreds of poor people, men, women and children, of all ages from the drivelling idiot of 90 to the babe just born, huddled together, without light, without air, wallowing in filth, and breathing a foetid atmosphere, sick in body dispirited in heart . . . the fevered patients lying between the sound in sleeping places so narrow, as almost to deny them a change of position . . . living without food or medicine except as administered by the hand of casual charity, dying without spiritual consolation and buried in the deep without the rites of the church."[19]

Robert Whyte was untypical too, a cabin passenger rather than one of the huddled masses in steerage, but his account of conditions belowdecks mirrors De Vere's. Whyte also tells the instructive story of the German immigrants who reached Grosse Île a couple of days after him. It is a description of the normal quarantine procedure at Grosse Île which casts the Irish experience in sharp contrast. One of the assistant medical officers, Dr. Jacques, boarded the German ship and inspected the five hundred passengers who had embarked at Bremen, "all of them (without a single exception) comfortably and neatly clad, clean and happy. There was no sickness among them and each comely fair-haired girl laughed as she passed the doctor to join the robust young men who had undergone the ordeal." Later that day, Whyte passed the same ship, whose "deck was covered with emigrants who were singing a charming hymn, in whose harmony all took part," as it set sail upstream to Quebec.[20]

As the summer wore on, Buchanan's complaint became a common refrain as the Canadians confronted shipload after shipload of malnourished, diseased, and even naked people. On June 25, the Legislative Assembly voted to urge the British government to ameliorate the conditions mandated by the shipping regulations, calling specifically for more space per passenger, more food, and better medical facilities.[21] Among those who wrote to the Colonial Office in London, increasingly angrily, were Adam Ferrie, chairman of the Legislative Assembly's emigration committee, who called the conditions of the Irish emigrants "as bad as the slave trade," and the Common Council of the City of St. John, New Brunswick.[22]

The Medical Commission

By May 31, forty vessels were at anchor in the St. Lawrence, in a line stretching over two miles downstream; more than a thousand fever cases were on the island, the overflow from the hospital housed in hastily erected sheds and tents and in the chapel; as many again were on the ships waiting to come ashore. The death toll was appalling: nine hundred deaths had been recorded in the two weeks since Ellen Keane's. With good reason, Dr. Douglas's reports to the Legislative Assembly became peevish. Conditions on the island were unbearable; he and his assistants, medical, clerical, and lay, were worn out and oppressed by the disease and mortality all around them. A poignant symbol of the dimensions of the epidemic is the case of Dr. Benson, a physician with experience in the fever hospitals in Ireland, who arrived on the *Wandsworth* on May 31, volunteered to assist Dr. Douglas, contracted typhus and died within a week. Douglas himself contracted typhus but survived, as did several of the priests. On June 5, the day when the Medical Commission arrived at Grosse Île, 21,000 emigrants were at Grosse Île and the daily death toll had tripled: 150 people were buried that day.[23]

On Buchanan's recommendation, the governor general, Lord Elgin, appointed a Medical Commission of three physicians, Painchaud of Quebec and McDonnell and Campbell from Montreal, to examine the crisis at Grosse Île. On arrival, they discovered the sick on the island "in the most deplorable condition, for want of the necessary nurses and hospital attendants," while on board the ships in the river they found "corpses lying in the same beds with the sick and the dying." The hardship was compounded by the demoralization of the victims: "common sympathies being apparently annihilated by the mental and bodily depression produced by famine and disease." The commissioners echoed Buchanan's criticism of "the crowded manner in which vessels were allowed to leave the British Ports." On the central issue of the management by Dr. Douglas of the quarantine station, they wrote:

> We entirely disapprove of the plan of keeping a vessel in quarantine for any period, however prolonged, whilst the sick and healthy are congregated together, breathing the same atmosphere, sleeping in the same berths, and exposed to the same exciting causes of contagion. This year's melancholy experience has in many instances proved that the number attacked and the mortality of the disease increased in direct ratio with the length of time the ship was detained under such circumstances. As an evidence of the truth of the above statement, we may be permitted to instance the case of the ship *Agnes* which arrived about 16 days ago, with 427 passengers, out of which number not more than 150 are now in a healthy condition, the remainder being dead, or sick on board, or in Hospital.

They were, however, unable to offer any concrete remedies for the problem beyond instructing Dr. Douglas to comply with the regulations; which was, by this stage, no longer possible.[24]

De Vere's description of the hospital sheds on the island echoes and amplifies the medical commissioners' remarks:

> They were very miserable, so slightly built as to exclude neither the heat nor the cold. No sufficient care was taken to remove the sick from the sound or to disinfect and clean the beddings. The very straw upon which

they had lain was often allowed to become a bed for their successors and I have known many poor families prefer to burrow under heaps of stones, near the shore, rather than accept the shelter of the infected sheds.[25]

Fr. Bernard McGauran, who led the first group of Catholic priests on the island that year, put the same point more graphically, when he told the Select Committee, "I have seen in one day thirty-seven lying on the beach, crawling in the mud and dying like fish out of water."[26] As the temperature climbed, conditions on the island continued to deteriorate. In July, when the temperature reached 37°C, more than 2,500 sick people, suffering from typhus, dysentery, and simple starvation, were on the island.

At the end of July, the Legislative Assembly's Special Committee of inquiry into the management of Grosse Île quarantine station delivered its report, which consisted primarily of the testimony of the witnesses, without commentary or recommendations. The witnesses testified unanimously to the awful situation on the island: the sheds, tents, and other buildings were overflowing; the beds, such as they were, were shared by as many as three people; many fever victims were lying on bare planks or on the ground, the more fortunate on a bedding of straw. The dead were buried in trenches, one on top of another; so many were interred and so close to the surface, Douglas had to arrange to bring soil from the mainland to cover the dead; even so, this failed to deter the rats that came ashore from the ships to feast on the cadavers.[27]

Testifying on July 13, Fr. William Moylan, parish priest of St. Patrick's in Quebec City, told of seeing corpses left lying overnight in the bunks in the hospital, "even when they had a companion in the same bed." He confirmed the Medical Commission's observations, saying "the sick would have been better ashore under tents, having medical attendance close at hand, and besides would not have affected the healthy Emigrants confined in the holds of the vessels with them." He estimated the mortality as a result of confinement on the ships was "at least twice as great as on shore."[28]

In his evidence before the Legislature on July 23, Fr. Bernard O'Reilly from Sherbrooke blamed the British government for the conditions on the emigrant ships, but he also warned the Canadians that unless they acted quickly they would "choose to consent to the wholesale murder of thousands who are just now on the ocean or preparing to leave home for Canada." He balanced praise for Dr. Douglas's unstinting efforts with reiteration of criticism of the policy of keeping people on board the ships.[29] De Vere, however, criticized the quarantine system, saying both "medical attendance and hospital accommodations were inadequate." Because the doctors were overwhelmed, the "medical inspections on board were slight and hasty," and this produced a "twofold ill effect": "Some were detained in danger who were not ill, and many were allowed to proceed who were actually in fever."[30]

Even those who escaped confinement in the holds of the ships were not safe. Father Jean Baptiste Antoine Ferland, Director of the College of Nicolet, reported that "in the greater part of the sheds on Grosse Île, men, women and children are found huddled together in the same apartment . . . many who have entered the shed without any serious illness, have died of typhus, which they have caught from their neighbours."[31]

The *Agnes*, cited by the Medical Commission, was an extreme but not extraordinary case. The *Larch* sailed from Sligo with 440 passengers; 108 died at sea and 150 had the fever on arrival. The *Lord Ashburton* brought tenants evicted by Lord Palmerston; 107 of the 477 passengers died at sea, 60 were ill; the *Sir Henry Pottinger* left Cork with 399 passengers; 106 died and 100 were sick.

The ships that brought more than one thousand people from the Mahon estate at Strokestown, county Roscommon, earned an unsavory reputation. Not without some justification, Major Denis Mahon acquired notoriety as a tyrannical clearing landlord, and a place in history as one of the handful of landlords assassinated in late 1847. He left behind, also, an unadorned summary of the landlords' economic point of view. "I think," he wrote to his agent, "the first class for us to send is those of the poorest and worst description, who would be a charge on us for the Poor House or for Outdoor Relief, and that would relieve the industrious tenant." Like scores of other landlords, Mahon undertook large-scale eviction—the Bishop of Elphin reported that he had evicted 3,006 people from his estate—but he also provided assisted emigration to about one thousand of his tenants at a cost of £4,000. But even the apparently humane part of the process was fraught with squalor and indignity: medical inspection of the prospective emigrants was hasty and rudimentary, they were sent to Liverpool to squalid lodging houses where fever was already rampant, and they took passage to Canada (the cheaper destination) in the holds of unsanitary, overcrowded merchant ships.[32]

The outcome, recorded in early August, was the first of Mahon's ships to arrive at Grosse Île, whose condition struck Dr. Douglas as noteworthy even after weeks of unrelieved horror:

> The *Virginius* sailed from Liverpool, May 28, with 476 passengers. Fever and dysentery cases came on board this vessel in Liverpool, and deaths occurred before leaving the Mersey. On mustering the passengers for inspection yesterday, it was found that 106 were ill of fever, including nine of the crew, and the large number of 158 had died on the passage, including the first and second officers and seven of the crew, and the master and steward dying, the few that were able to come on deck were ghastly yellow looking spectres, unshaven and hollow cheeked, and, without exception, the worst looking passengers I have ever seen; not more than six or eight were really healthy and able to exert themselves.[33]

Nineteen more passengers died while the *Virginius* was at anchor, and 90 died in the sheds. As he was writing this report, two more ships commissioned by Mahon arrived. After boarding the *Naomi*, Dr. Douglas said, "the filth and dirt in this vessel's hold creates such an effluvium as to make it difficult to breathe"; 196 of her 421 passengers died before she reached Quebec. The *Erin's Queen* sailed with 493 people, of whom 136 died at sea; on arrival at Grosse Île, the ship's master had to bribe his crew, at the rate of a sovereign per corpse, to remove the dead from the hold.[34]

Although they disapproved of the quarantine arrangements, neither the medical commissioners nor other witnesses were able to provide an alternative. There were no resources available and the flood of Famine refugees was simply too great. It fell again on the shoulders of Dr. Douglas to seek a remedy. In the first half of July, before testifying at the Special Committee hearings, Douglas attempted to deal with part of the problem identified by the commissioners by establishing a regime based on the eminently sound medical principle of preventing the spread of disease by segregating the healthy from the sick. He began by setting up a tent camp at the eastern end of the island where the healthy could be sheltered while remaining in quarantine. This new hospital area was made permanent by the rapid construction of a dozen wooden hospital sheds. By August, the hospital sheds and tents could accommodate some 2,000 sick people, 300 convalescents, and as many as 3,500 people deemed healthy but held in quarantine. By the end of the year, the summary report of public works effected on the island listed a total of twenty-two hospital sheds.[35]

UNFORTUNATELY, THE difficulties of diagnosis and epidemiology which had been evident in 1832 remained, and were compounded by the sheer

size of the task. Despite good intentions, segregation was at best a palliative measure; at worst it exacerbated the situation, spreading the disease
even more widely. Father O'Reilly told the legislative inquiry that he had
given the last rites to fifty people, on one July day, among the so-called
healthy in the east-end tents. The extent of the problem was underlined
by a report of twenty-seven deaths among the healthy on July 31, and a
month later when the *Montreal Gazette* reported eighty-eight deaths in
one week among the healthy at the east end of the island. As late as September 16, the *Quebec Mercury* reported a large number of dysentery cases
among the healthy.[36]

Although it is estimated that only 10 percent of the Irish emigrants in
1847 were Anglican, the Anglican bishop of Montreal, George Jehosha-
phat Mountain, worked tirelessly that summer, traveling back and forth
between Montreal, Quebec, and the island, spurring on his flock to the
charitable work of offering assistance to the Famine victims and recruit-
ing at least fifteen volunteers from his clergy. He visited the island twice.
On his second trip, in August, when he recounted "scenes of loath-
someness, suffering and horror, in the holds of the ships and in the recep-
tacles for the patients,"[37] more than 2,500 fever cases were housed in the
island hospitals. A month later, as the shipping season was drawing to a
close, there were still 14,000 people held in quarantine aboard the ships
at anchor off Grosse Île. Twelve hundred of the sick were transferred to
the hospitals at the east end of the island on September 13, to allow Douglas and his staff to fumigate the sheds and tents at the western end. In the
first three weeks of October, the parish register of St. Luke's church on
the island recorded 97 anonymous burials. At the end of October, after
the first snowfall of the winter, the final 60 patients on the island were
transferred to hospitals at Quebec and Montreal, and the Grosse Île quarantine station closed for the winter.

The Ocean Plague

The implications of failure of the quarantine system were clearly recognized by several witnesses, including Dr. Douglas and Father O'Reilly. As
early as Tuesday, June 8, Douglas had written to Buchanan warning of
the imminent danger of the spread of disease throughout the colony:

> Out of the 4,000 or 5,000 emigrants who have left this island since Sunday,
> at least 2,000 will fall sick somewhere before three weeks are over. They

ought to have accommodation for 2,000 sick at least at Montreal and Quebec, as all the Cork and Liverpool passengers are half dead from starvation and want before embarking; and the least bowel complaint, which is sure to come with change of food, finishes them without a struggle. I never saw people so indifferent to life; they would continue in the same berth with the dead person until the seamen or captain dragged out the corpse with boat hooks. Good God! what evils will befall the cities wherever they alight. Hot weather will increase the evil. Now give the authorities of Quebec and Montreal fair warning from me. I have not time to write, or should feel it my duty to do so. Public safety requires it.[38]

Six weeks later, Father O'Reilly told the inquiry the same thing:

... those who are healthy, if sent up as hitherto to Montreal, must bring with them the seeds of sickness ... while out of the numbers who can leave Montreal for a further destination, the large majority are predoomed to expire on the wharves of Kingston or Toronto, and to carry with them whithersoever they direct their steps, the dreadful malady that now hangs over the country like a funeral pall.[39]

Looking further ahead, Robert Whyte anticipated more deaths, as his fellow passengers "wandered over the country, carrying nothing with them but disease, and that but very few of them survived the severity of the succeeding winter, ruined as their constitutions were, I am quite confident."[40]

These gloomy predictions were all too accurate, but it took some time for Douglas's fair warning to be heeded. At first, in Montreal, the Irish were housed in the sheds erected in 1832, in the center of the city. The growing danger of further contagion, evident in the fact that the death toll in Montreal reached thirty people a day in June, led to demands for what was effectively a second quarantine station. After considerable debate, Point St. Charles was chosen as the site; hospital sheds and open-sided shelters for the healthy were built. The new establishment formed "a large square with a court in the centre where the coffins were piled, some empty waiting for the dead, some full awaiting burial."[41] Twelve years later, when the site of the fever sheds and mass graves at Point St. Charles was cleared to begin construction of the Victoria Bridge across the St. Lawrence, the workers, mostly Irishmen, downed tools and refused to continue until a proper memorial was built. They dredged a huge black stone out of the river and had carved on it this inscription:

To preserve from desecration the remains of 6000 immigrants who died from ship fever AD 1847–48 this stone is erected by the workmen of Messrs.

Peto, Brassey and Betts employed in the construction of the Victoria Bridge AD 1859.

What happened in Montreal was the Grosse Île experience writ small; and it was repeated as the epidemic swept down the St. Lawrence from Quebec to Hamilton at the western end of Lake Ontario. In Quebec, Montreal, Kingston, Toronto, and Hamilton, the emaciated, starving, destitute, and febrile Irish brought disease and misery with them. They caused alarm and fear, but, for the most part, generosity outweighed xenophobia in the Canadian response. Indeed, the story of 1847 is as much one of Canadian heroism as it is of Irish suffering. In the face of unspeakable horror, hundreds of Canadians demonstrated remarkable generosity of spirit. Fever sheds were built, the victims were hastily segregated, and they were tended, tirelessly and heroically, by clerical and lay authorities in each community, but still they died, in their thousands.

Some of the Canadian heroes are well known, but most remain anonymous. At the end of the year, Dr. Douglas raised a monument at the mass graveyard at the western end of the island to mark the sacrifice of the four doctors, Benson, Pinet, Malhiot, and Jameson, who "died of typhus fever contracted in the faithful discharge of their duty upon the sick." The monument bears this inscription:

> In this secluded spot lie the mortal remains of 5424 persons who fleeing from Pestilence and Famine in Ireland in the year 1847 found in America but a Grave.

Of the seventeen Anglican clergymen who worked as volunteers on Grosse Île in the summer of 1847, two—Rev. Richard Anderson and Rev. Charles Morris—died of fever contracted from those they helped. Similarly, four of the forty-two Catholic priests who tended the sick at Grosse Île paid with their lives for their charity: Frs. Hubert Robson, Pierre Roy, Felix Severin Brady, and Edouard Montminy. The same fate befell Fr. Hugh Paisley and the Anglican Rev. William Chaderton in Quebec City. In addition, Dr. Douglas reported the deaths on Grosse Île of thirty-four workers: stewards, nurses, orderlies, cooks, policemen, and carters.[42]

In Montreal, as elsewhere, the "ocean plague" exacted its price among the Canadians. Tending the sick fell largely to the Catholic church. The Order of Grey Nuns provided nurses, almost all of whom became ill; several died. Father Hudon, vicar-general of the diocese of Montreal, died in August, as did eight other priests. In November, John Mills, the mayor of Montreal whose energy and magnanimity ensured relatively safe and healthy conditions for the famine victims, caught the fever at the sheds and died. Toronto's first Catholic bishop, Michael Power, tended the sick in that city and fell victim to the fever.

Like other witnesses, Bishop Mountain was particularly touched by the plight of the hundreds of children left orphans by the epidemic. Among the dozens of miserable waifs, a couple particularly caught his attention: a dying child, huddled under a pile of rags in one of the tents, and the body of a little boy who was walking with his friends, sat down to rest under a tree, and died.[43] It fell, however, to Father Moylan and to Fr. Charles-Félix Cazeau, "priest to the Irish" and future vicar-general of the diocese of Quebec, to ensure the future of the children. Lord Elgin reported the presence of more than a thousand orphaned children in Montreal. In Quebec City, the Catholic Ladies' Charitable Society took charge of 619 children, and the priests went on the circuit of parishes in Quebec urging the faithful to adopt the orphans. One priest, Fr. Thomas Cooke of Trois Rivières, wrote that his parishioners were arguing over the right to adopt the orphans. As many as two thousand children were welcomed into Québecois families and, in another remarkable display of generosity, many of them were allowed to retain their Irish names.[44]

Hallowed Ground

The assertion that Grosse Île is the most important Great Famine site outside Ireland begs a critical question: How many Irish men, women, and children are buried in the mass graves at Grosse Île? A completely accurate answer is not within our grasp. It was in the interests of many—the British government and politicians, English landlords, and, apparently, the colonial administration in Canada—to minimize the extent of what happened in 1847. Moreover, it is clear beyond a doubt that all the statistics for 1847 are muddled, incomplete, internally inconsistent, and contradictory. The best we can do is reach an approximation.

In March 1848, the British government reported that 258,000 people, the vast majority of whom were Irish, set sail in 1847 from British and Irish ports: 143,400 for the United States and 106,812 for British North America. Norman Anick, citing the same report, gives 138,000 passengers bound for the United States; Terry Coleman, citing yet another parliamentary paper, gives 109,680 people embarking for Canada.[45] Whether it was 106,000 or 109,000, the number is an underestimate, by as much as 10 percent, for two reasons. First, a number of the ships destined for American ports were turned away on arrival and made their way to Halifax, St. John, or Grosse Île.[46] Second, the official manner of reckoning passengers counted "statute adults" as defined in the British shipping regulations; in other words, one person over the age of fourteen, or a mother and dependent child under one year, or two children between one and fourteen years old. So, for example, the master of the *Greenock* was legally correct to declare he carried only 633 "statute adults" though his vessel was crammed with 816 persons: 528 adults, 210 children between the ages of one and fourteen, and 78 infants.[47]

In his first report, Alexander Buchanan, the Canadian emigration agent, said 97,002 people arrived at Quebec City from British, Irish, and Canadian ports by October 31, 1847. The report approved in December 1847 by the Committee of the Executive Council gives 98,106 as the total number of immigrants landing at Quebec. While this document specifies a figure of 54,329 as those who sailed from Irish ports, this fails to take into account the obvious fact that virtually all of the 134,524 people who embarked at Liverpool were Irish. Another account by Buchanan, also written in December 1847, reduced the number of Irish immigrants to 89,738, of whom 5,293 died before arriving, leaving only 84,445 who actually reached Canada. Finally, a year later, in his annual report for 1848, Buchanan had lowered the number again to 82,713 or 82,694 immigrants who had arrived at Quebec in 1847 from Irish or British ports.[48]

With discrepancies of this magnitude in the computation of the number of those who survived the passage in the coffin ships, it is no surprise to find the same difficulties in the numbers given in the official records of deaths in 1847. As noted, Buchanan's December 1847 report gives 5,293 as the number who died during the passage. Further deaths occurred in Canada. Dr. Douglas reported 3,238 deaths at the quarantine station; Buchanan reported 3,389 deaths at Grosse Île; the colonial commissioners reported 3,452 deaths at quarantine. More deaths occurred in Quebec and Montreal: 1,041 of the 2,500 people admitted to the Quebec Emigrant Hospital and 3,579 out of 11,000 admitted to Montreal Emigrant Hospital—these figures account for some 80 percent of the 10,037 reported deaths in Canada.[49] It is immediately apparent that these numbers must be considered no better than notional. The number of patients brought to the hospital tents and sheds at Grosse Île in 1847 must have been considerably larger than eight thousand; all the accounts report at least two thousand people on the island at all times from the end of May until the end of September, with a very high rate of turnover given the mortality rate, which was certainly fifty per day, and often higher. The overall figure must be augmented by those who were brought for burial directly from the ships.

Approaching the matter from Grosse Île itself is no more helpful. The officials, doctors, priests, and lay attendants were so overwhelmed they lost count of the dead within the first month. Deaths and burials were recorded at 50 per day very soon after the first ship arrived; on June 5, 150 people were buried. In July, Dr. Douglas told the Special Committee that "six men are constantly employed digging large trenches from five to six feet deep, in which the dead are buried." This mass grave, at the western end of the island, occupied an area of six acres. In his official report to the government, at the end of the year, Dr. Douglas gave a total of 3,238 deaths on the island, but plainly carved on the monument he erected overlooking the mass grave is the statement that it contained the remains of 5,424 people.[50] Again, the best we can say about these figures is they approximate the truth.

It is clear that the records on the island are both fragmentary and internally contradictory. Thus, for instance, Fr. Phillipe Jean recorded in the parish register of St. Luke's, the Catholic chapel on the island, that he buried 21 people on June 23; the summary of burials, from the same parish register, however, says 112 people "whom it was not possible to name" (*sans qu'il ait été possible de mentionner les noms*) were buried that day. The summary of burials gives a global figure of 2,900 people buried between June 16 and October 20; but the preceding four weeks, from May 17, when at least the 1,050 deaths noted above occurred, are unrecorded. If the average number of people buried in each trench (120) is extended backward to fill in the gap to May 17, when Ellen Keane died, then this one mass graveyard probably holds the remains of no fewer than 7,000 people.[51]

If there is confusion about the number of people buried in the mass graves at the western end of the island, the rest of the puzzle is even more convoluted. While the six-acre field was the principal and formal cemetery in 1847, it was only one of the burial sites on the island. The testimony of Bishop Mountain and Robert Whyte, among others, underlines two critical facts: first, that Dr. Douglas's hospital records are necessarily incomplete, since they did not record all the dead who were winched out of the holds of the ships and "stacked like cordwood" on the shoreline to await burial; and second, that many of the sick, febrile and hallucinating, wandered away from the sheds, tents, and other buildings to die in the bush and to be buried wherever they fell. Furthermore, there is the issue of the 1847 cemetery at the eastern end of the island, identified by the Canadian Parks Service as "Catholic" and "Protestant" (following later practice).[52] In light of the evidence of substantial numbers of deaths among the so-called healthy accommodated first in tents and then in the hospital buildings erected in July 1847, of which the Lazaretto is the sole remaining example, this area too contains the remains of Famine victims. The alternative explanation, that the bodies of those who died at the east end of the island, of fearsome contagious fevers, were transported across the island for burial south of Cholera Bay, defies logic and reason alike. Moreover, oral tradition in the immediate region of Grosse Île tells the story of the bulldozer driver, employed by the Canadian Department of Agriculture in 1964 to grade the land for an airstrip, who uncovered human bones. Unlike the main mass grave site at the west end of the island, this area is less well known and, despite clear evidence of its existence and extent in the archival survey maps, it is only grudgingly acknowledged by the Canadian Parks Service in its recent publications.[53]

When all the pieces of this puzzle are assembled, the best point of departure for estimating the importance of Grosse Île as a Great Famine site is the difference between the most realistic number of Irish Famine refugees who actually came up the St. Lawrence in 1847, about 110,000, and the number reported as arriving, alive, in Canada. Given the contradictions in the primary sources, the latter number is also an estimate, and 85,000 is the round number that best accords with the estimates offered by Buchanan, Douglas, and others. In other words, at a minimum, the death toll in the coffin ships and at Grosse Île must be reckoned at about 20,000 Irish men, women, and children; it may even be as high as 30,000. It must be emphasized that this number does not include the thousands of others who, having survived Grosse Île, reached Quebec City, Montreal, Kingston, Toronto, and Hamilton, only to die there in fever hospitals and emigrant sheds.

We shall never know exactly how many Irish people are buried at Grosse Île. Early accounts, by J. F. Maguire and A. Béchard, estimated the number of Irish people buried on the island in 1847 at 12,000; a later local history put the figure at 11,000;[54] to which, of course, must be added the minimal estimate of 3,000 cholera victims of 1832. In the end, it is probably less significant to arrive at a definitive number than it is to acknowledge the sanctity of the site. Let the estimate stand, conservatively, at between 12,000 and 15,000, and recognize that their presence makes Grosse Île hallowed ground.

The special significance of Grosse Île for the Irish community, in Canada, the United States, and, increasingly, in Ireland itself, was demonstrated over eighty years ago when the Irish community in Quebec marked the fiftieth anniversary of Black '47 with a pilgrimage to the island. This initiative was followed by a campaign launched by the Ancient Order of Hibernians to mark the site, and on August 15, 1909, a forty-six-foot-high Celtic Cross was unveiled on Telegraph Hill, the highest point on Grosse Île, 140 feet above the river. It faces west, toward Quebec City and the new life the thousands who died there never saw. The Irish inscription on the panel on the eastern face of the cross declares:

> Cailleadh Clann na nGaedheal ina míltibh ar an Oileán so ar dteicheadh dhóibh ó dlíghthibh na dtioránach ngallda agus ó ghorta tréarach isna bliadhantaibh 1847–48. Beannacht dílis Dé orra. Bíodh an leacht so i gcomhartha garma agus onóra dhóibh ó Ghaedhealaibh Ameriocá. Go saoraigh Dia Éire.

> Children of the Gael died in their thousands on this island having fled from the laws of foreign tyrants and an artificial famine in the years 1847–48. God's blessing on them. Let this monument be a token to their name and honour from the Gaels of America. God Save Ireland.

This monument was paid for by public subscription raised by the Ancient Order of Hibernians (AOH) in Canada and the United States. The opening ceremony drew nine thousand people from all over North America. The cross was unveiled by the papal legate to Canada, Mgr. Antonio Sbaretti; sermons were delivered by Monsignor Sbaretti, Archbishop (later Cardinal) Louis-Nazaire Bégin, and Fr. A. E. Maguire, chaplain to the AOH. Among those present at the ceremony were Father McGuirk, the last survivor of the forty-two priests who tended the victims of 1847, and Madame Roberge, one of the many children orphaned that year and adopted by a local family. In addition to spokesmen for the AOH, the dignitaries included Canada's Chief Justice, Sir Charles Fitzpatrick, and Secretary of State Charles Murphy, as well as members of both the federal and provincial parliaments.[55]

In August 1989, at a ceremony marking the eightieth anniversary of the unveiling of the High Cross, His Excellency Dr. Edward J. Brennan,

Ireland's ambassador to Canada, recalled the Famine in words evocative of both contemporary and modern Irish understanding of the Great Hunger:

> During the years 1845–47, with the failure of the potato crop, which was their principal means of sustenance, the Great Famine struck the people of Ireland. As an immediate consequence over a million people were to perish from hunger, disease and lethal fever. And in the short space of five years around a million people were to flee to the New World, seeking there the liberty and better conditions of life denied them in their own native land. Emigration became a permanent feature of Irish society under colonial rule. The Great Famine was Ireland's holocaust, and the slow-sailing vessels . . . Became coffin ships in which many would-be emigrants died a lingering and painful death. The Great Famine condemned the Irish to be the first boat people of modern Europe. . . . [56]

Dr. Brennan's words were echoed in 1994 by Mary Robinson, president of Ireland, who noted that while the failure of the potato was a "natural disaster" across Europe, "in Ireland it took place in a political, economic and social framework that was oppressive and unjust." Speaking to some four hundred people gathered on the island to commemorate the victims of 1847, she said, "Grosse Île—Oileán na nGael—l'île des irlandais—is special. . . . This is a hallowed place." [57]

Notes

1. Rt. Hon. Sheila Copps, deputy prime minister and minister of Canadian heritage, "Speaking Notes: Declaration of Grosse Île and the Irish Memorial," Québec, Mar. 17, 1996, 3.

2. Robert Whyte, *The Ocean Plague* (Boston, 1848), reissued as *Robert Whyte's 1847 Famine Ship Diary* (Cork: Mercier Press, 1994), 62, 67.

3. Testimony of John Wilson, shipping agent at Quebec, Report of the Special Committee appointed to inquire into the management of the Quarantine Station at Grosse Île, *Journals of the Legislative Assembly of the Province of Canada*, 1847, vol. 6, Appendix RRR.

4. Chas A. Mitchell, "Events leading up to and the Establishment of the Grosse Île Quarantine Station," *Medical Services Journal* [Canada] (1967): 1436.

5. Marianna O'Gallagher, *Grosse Île: Gateway to Canada 1832–1937* (Quebec: Carraig Books, 1984), 24.

6. Mitchell, "Grosse Île Quarantine Station," 1443.

7. O'Gallagher, *Grosse Île*, 26.

8. Suzanne Kingsmill, "Isle of Irish Despair," *Canadian Geographic* (Jan.–Feb. 1992): 80.

9. O'Gallagher, *Grosse Île*, 40; Norman Anick, "Grosse Île and Partridge Island Quarantine Stations," *Agenda Papers* (Moncton, N.B.: Historic Sites and Monuments Board of Canada, 1984), 83–84.

10. Donald MacKay, *Flight from Famine: The Coming of the Irish to Canada* (Toronto: McClelland & Stewart, 1990), 263; Cecil Woodham-Smith, *The Great Hunger: Ireland 1845–49* (London: Hamish Hamilton, 1962), 218.

11. Woodham-Smith, *Great Hunger*, 219–20.

12. Ibid., 219.

13. Letter from Douglas to Provincial Secretary, Dominick Daly, *Journals*, App. L.

14. Terry Coleman, *Passage to America* (Quebec: Pigwidgeon Press, [1972], 1991), 84; Marianna O'Gallagher, "Island of Sorrows," *Irish America* (April 1991): 27; Woodham-Smith, *Great Hunger*, 222–30; MacKay, *Flight from Famine*, 198–99.

15. *Journals*, App. L.

16. Whyte, *Ocean Plague*; Coleman, *Passage*; De Vere cited in MacKay, *Flight from Famine*; Medical Commission and Select Committee in *Journals*, etc.

17. Coleman, "Hard-driven Ships & Brutal Crews," *Passage*, chap. 6, 82–99 passim; MacKay, *Flight from Famine*, 198–215.

18. Coleman, *Passage*, Appendix A, 324–32.

19. Stephen De Vere, cited by Woodham-Smith, *Great Hunger*, 226.

20. Whyte, *Ocean Plague*, 76–77 and passim.

21. Padraic O Laighin, "Grosse Île: The Holocaust Revisited," in *The Untold Story: The Irish in Canada*, ed. Robert O'Driscoll and Lorna Reynolds (Toronto: Celtic Arts, 1988), vol. I, 85.

22. Woodham-Smith, *Great Hunger*, 228–29.

23. *Morning Chronicle* (Quebec), June 10, 1847, cited in O Laighin, "Holocaust Revisited," 84.

24. Report of the Medical Commissioners, *Journals*, App. L.

25. Stephen De Vere, cited in Whyte, *Ocean Plague*, Appendix 3, 114; Anick, "Grosse Île and Partridge Island," 85.

26. Report of the Select Committee, *Journals*, App. RRR; cited by MacKay, *Flight from Famine*, 269.

27. Report of the Select Committee, *Journals*, App. RRR; Coleman, *Passage*, 150.

28. Report of the Select Committee, *Journals*, App. RRR.

29. Ibid.

30. De Vere, cited by MacKay, *Flight from Famine*, 267; Anick, "Grosse Île and Partridge Island," 85.

31. Report of the Select Committee, *Journals*, App. RRR.

32. Stephen J. Campbell, *The Great Irish Famine* (Strokestown: Famine Museum, 1994), 40–42; Woodham-Smith, *Great Hunger*, 324–25.

33. British Parliamentary Papers, *Colonies—Canada*, vol. 17, 385.

34. Coleman, *Passage*, 160.

35. *Quebec Mercury*, Aug. 7, 1847; Christine Chartré, *Chronologie des Aménagements de Grosse Île, 1796–1990*, (Quebec: Canadian Parks Service, 1992), 39–51; Anick, "Grosse Île and Partridge Island," 86.

36. Report of the Select Committee, *Journals*, App. RRR; *Montreal Gazette*, Aug. 20, 1847, cited by Woodham-Smith, *Great Hunger*, 222; *Quebec Mercury*, July 31, 1847, and Sept. 16, 1847, cited by Chartré, *Chronologie*, 43, 48.

37. Report of the Select Committee, *Journals*, App. RRR, cited in O Laighin, "Holocaust Revisited," 88.

38. Cited by MacKay, *Flight from Famine*, 265; Coleman, *Passage*, 149.

39. Report of the Select Committee, *Journals*, App. RRR, cited in O Laighin, "Holocaust Revisited," 88.

40. Whyte, *Ocean Plague*, 84.

41. Cited by Woodham-Smith, *Great Hunger*, 235.

42. O'Gallagher, *Grosse Île*, 88–89; Coleman, *Passage*, 160–61.

43. Cited by Woodham-Smith, *Great Hunger*, 222.

44. O'Gallagher, *Grosse Île*, 56–57, 115–43; Coleman, *Passage*, 156–57.

45. *Report of the Select Committee of the House of Lords on Colonization from Ireland*, vol. 5, 42; Anick, "Grosse Île and Partridge Island," 81, citing ibid., 55; Coleman, *Passage*, 161, citing *Reports of Colonial Land and Emigration Commissioners*, 1848 and 1873.

46. Woodham-Smith, *Great Hunger*, 239–40.

47. *Colonies—Canada*, vol. 17, 422, cited in O Laighin, 89.

48. *Colonies—Canada*, vol. 18, 449; ibid., vol. 17, 384; ibid., 4; vol. 18, 463–69; *Journals*, 1849, App. EEE; see Anick, "Grosse Île and Partridge Island," 84; O Laighin, "Holocaust Revisited," 88–89; Coleman, *Passage*, 160–61; cf. Commission on Emigration and Other Population Problems, 1948–1954, *Reports* (Dublin: Stationery Office, 1954), Statistical Appendix, 314–20.

49. Anick, "Grosse Île and Partridge Island," 86, citing Report of a Committee of the Executive Council, *Colonies—Canada*, vol. 17, 385; cf. Coleman, *Passage*, 161, citing Eighth Report of the Colonial Land and Emigration Commissioners.

50. *Colonies—Canada*, vol. 17, 383–87; see n. 62.

51. O'Gallagher, *Grosse Île*, 169, 173; see n. 37.

52. Christine Chartré, *Rapport synthèse sur les aménagements de Grosse-Île 1832 à nos jours* (Quebec: Canadian Parks Service, 1992), 61.

53. Ibid., 116, 196, 328, 348, 360; Pierre Dufour et al., *Inventaire sommaire du patrimoine architectural de la Grosse-Île* (Quebec: Canadian Parks Service, 1983), 98–99; *Grosse Île: Development Concept and Supplement* (Quebec: Parks Canada, 1992). The *Supplement* says the cemetery at the east end of Grosse Île was not opened until 1848 or at the earliest "the end of 1847," 13–17.

54. John Francis Maguire, *The Irish in America* (London: Longmans, Green, 1868); A. Béchard, *Histoire de l'île-aux-grues et des îles environnantes* (Quebec, 1879); J. A. Jordan, *The Grosse Île Tragedy* (Quebec: Telegraph Printing Company, 1909); Damase Potvin, *Le Saint-Laurent et ses îles* (Montreal: Editions Bernard Valiquette, 1940), cited by Coleman, *Passage*, 150–56; see also Padraic O Laighin, "Grosse Île:

The Irish Island," *Public Consultation: Briefs Presented in Montreal* (Quebec: Parks Canada, 1992), n. 5.

55. O'Gallagher, *Grosse Île,* 85–88.

56. Ireland Fund of Canada, *Journal* (1992), 14. The classic contemporary accounts are Canon John O'Rourke, *The Great Irish Famine* (1874, reprinted Dublin: Veritas, 1989), and John Mitchel, *The Last Conquest of Ireland (Perhaps)* (1861); for a valuable reassessment of contemporary Irish views of the Famine by a modern historian, see James S. Donnelly, Jr., "Mass Eviction and the Great Famine," in *The Great Irish Famine,* ed. Cathal Póirtéir (Dublin: Mercier Press, 1995), 155–57; also the overview by Cormac O Gráda in *Ireland: A New Economic History, 1780–1939* (Oxford: Clarendon Press, 1994), 171–209.

57. "Address by the President, Mary Robinson, at Grosse Île, 21st August, 1994" (Dublin: Department of Foreign Affairs), 1–2.

8

The Famine Beat
American Newspaper Coverage of the Great Hunger

O N WEDNESDAY, OCTOBER 1, 1845, the British Royal Mail Ship *Cambria* steamed into Halifax, Nova Scotia, eleven and a half days out of Liverpool. *Cambria* had no time to linger. Twenty-three passengers came down the gangplank; eleven passengers boarded; cargo was quickly unloaded and the steamship, the fastest of the Cunard line mail packets that plied the North Atlantic, sailed off for Boston.

Among the cargo was a leather sack filled with the latest newspapers from Europe—those from Paris up to September 16, from Ireland and London as late as September 18, and from Liverpool up to the morning of September 19, printed just hours before *Cambria* sailed. A printer's apprentice lugged the sack to the office of Halifax's weekly newspaper, the *Nova Scotian,* and when the excitement of the mail ship's arrival subsided that evening, editor William Annand pored over the newspapers. His task was a classical rewrite assignment—boil down the contents of half a dozen or so European newspapers into a few lively paragraphs of the most interesting and important "advices" or "intelligence," as the news often was called in those days, from the other side of the Atlantic.

Overall, the news brought by *Cambria* was not earthshaking, and, in the honest custom of editors of those days, Annand told his readers so. "Unusually uninteresting," he wrote at the top of his summary. But there was an item from Ireland that caught his eye. And with the instinct of a veteran newsman for a potentially big story, he inserted a paragraph in the summary: "As in other parts of the United Kingdom and on the European Continent, the potatoe crop has suffered an epidemic, and the effect of such a disaster to Ireland will be very serious." [1]

Annand probably did not realize it, but he had just written the lead for what was to be one of the most significant stories of the nineteenth century for Canadian and United States newspapers—the story of the Irish Potato Famine. The grim accounts of starvation, emigration, and eviction were yet to come, but only a few weeks after the first rotting potatoes were discovered in Irish fields, the situation of that island and its people had leapt onto the front pages of American newspapers. It would remain there not just for days or weeks, but for all the years of the Famine era. Working without benefit of high-speed transmission, camera crews, teams of reporters, and other tools of modern journalism, American newspapers managed not only to cover the Irish Famine, but to bring it to their readers in vivid detail, providing depth and perspective and an amazing variety of news angles. For students of the Famine and for anyone who seeks to experience it close up rather than from afar, American newspapers are a rich lode of information and insight into what occurred in Ireland and into the shock waves that rippled across the Atlantic. In many ways they provide a first draft of history.

As Fast as the News Could Travel

The news did not travel instantaneously in those days, but in legs—not unlike a relay race—whose time and distance were determined by the speed and the staying power of a ship, a locomotive, a horse and rider. From Halifax, the first landfall in the New World for British mail steamers, European news was carried south to the United States and west to Canada. The *Philadelphia Public Ledger* boasted of having a "special and extraordinary express" that ran nearly one thousand miles from Halifax by horse, steamboat, and locomotive.[2] Its competitor, the *North American,* claimed that it was forced to establish a similar network because of "the monopoly which has existed on the Long Island Railroad for the benefit of portions of the New York press and latterly a part of the Philadelphia press which shut us out from all participation."[3] And another Philadelphia paper, the *U.S. Gazette,* grumbled on one occasion that its news from Halifax arrived at 10:45 P.M. "and would have been in somewhat sooner, but that within a short distance of the office, the horse stumbled and threw his rider, who though considerably bruised . . . ran on and delivered his package safely!"[4]

Cambria, which had given editor Annand the first shot at a major news development, docked at East Boston at 5:30 P.M. the next day, Thursday, October 2, 1845.[5] From there, couriers raced across southern New England all night to deliver the news to New York papers in time for Friday's editions. Newspaper editors knew the schedule of the mail steamships and were waiting anxiously. The *New York Herald* acted every bit like an expectant father whose mood became more tense with each passing day. On Wednesday, October 1, it told readers, "The *Cambria,* remarkable for speed . . . is now in her twelfth day."[6] On October 2 it fussed, "This steamship is fully due and we ought to receive her news this morning."[7] And by October 3, it scolded, "The *Cambria* is losing in reputation for speed what she gained in her last trip. She is now in her 13th day, she has crossed the ocean in 11 days."[8]

Its courier having finally arrived at midday Friday, October 3, the *Herald* was on the streets at 5:00 P.M. with an extra edition. After all that waiting, however, its sophisticated editors proved less perceptive than their Halifax counterpart. The *Herald* extra sported an eighteen-deck headline:

Two Weeks Later
From Europe
Arrival of the
Steamship *Cambria*
at Boston
The Harvests in Europe
State of the Grain Markets
The Cotton Market
Affairs in Spain
The New Religious Impulse on the Continent
Great Battle in Circassia
Arrival of the Monster Steamer
The Great Fight in England
Between Caunt and Bendigo
for Two Thousand Dollars
Bendigo the Champion
Markets
&c., &c., &c.[9]

But it failed to mention the potato blight. The next day, when they had had more time to study the European papers, the *Herald's* editors corrected that oversight by inserting a paragraph—even then below the account of Queen Victoria's visit to Germany and that of the boxing match for the championship of England—stating, "The disease among the potato crop in Europe appears to be almost universal." [10]

It was Tuesday, October 7, before readers of the *Richmond Enquirer* got the news from the *Cambria:* "The potato disease had prevailed to an alarming degree in some parts of England and also in Belgium, France and other parts of Europe." [11] The same day, the *Montreal Gazette,* having received its European papers by steamboat from Halifax, noted, "It is reported that not merely in England, but in Europe the potato crop was likely to be a general failure. . . ." [12] The *Cincinnati Daily Enquirer* reported on October 10, "The malady which has attacked the potato crop in Belgium has also made some ravages, though nothing like so extensive, in the northern provinces of France." [13]

By modern standards, this step-by-step progression of news across the continent was slow and ungainly. Even during the Famine period, the search for speedier technology would introduce wireless networks, the predecessors of our modern instantaneous transmission. But for the moment, those who had a stake in European news—whether through family, political, or business ties—had nothing to do but keep track of the steamer schedules and wait as patiently as possible for the news they carried.

Betting on a Famine

The haste to deliver that news to readers was not all just journalistic zeal. American newspapers were to a large extent organs of the business community, published by and for businessmen. And to businessmen, investors, traders, and entrepreneurs, the news was first and foremost a matter of dollars and cents. The effect of the European potato crop failure on New York markets, according to the *Philadelphia Ledger,* was "immediate and important . . . Several thousand barrels of flour were taken yesterday at an advance of 25 cents to 37 1/2 cents. Rice went up, too, from 25 to 50 cents." [14]

In Houston, where the major story that autumn was whether Texas would remain a republic or become a state and where the news came by steamship from New Orleans to Galveston and then overland, the *Telegraph and Texas Register* of October 22 put things in proper economic order from a Southern point of view: "The news from Liverpool by the

Cambria was received at New Orleans on the 12th, but it had no sensible effect on the cotton market. The day after the arrival of the *Cambria* at New York, the price of flour advanced 25 cents a barrel." [15]

The next royal mail steamer that reached America, the *Great Britain*, brought more alarming reports, causing the *New York Tribune* to state on October 16:

> Now that circumstances render it painfully apparent that supplies of food must be had from some quarter, all eyes are turned across the Atlantic and fears prevail that the late orders which have been sent to Canada will miss the season and arrive after the navigation of the St. Lawrence has been closed by the ice . . . If the weather is favorable there is little doubt that handsome fortunes will be made by those who have speculated largely in bread stuffs. [16]

With the arrival of each mail steamer the news became more distressing and the speculation in the markets more frenzied. In late November, the *Hartford Courant* in Connecticut reported:

> We understand that several Flour dealers from Springfield, came down in the train of cars yesterday which brought the Foreign News, with the expectation of getting some bargains out of our merchants before they heard of the rise in Flour. They found them too wide awake, however, to be caught, and went home disappointed. [17]

The publisher of the *New York Herald*, James Gordon Bennett, was even accused of delaying publication of news about the crop failure to make a profit for himself. The *Cincinnati Gazette* of December 1, 1845, reported

> Mr. Bennett has been censured very severely for the last two days respecting his transactions with the foreign news by the last Boston arrival. He received it on Friday at 2 o'clock several hours in advance of the mail by a private express. Instead of publishing it immediately, he held it back some 3 or 4 hours, and sold it to some speculators, and by that means cleared about $5,000 in the transaction. Of all the infamous tricks the *Herald* has practiced this caps the climax. [18]

The suspicion that Bennett was involved in chicanery illustrates the fact that newspaper publishing in America has always mingled public and private, social and entrepreneurial purposes. Followed closely and influenced greatly by the business community of which they usually were leading members, publishers catered to that community's needs. Market news found a prominent place in the columns of most papers, and news from distant cities and countries often was treated as important to the degree that it influenced local business.

Links in the News Chain

The most frequently used sources of such news in that era were other newspapers. South Carolina readers, for example, first learned of the failure of the potato crop in Ireland through an eyewitness account that the editor of the *Charleston Courier* culled from the Dublin *Freeman's Journal*—among the papers brought over by the *Cambria*—and published on October 9:

> We regret to have to state that we have had communications from more than one well informed correspondent announcing the fact of the appearance of what is called 'cholera' in potatoes in Ireland, especially in the north. In one instance the party had been digging potatoes—the finest he had ever seen—from a particular field, and a particular ridge of that field up until Monday last. On digging in the same ridge on Tuesday, he found the tubers all blasted and unfit for the use of man or beast.[19]

Such accounts from foreign newspapers were an excellent source of news, but men and ships were subject to nature in a way satellite dishes are not. News items, therefore, often got into print in unexpected ways and places. In November 1845, the steamship *Massachusetts*, which sailed from Liverpool for New York on October 22 and which "met with a succession of head winds and gales," struck on shoals off Holmes Hole, Massachusetts. The ship's passengers were taken off by a coastal steamer and brought into New Bedford. Not normally having an opportunity to get first crack at European news, the *New Bedford Mercury* buttonholed some of the passengers carrying Irish and English papers and was able to beat both New York and Boston papers. On the morning of November 20, it reported:

> The potato disease has extended almost throughout Ireland. According to the accounts the crop has been almost entirely destroyed in some instances, but more generally the injury is partial, extending to a third or fifth part of the crop. In some districts, fields seem to have escaped the pestilence when all around has been affected. Taken together, says the Dublin correspondent of the *London Morning Chronicle,* at least a fifth of the potato crop must have been destroyed and there are well-grounded apprehensions of a further extension of the rot.[20]

The vagaries of weather and transportation notwithstanding, the practice of picking and choosing items from foreign newspapers enabled American papers to give their readers a comprehensive picture of Famine developments. The *Boston Pilot*, an Irish-American paper, played to its readership's interest in back-home news. A typical summary of Irish happenings in the *Pilot* provided Famine accounts from the *Limerick Reporter, Limerick and Clare Examiner, Limerick Chronicle, Kilkenny Journal, Tipperary Vindicator, Cork Examiner, Tuam Herald,* and *Mayo Constitution.*[21] The accounts were filled with the names of people and townlands that might strike a chord with *Pilot* subscribers. The *Pilot's* summary, for example, included this item from the *Mayo Constitution,* published in Castlebar:

> On last Wednesday, a young man named James Toole who lived about four miles back of Louisburgh came to this town to get into the poorhouse and after remaining all day, was at length told he could not be admitted. The poor creature attempted to make his way home, but from fatigue and hunger he lay down on the road side where he was found dead.[22]

American papers too distant to receive newspapers directly from Europe relied on exchange subscriptions with the large dailies in major cities. Such exchanges were encouraged by the U.S. Postal Service, which delivered without charge newspapers exchanged between publishers.[23] As far away as the Pacific Northwest, subscribers of the *Oregon Spectator* learned in that paper's edition of April 1, 1847:

> By the *New York Sun* of the 9th of November last . . . that the steamer *Britannia* arrived at Boston on the day previous from Liverpool. . . . The intelligence of most moment relates to the deplorable condition of Ireland, in consequence of the failure of the potato crop . . . The famine continues to spread over that unfortunate country. Diseases of a malignant type are also adding to the horrors of the scene.[24]

The *Spectator's* readers were constantly about half a year late getting news of the Famine. On November 25, 1847, it reprinted a March 25 summary from the *Boston Atlas:*

> The quays of Dublin are every day crowded with emigrants, principally natives of Tipperary, Kilkenny, King's and Queen's County, Westmeath, Longford, Cavan and Leitrim. They invariably appear to be of that class known in Ireland by the description of "snug people" or fine able young fellows of the laboring classes, whose energies do not seem to have been much impaired by the prevailing destitution. About three hundred daily is

the number of those who fly from the scenes of misery which exist to such a fearful extent. . . . [25]

Stories from exchanges even bounced back and forth across the Atlantic in most unusual ways. The weekly *Litchfield Enquirer* in a county seat in rural northwestern Connecticut reprinted on March 9, 1848, this tragic story from a Liverpool newspaper, which got it from a letter sent back to England by a passenger who arrived at New Orleans in the ship *Constitution* from Liverpool:

> We were towed out of the river by a steamboat during which our ship was searched for persons who might have secreted themselves in order to pass across the ocean free. Well, eighteen were found, fifteen of whom the master sent back by the steam tug. The rest he allowed to work their passage. After the tug had left and we were in the channel, a large sea chest was secretly opened by the owner of it, an Irishman, who found within, not his living, but his dead brother! He had secreted him and the poor fellow was suffocated. He was thrown overboard that night. [26]

In the absence of international news services, the practice of exchanging newspapers was a remarkably efficient method of spreading the word of happenings in distant places. In the case of the Famine, it gave editors across the American continent a large and diverse selection of items from Ireland itself as well as from England and from American ports of entry to pass along to their readers.

Johnny on the Spot

As efficient as that network was, newspaper professionals still wanted to have their own reporters at the location of the action. To that end, larger and more affluent American papers retained correspondents to fill gaps in the Famine story with on-the-spot coverage. In the always highly competitive news business, such correspondents could provide eyewitness accounts that were not available to readers of competing papers. The correspondents handled their assignments with varying degrees of skill.

The *New Orleans Picayune's* correspondent in Liverpool was sitting in the middle of one of the major stories of the Famine—the arrival and departure from that port of tens of thousands of destitute Irish bound for America—but managed to miss that story almost completely. The *Picayune* reporter seems to have fallen into that trap which even today snares its share of otherwise competent reporters—getting the news mostly from government officials in whose interest it is to paint a rosy picture even in the midst of disaster. In April 1847, when thousands were dying in Ireland just across St. George's Channel and other thousands were fleeing into Liverpool, the *Picayune* correspondent reported encouragingly:

> From Ireland we have more cheering accounts. Grain and breadstuffs are pouring in abundantly . . . Deaths from starvation are less heard of. The men employed on the public works, the number of which had increased to 300,000 . . . have been reduced by one-fifth without any disturbance being created . . . In short, affairs in 'Old Ireland' begin to wear a brighter aspect.[27]

In stark contrast to the mediocre reporting of the *Picayune* man was that of the London correspondent of the *Boston Traveller,* who wrote in a dispatch dated June 31, 1847:

> I am compelled to write about famine, disease and death in Ireland. The picture that I shall hold up to your view is a frightful one; far exceeding in its vividness and horror anything that the pen of the romancer has ever produced . . . It is said that death is mowing down the poor in all directions and the affluent are falling in numbers far above the proportion which they bear to the humbler classes of sufferers. . . . [28]

The *New York Tribune's* London correspondent wrote a similarly shocking description in a dispatch dated January 28, 1848, regarding the impact of the Famine on England:

> London and all the large towns of England are crowded with Irish beggars. In the metropolis their ragged and forlorn appearance boggles description. The group generally consists of a tall, lank man, a woman with a child fastened to her back, another at her breast, and from two to four children almost naked, creeping at her side. They all move at a snail-like pace and beg in the most distressing voice every person who passes . . . [29]

The *Tribune's* Washington correspondent during the Famine was an Irishman, William Robinson, and his ardor for his native land added a dimension—not entirely objective, but papers in those days placed a good deal less importance on objectivity—to his coverage of Famine-related topics in Congress. A Scots-Irish Presbyterian from county Tyrone, Robinson wrote under the pseudonym "Richelieu."[30] He followed closely the debate in Congress on the question of aid to the starving Irish, and when the next election approached he vehemently called for the defeat of a

Nativist congressman, Orville Hungerford, who, Robinson said, had played a major role in the defeat of the legislation. Robinson wrote:

> [The bill] was defeated in the House by Orville Hungerford and one or two other members of the committee on ways and means. I recollect how I appealed to the members of that committee not to strangle the bill in the committee room. I begged of them, if they were opposed to it to vote against it, but not to stab it in the dark. The Irish papers and the Irish citizens of both parties were in favor of its passage and it would have passed by a large majority if Hungerford and company had given it back. He was deaf to our cries then; shall we remember him now? He was not contented with voting against it. He undertook to veto if by the meanest kind of a veto. . . . I would not dictate to any man how he should vote, but I could not vote for the Loco Foco ticket with Orville Hungerford on it without feeling the guilt of Irish deaths upon my soul.[31]

The *Cincinnati Gazette* had a crackerjack of a correspondent in New York when it came to the financial aspects of the Famine story. In a dispatch dated November 23, 1845, the *Gazette's* reporter described the scene in New York:

> A lively place yesterday was the great flour depot of the city; all along South street in the vicinity of Broad were seen grouped together not only the regular Flourists, but many who came to speculate in the article for the first time. Vast quantities changed hands at prices ranging from $7.06 to $7.25, though very few sales were made at the last named price, and those were in small lots and of favorite brands. It was quite amusing to a looker-on to hear the fancy offers of some of the new operators; for example: A Wall street Stock-broker offered $150 for the privilege of taking or leaving, at the expiration of three days, a lot of 2,000 barrels at 7.25, on forfeiting the amount of the advance. . . . Speculators in flour must have great confidence that the British government will accommodate them by an abatement of the duty; for surely there is no margin for profits at present prices. This mode of trading appears to be very much like gambling.[32]

Even some small regional papers put correspondents to good use—or had correspondents who put their opportunities for coverage to good use—in the story of the Famine. The *New Haven Palladium* in Connecticut employed a correspondent who signed his dispatches "Trumbull" and who provided some of the best coverage of the immigrant side of the Famine story simply by hanging around the docks of New York City. On January 20, 1848, for example, Trumbull wrote:

> The packets which arrived on Sunday with such an army of emigrants were in a terrible filthy condition, having been out so long. On board of

one of them, which had nearly five hundred steerage passengers, some
dozen died on the passage. In answer to my inquiry as to the nature of
their disease, one of the mates said, 'starvation!' 'But you wouldn't allow
people to starve on board of your ship when you had enough and to spare?'
'Certainly not,' said Jack, 'if we knew it. But these people crowd into the
ship, many of them are alone and total strangers and nobody knows or
cares about them, and they hunger and die; the steerage passengers find
their own provisions and their food is no concern of the officers of the
ship.' The greater part of these passengers were of the very poorest class
from Ireland—in a state of destitution—without decent clothes or food;
they began begging the moment they landed on the dock.[33]

The *Boston Pilot* had a correspondent with a very specialized purpose.
Its Thomas Mooney traveled throughout the western parts of the United
States and wrote glowing reports about them in the hope that immi-
grants would leave the crowded eastern cities and move westward. On
February 5, 1848, the *Pilot* published a typical Mooney dispatch from Iowa
City, Iowa:

> The more I see of those western states the more I am enamored of them—
> the more I am convinced that they offer the emigrant from Ireland the real
> and safe asylum which he has heard of at home, but which he never can
> realize till he comes out west. Here is this new state of Iowa, far bigger
> than Ireland, highly fertile, generally healthy, partly prairie meadows and
> oak openings, so well mixed that the emigrant can find a farm with just
> enough of timber land to afford him fuel and building wood, yet scattered
> over this beautiful state there are not yet more than one hundred and fifty
> thousand inhabitants of all ages and sexes though it will support many
> millions.[34]

Thus did American newspapers put correspondents to good use focusing on particular aspects of the Famine story—commercial, legislative,
social—that they believed were of special interest to their subscribers.
That such correspondents brought their own biases and journalistic
shortcomings to their reporting was more than offset by the extra dimension they were able to add to coverage.

The Local Scene

Ironically, while Famine-era newspapers employed correspondents to
supplement accounts of the news from afar, they often were less attuned
to the possibilities of local angles. Local reporting was not a strong suit
of pre–Civil War American newspapers, and the covering of local beats

seems to have been haphazard at best. However, when reporters or editors did tap local sources, the result often was the publication of wonderfully personal and moving accounts. The *Boston Transcript's* May 24, 1847, report of a "disturbance on an immigrant ship" tells much about the conditions under which many of the starving Irish crossed the ocean:

> A disturbance occurred on board the British brig *Mary* on Saturday last, originating in the following reasons: the brig brought 46 steerage passengers but owing to their destitute condition, the city authorities would not suffer them be landed unless the master gave bonds that they should not become a burthen to the city. This he was unable or unwilling to do, and came to the conclusion that he must take them to Halifax for which port he accordingly cleared on Saturday. The passengers were exasperated at this and swore they would remain in Boston and when orders were given to weigh anchor, they opposed the crew and would not suffer them to proceed with their duty. Capt. Joseph Sturgis with a portion of the Cutter Hamilton's crew was called on board the brig and after some resistance during which he had a personal recontre with one of the passengers, succeeded in putting a stop to the disturbance and got the vessel under weigh and went to sea.[35]

The *Gleaner* in the seaport town of Miramichi, New Brunswick, provided excellent spot news coverage of a "coffin" ship in distress in its June 8, 1847, edition:

> The usual quiet of our little town was considerably disturbed on Thursday afternoon last, by the appearance of a ship's boat off Henderson's wharf and one of the parties hailing some of the persons thereon, stated he wished to be put in communication with the public authorities. A number of individuals speedily congregated, among them two or three Magistrates. The person in the boat then said his name was Thane, that he commanded the ship *Looshtauk*, belonging to Dublin, of upwards of 600 tons from Liverpool bound for Quebec, out 7 weeks; that he had, when he left port 467 passengers, 117 of whom died on the passage; that there were now 100 unable to help themselves and that the crew, from exhaustion were not able to work the ship. He craved medical attendance, fresh provisions, bread, &c. Two of the Poor Commissioners being present, immediately set about collecting necessaries and to the credit of the inhabitants of the town, the appeal to their humanity was spontaneously responded to. In a short time, a large quantity of beef, bread and other supplies were collected and put on board the boat. The Honorable Joseph Cunard furnished the Captain with written instructions to the Commander of his Steamer, which was hourly expected from below, to tow the vessel up to the Quarantine ground. On Friday evening, she was brought up to the station, near

Middle Island, and yesterday the passengers were landed on that Island, where temporary sheds had been erected for their reception on Sunday. The number of deaths, as far as we have been able to ascertain, since she put into this port up to yesterday evening was forty!—a shocking mortality . . . [36]

The Saint John, New Brunswick, *Courier* told of the plight of another coffin ship on May 22, 1847. Thirty-four of 418 passengers died on board the *Alderbaran,* which sailed from Sligo on March 22. And when it arrived in Saint John, another 100 passengers were ill with fever and dysentery. The paper blamed bad water and a scarcity of soft food for the children for the high rate of death and sickness.[37] Later, the *Courier* printed a list of the names and ages of those emigrants who had died at Saint John's quarantine station on Partridge Island. The list makes grim reading, containing as it does the names of infants, elderly, and those in the prime of life. From just one ship, the dead included:

From Barque *Amazon* from Liverpool—Winfred Cummidy, aged 46; Bridget Marren, 25; Ann Dugan, 2 1/2; Mary Hobin, 27; Rachael Gypsum, 22; Norry Sullivan, 20; Charles McGuire, 8; James Gibson, 30; Patrick McDonagh, 25; Patrick M'Donough, 20; Catherine Curryan, 16; Martin Aikin, 16; John Coffee, 40; Catherine Owen, 56; Thomas McGraugh, 30; Bernard Morin, 4; William Kennedy, 50; James Gill, 4; Joseph Martin, 2 . . . [38]

The *New York Tribune* on May 1, 1847, printed an account of a visit to the quarantine hospital on Staten Island where one of its reporters found that of 250 patients, all were Irish and all were suffering from ship fever.[39]

Occasionally, the Irish emigrants found a friend in an investigative reporter. The *Montreal Baptist Register,* for example, refused to accept assurances of authorities in that city about the condition of emigrants arriving there. It commented:

It is difficult to obtain accurate information from an unwillingness on the part of those in office to divulge particulars. Against this concealment we must utter our decided protest. Surmises founded on an unwillingness to disclose facts, will have a more widespread and pernicious influence than the truth, however startling. From sources, however, on which we can rely, we learn that 30 corpses were buried on Saturday and 27 on Sabbath and that the average number of deaths is about 25 per day. Many cases of extreme distress came to our knowledge during a recent visit to the sheds. We met with one poor heart-broken man whose children were in the hospital at Grosse Isle and whose wife was uttering her last sighs in our sheds.

An interesting girl with tears in her eyes entreated us to visit her dying sister—her only relative in this continent. Lonely was she amongst multitudes. Numbers were lying about on their wet bedding and boxes, the subjects of excessive weakness, brought on by violent dysentery. They manifested a state of apathy and indifference to personal cleanliness ever the result of great and protracted suffering . . . [40]

Touching examples of family loyalty did not go unreported. The Washington, D.C., *National Intelligencer,* for instance, learned from a merchant in that city that an impoverished Irish immigrant had come to him with five dollars in gold. The immigrant said it was the first money he had earned in America and that rather than spend it, he wanted it sent to his brother who was starving.[41] And the *Cincinnati Commercial* reporter dug up this fascinating story of another young Famine immigrant determined against all odds to find his family:

A lad about thirteen years of age arrived in this city by the cars night before last, and exhibits a strength of close clinging affection, which it is a pleasure to record. His mother and sister left Ireland about a year ago for America and the boy being then a bound apprentice was not permitted to accompany them, although he desired to do so. Some eight months after their departure, the fellow, without a penny in his pocket, ran away from his master, walked to Dublin City, told his story to the captain of an American ship, and tearfully solicited his aid in taking him to his mother. The captain told him that the United States was a very large country and should he get there he might not find the object of his search, but the little Japhet was determined to try and finally got the captain's consent to take him over the ocean in the capacity of a second cook.

The vessel arrived at New York and the little fellow, all alone, searched the great Metropolis throughout, inquiring of the Irish families of the whereabouts of his mother, but to no purpose. No one knew her. During the search which continued more than a week, the little fellow met his current expenses by doing chores in the streets such as holding horses, etc.—for a lad of that kind could not be dishonest. Failing in New York, he worked his passage on a steamboat to Albany, reached that city and worked his way to Buffalo, thence to Sandusky and on to Cincinnati, making a journey in all of about four thousand miles in search of his mother! Upon his arrival here, he immediately sought out the Irish residents and for the first time heard of the object of his long and singular pilgrimage. He learned that his mother and sister had lived in Cincinnati, but about a month since had moved to Vanceburg, Ky.

The little Japhet in the fullness of his joy was determined that an hour should not be lost, and went to Capt. Grace, *Brilliant,* yesterday and told his story. The captain took him on board, gave him some money and pro-

vided him comfortably for the passage and doubtless ere this, the little
fellow is in the arms of the loved ones of his search.[42]

Such accounts are wonderful testimonies to what newspaper people
even today call "enterprise," that practice followed by really good reporters who just wandered about town talking, not to political leaders, but to
the common people. From storekeepers and bartenders and trolley car
conductors, they picked up leads which when chased down and fleshed
out caught the heartbeat and the heartache of the Famine story.

Letters to the Editor

Another way that editors had of getting to the grass roots of the news at
the time of the Famine was the letter to the editor. Today, such letters are
consigned to the editorial page, their value seen in their expression of
opinions by citizens on questions of public policy. In the Famine era, editors treated their letters as news items rather than opinion pieces. They
placed them in news columns, often even on page one. Turned into reporters, letter writers frequently responded by providing remarkably
graphic and moving accounts.

Early in the Famine years, the *New York Tribune* printed a letter from a
Dublin observer that accurately predicted what was about to happen:

> Ere this letter will have reached you, the famine will actually have com-
> menced and whatever may be done in the interim to avert its evils, im-
> mense suffering must ensue. Could I detail to you the many cases of
> wretchedness and want daily under our observation, I believe it would
> arouse our country to immediate and energetic action. But I need not de-
> tail them. Is it not enough that six millions of human beings in England
> and Ireland are within eight weeks of starvation?[43]

In early July 1847, the New Orleans firm of McDowell & Peck received
from a business acquaintance in Galway, Henry Barry Hyde, a letter containing a copy of a report that Hyde had prepared in his capacity as secretary of the Galway Industrial Society, detailing the suffering on the west
coast of Ireland. McDowell & Peck passed the report along to the *Picayune*, which printed it. It told how laborers in Galway had hardly the
strength to do the work of boys, how fishermen were so emaciated that
they could not work their boats and how the town was full of orphans,
boys and girls ten or twelve years old, tottering under the weight of

smaller children.[44] That letter prompted another from a New Orleans woman just back from Ireland:

> Gentlemen, permit a lady who has recently spent a year in Ireland and who has witnessed from the Giant's Causeway to Cape Clear the miseries of its inhabitants to corroborate the late testimony contained in a circular addressed to a mercantile house in this city . . . Language is inadequate to give even a faint idea of the horrors endured by the sons and daughters of that most beautiful portion of God's earth . . . The writer . . . has seen tears of gratitude course each other down the furrowed cheek of the once strong and stalwart man receiving a trifle too pitiful to name with which to appease the hunger gnawing at his vitals and reducing his Herculean frame to a skeleton; this man with thousands of his class with more than Spartan firmness resisting all impulses of self-relief going at early dawn fasting, to his work on the public roads and returning at night exhausted to cast his weary limbs on the damp floor of his cheerless hovel, naught having passed his lips for the day but a drink of water or, perchance a raw turnip, his only comfort the hope that miserable earnings had afforded in his absence a mouthful a piece to his numerous little ones and loved wife—a wife who in her turn had been practicing a touching lesson of self denial, by tasting only of the food which she apportioned to her famished children . . .[45]

Letters describing aspects of the Famine pop up in the most unlikely journalistic places. Rev. William Livesey, an American Methodist minister, sailed to England in 1846 to confer with Methodist clergymen. While there, he crossed over to Dublin to attend a church conference. In a letter to *Zion's Herald and Wesleyan Journal,* a church paper published in Boston and Portland, Maine, he left a vivid description of the plight of Famine immigrants on the Dublin to Liverpool steamboat:

> Every berth in the cabin was taken up and the whole of the deck was occupied with cattle and passengers. The number crowded together upon the deck was incredible; so close was the jam that it was almost impossible to change their position without treading on someone. No chair or bench of any kind was provided . . . Here were hundreds of passengers, male and female, many on their way to Liverpool and from thence to America, children and baggage stowed together upon the deck of a steamboat like cattle and with cattle, many of whom left their native country with great emotion, for we saw them weep as they parted from their friends and many an anxious look was cast upon the highlands as they receded from their view . . .[46]

Another clergyman, Fr. B. O'Hara, gave the *Boston Pilot* a copy of the diary he kept of his voyage to America on an immigrant ship, the *Granada*, in the summer of 1849. The diary provided graphic descriptions of life on board an immigrant ship, including this narration of a storm at sea:

The ship bent and bowed and groaned, she heaved and rolled but up again she stood after a trying and glorious struggle . . . and although one's heart grew faint and sunken as the chances became more and more uneven and the gloomy horrors of death stared him more and more nearly, yet, his attention was unavoidably arrested by the piercing cries of grief which issued from the hold of the vessel. Here were two hundred and fifty human beings in a narrow space rendered still more intolerable now that it was darkened; for as each tremendous wave struck the ship it swept across the decks and bursting through the hatchways rushed impetuously amongst the poor, terrified passengers. They screamed aloud, frantic in despair and forgetting that the ship was still riding above the storm they fancied that the angry ocean in all its fury had ruthlessly burst in upon them. To save and quiet them, they were shut in and the hatches closed down but, poor creatures, this augmented their desolation and their cries were loud enough to rise above the storm and reach to heaven.[47]

A traveler visiting "Canada East" sent letters back to the *Toronto Globe* including one in which he or she gave from the deck of an excursion boat a haunting description of Grosse Île, the quarantine station in the St. Lawrence just above Quebec City:

Thus were we employed when the words Grosse Isle, Grosse Isle sounding in our ears—all arose, intent upon getting a sight at this isle of graves. Its shores were covered with shining tents, without all beautiful and fair— within the abode of sighs and moans and death; around it lay, at anchor, eighteen ships whose passengers were now ashore and on our way we afterwards met four others crowded with immigrants to add their quota to the scene of death . . . [48]

Occasionally letters from celebrities turned up in the columns of American papers. On March 18, 1847, the *Boston Pilot* printed a letter from the famous Irish novelist Maria Edgeworth, who stated:

I assure you that during my sixty-six years resident in Ireland, I never knew of distress equal to the present. . . . At this moment a vast quantity of the land in Ireland is untilled for want both of men to till and of seed to sow it. The men who have been employed in public works, now when almost too late they are turned back to till the ground as tenants or as laborers for themselves or others, have merely and hardly been supported by their wages at the public works and cannot now without wages or with lowered wages feed themselves or work to prepare the crop for next season.[49]

Some letters were prescriptive rather than descriptive. Having experience with the potato blight, American agriculturalists took great interest in the causes and remedies of that disease in Ireland. A Hanover, New Hampshire, gentleman, Mr. J. Pinneo, told the *Boston Cultivator* of his experience that "the potato rot did not affect the hills which were planted in the immediate neighborhood of shade trees, though all other parts of the same field were seriously affected with the rot."[50]

And up in the potato country of Maine, the *Calais Advertiser* on November 12, 1846, reprinted a letter from the *Maine Farmer,* which had picked it up from the *Berwick Advertiser,* which had copied it from the *Farmer's Cabinet.* The correspondent said he had produced an excellent crop by planting the cuttings of the green stalks of early potatoes. He suggested that if everyone in the United Kingdom tried that method they would enjoy more abundant and healthier crops.[51] Another letter writer to the Calais paper on April 8, 1847, chided people in that area for not lifting a finger to aid the suffering Irish. The writer said there was hardly a town in New England that had not lent a helping hand and urged Calais residents to call a town meeting and collect money for the Irish.[52]

Letters appealing for aid for Famine victims were common. A letter to the *Philadelphia Pennsylvanian* printed on April 9, 1847, pointed out that those who had visited Ireland had reported a great need for clothing and suggested that instead of giving money Philadelphians search their wardrobes for used garments that still were good enough to be sent to the sufferers.[53]

Some letters were written on behalf of specific Famine victims. In a letter to the editor in the *New York Tribune* of April 17, 1847, a Miss Wood related this sad tale:

Catherine Haggerty from Castletown, parish of Killbridge and County of Meagh or Mayo—came in search of a sister who had sent for her repeatedly . . . she landed at Quebec and thence proceeded to New York. Imagine a simple, ignorant girl left alone probably at dark in such a scene of discord and confusion as always occurs on the arrival of a steamboat. A trunk containing her clothing and everything she possessed was placed on a cart and while she was standing on the dock talking to a woman, the cart drove off. When she looked around and discovered her loss, her cries of disappointment and despair attracted the bystanders. Being literally penniless and friendless, she was lodged in the tombs and the next day sent as a vagrant to Blackwell's—there she remained until observed by some charitable visitor who procured admission for her at the Home. She is industrious and well disposed, but subject to violent paroxysms of grief at the recollection of her parents who endeavored to dissuade her from leaving them and the hopelessness of meeting the sister for whom she has braved all the hardships of a long voyage to a strange land. Her sister is residing, she believes, in Danville, Ohio; her husband's name is Peter Powers. If this article were republished in the Ohio papers it might reach the eye of someone capable of furnishing information . . . [54]

Moved only by compassion, Miss Wood probably had no thought of writing history when she penned her appeal on behalf of Catherine Haggerty. Yet, the few lines of her letter are vibrant with details about the immigrant experience—routes traveled, hazards faced, the terrible uncertainty of being alone in an alien land. Her letter, along with countless others printed in American papers, added depth and dimension to Famine coverage.

The Power of Advertising

Catherine Haggerty was not alone in losing track of relatives during the often hastily arranged emigration of the Famine years. The situation was exacerbated because funds frequently were insufficient to pay passage for entire families, so that Irish immigrants came one at a time or in small groups. In the process, thousands of immigrants were separated from their families. For them, American newspapers were not so much a source of information but a lifeline. Immigrants and Irish people already settled in the New World used the advertising columns of those newspapers as a continent-spanning bulletin board to reunite them with loved ones. The *Nova Scotian* of February 6, 1848, for example, contained a typical immigrant advertisement placed by Ellen Marah of Halifax seeking information about her brother Daniel, whether dead or alive. A native of Killinane, county Kerry, he had sailed from the Cove of Cork in May 1847 and landed in Quebec in June.[55]

Secular papers carried some of these advertisements, but Irish and Catholic newspapers were favored by immigrants and their families, probably because such papers had a wider circulation in the Irish community and had the most chance of producing results. The *Catholic Herald* in

Philadelphia on December 7, 1848, ran a series of such ads, including this one, which suggested how easy it was for immigrants in a strange land to miss connections with each other:

> Information wanted of Joseph Byrne, who left Pittsburgh about the 20th of June and came to Philadelphia to meet his wife and six children from Ireland. This is to inform him that they arrived in Pittsburgh shortly after he left there. The said Joseph Byrne informed his family by letter that he was going to settle on land in Knox County, Ohio.[56]

Advertisers used newspaper columns in other ways during the Famine period. A shipping agent in Philadelphia advertised in the *Pennsylvanian* on November 18, 1846:

> Passage from Londonderry—Persons wishing to engage passage for their friends in first rate ships to sail from Londonderry to Philadelphia the ensuing spring . . . may now do so by applying to Robert Taylor, no. 32 Walnut st.[57]

Tapscott's General Emigration and Foreign Exchange Office advertised that it could handle drafts to all parts of England, Ireland, Scotland, and Wales from those wishing to bring their friends across the Atlantic.[58] A competitor, Roche Brothers, advertised that its drafts on the Royal Bank of Ireland were free of discount or any charge whatever in all the principal towns of the United Kingdom.[59]

As always there were hucksters and hustlers waiting to squeeze a buck out of immigrants. The *New York Herald* of June 1, 1848, ran this ad:

> Emigrants!—The Miseries and troubles of sickness from change of climate can, in a great degree, be saved you if you procure and keep by you the Brandeth Pills to be immediately resorted to should your health become affected. Days, months, nay years of sickness may be thus prevented . . . [60]

And taking Dr. Townsend's sarsaparilla to ward off ship fever was touted as almost a civic responsibility in one ad:

> That this disease is contagious there now can be no doubt and is spreading throughout the city. It is the duty of everyone as well as the authorities to guard against it. Dr. Townsend's sarsaparilla will prevent the ship fever. If the blood is pure and healthy it is impossible to take this fever or any other. Let all such as have impure blood or are in any way debilitated and especially weakly children, take the sarsaparilla and protect them from the pestilence and the hot season before it is too late.[61]

American newspaper advertising, then, made its own contribution to coverage of the Famine saga, a contribution as intriguing as that of newspaper reporting. Whether as a means of reuniting families or of fleecing unsuspecting immigrants, it became one colorful thread in the fabric of the great mass migration triggered by the starvation.

A Light Side to the Gloomiest News

An equally colorful but far less likely thread in that fabric was humor. From colonial times, humor was a staple of American newspapering. Indeed, newspapers of the 1840s were filled with tall tales and yarns making the rounds in an age without televised sitcoms. As horrifying a story as the Famine was, journalists were able occasionally to lighten it with humor. Perhaps they did so out of the very human need to relieve the seemingly endless tragedy. Or perhaps they did so because they appreciated the ability of lampoon and satire to cut through sophistry and pretensions to lay bare the real causes and effects of the disaster.

A humorous story published on April 11, 1848, in the *New Haven Palladium* used a play on words to summarize the reaction of a Famine-era Irishman to the news that there had been a revolution in France that year:

> A native of the Emerald Isle the other day, on hearing of a revolution in France, the flight of the King and his family, the triumph of the democracy and the establishment of a provisionary government, exclaimed, By St. Patrick and is not that just the thing that sweet Ireland wants? A provisionary government for ever! By the powers, the only government she now has is a starvationary one.[62]

The *Woburn (Mass.) Guide-Post* printed what it described as a bona fide letter transmitted by an Irishman living at Craigie's Point or East Cambridge to his brother in Ireland:

> Dear Pathric—Americay is a vary fine counthry. There is no hangin' fur stealing and portatoes is 40 cents a booshl and New Rum the same. Yez can cum by the way of Canydtha an' when yez git to Canydtha inquare for Lowl Raleroad. Ye'll buy a loaf of brid and the Raleroad before yez, and inquare for George Dunlaree at the Pint; any one'll shoo yez. I'm an agent for Lowl Raleroad and kape the key of the swetch in me pocket an' no one can pass widout me knowin' it.[63]

The *Niagara Mail*, published at Niagara on the Lake in what is now Ontario, regularly reprinted columns written for the *Dublin Warder* by a satirist who signed his pieces "Terry Driscoll." Driscoll wrote much in the manner of the more famous and later Finley Peter Dunn of the *Chicago Evening Post*. His columns were in the form of letters from Stoneybatter, near Dublin, to "my dear Thady." Driscoll found much to satirize in the response of government and church to the Famine and spared no one in his satires. In a column printed in the *Mail* on February 2, 1848, he spoke of his hesitancy in writing on a Friday, when

> The blessed Catholic biships . . . are sittin' this present minit, takin' their fried fish and the least taste o' brandy in their tay, at Misther Coffey's hotel an' plannin' how they'll take a start out o'Lord John Russell in regard o' the comin' scarcity . . . as regards intelligence in a general sinse, we're followin' the beaten thrack. Public meetin's an' nothin' out o' 'em, Ireland lyin' down like a crathur in the typhus an' all the quacks about her, advisin' an' prescribin', but perdition to the two of 'em agreein'—an' signs of the patient's sinkin' day by day.[64]

If Driscoll's quacks had no answer for Ireland, a gentleman named Timothy O'Reardon did in what was offered, apparently at least partly tongue in cheek, in a letter printed in the *New York Tribune* on June 18, 1846. O'Reardon, who claimed to be a resident of Navan, county Meath, addressed his letter to the House of Representatives in Washington and begged that body to work out a deal whereby the United States could lease Ireland from England:

> The population of Ireland is . . . in round numbers eight millions. The larger half is described by royal commissioners as being badly housed, badly clothed and badly fed. I am one of these. The English say it is our fault, we say it is theirs. Let them only give a lease of us to your government for thirty-one years, almost on any terms and it will settle the question. They acknowledge that we give them a great deal of trouble and we know that they inflict on us a great deal of hardship and suffering. Try, then, honorable sirs, to get the treaty passed, the lease made perfect, so that there shall be no squabbling afterward about it and see if Ireland will not improve. That she should retrograde is impossible. She cannot be lower . . . [65]

Conclusion

When editor William Annand wrote his lead story in the *Nova Scotian* on October 1, 1845, little did he realize its true significance. As fate would have it, a single but key sentence of his story was likely the first line in a long literature on the Great Famine. And so with the brush of humor as well as that of pathos did American newspapers sketch the portrait of the first terrible starvation of modern times. Their strokes came in bits and pieces garnered from across an ocean that was still a major barrier to communication, filtered through the eyes of correspondents and letter writers from all walks of life and served up in the colorful, personal style of mid-nineteenth-century journalism.

Those who contributed to Famine coverage brought to their task their own viewpoints, biases, and agendas. Among them were hard-nosed editors scrapping to scoop the competition, crusaders determined to ease the suffering, calculating entrepreneurs looking for a quick profit, advertisers bent on making a sale, thoughtful observers pondering the implications of a Famine that killed a million human beings and sent another million or more in headlong flight to the New World.

As inadequate as any of their individual observations may have been, together they gave American readers a compelling portrait of the tragedy that was unfolding in Ireland and producing a profound effect on life in America as well. If newspapers provide the first draft of history, then American newspapers served their purpose well in their coverage of Ireland's greatest tragedy, the Famine.

Notes

1. "The English Mail," *The Nova Scotian* (Halifax), Oct. 6, 1845.
2. "Arrival of the Steamship *Hibernia*," *Catholic Herald* (Philadelphia), Mar. 26, 1846.
3. Ibid.
4. Ibid.
5. "Arrival of the *Cambria*," *Montreal Gazette*, Oct. 7, 1845.
6. "The *Cambria*," *New York Herald*, Oct. 1, 1845.
7. "Steamship *Cambria*," *New York Herald*, Oct. 2, 1845.
8. "The *Cambria*," *New York Herald*, Oct. 3, 1845.
9. "Two Weeks Later from Europe . . . ," *New York Herald*, Oct. 3, 1845.
10. "Two Weeks Later from Europe . . . ," *New York Herald*, Oct. 4, 1845.
11. "Arrival of the *Cambria*," *Richmond Enquirer*, Oct. 7, 1845.
12. "Arrival of the *Cambria*," *Montreal Gazette*, Oct. 7, 1845.
13. "Foreign Intelligence," *Cincinnati Daily Enquirer*, Oct. 10, 1845.
14. "By the Last Mails," *Cincinnati Daily Enquirer*, Oct. 11, 1845.
15. "By Steamship *Cincinnati*," *Telegraph and Texas Register* (Houston), Oct. 22, 1845.

16. "The Crops," *New York Tribune*, Oct. 16, 1845.

17. (No heading) *Hartford Courant*, Nov. 22, 1845.

18. (No heading), *Cincinnati Gazette*, Dec. 1, 1845. See also "Newspapers and Speculators," *New York Tribune*, Nov. 24, 1845.

19. "Later from Europe," *The Courier* (Charleston, S.C.), Oct. 8, 1845.

20. "Arrival of the Steam-Propeller *Massachusetts* at Holmes Hole," *Evening Transcript* (Boston), Nov. 20, 1845.

21. "Ireland," *Boston Pilot*, Dec. 30, 1848.

22. Ibid.

23. Frank Luther Mott, *American Journalism, A History: 1690–1960* (New York: Macmillan, 1962), 305.

24. "Late and Important European News," *Spectator* (Oregon City, Ore.), Apr. 1, 1847.

25. "Foreign Intelligence," *Spectator*, Nov. 25, 1847.

26. "An Emigrant Suffocated in a Tea Chest," *Litchfield Enquirer*, Mar. 9, 1848.

27. "European Correspondence," *Daily Picayune* (New Orleans), May 2, 1847.

28. "Horrid State of the Irish," *Calais (Maine) Advertiser*, July 15, 1847.

29. "Foreign Correspondence of the *Tribune*," *New York Daily Tribune*, Feb. 18, 1848.

30. Neil Hogan, *Wearin' O' the Green* (Hamden, Conn.: Impression Printing, 1992), 7.

31. "The Irish and O.' Hungerford," *New York Daily Tribune*, Nov. 1, 1847.

32. "Correspondence of the *Cincinnati Gazette*," *Cincinnati Gazette*, Nov. 29, 1845.

33. "Correspondence of the *Palladium*," *New Haven Palladium*, Jan. 22, 1848.

34. "Emigration," *Boston Pilot*, Feb. 5, 1848.

35. "Disturbance on Board an Immigrant Ship," *Boston Transcript*, May 24, 1847.

36. "More Emigrants," *Nova Scotian* (Halifax), June 14, 1847.

37. (No heading), *Courier* (Saint John, N.B.), May 22, 1847.

38. "The following is a return of the persons . . ." *Courier*, July 10, 1847.

39. "Quarantine Hospital," *New York Daily Tribune*, May 1, 1847.

40. "The Emigrant," *Montreal Gazette*, June 18, 1847.

41. "Irish Generosity," *New Haven Palladium*, July 23, 1847.

42. "Youthful Perseverance," *New Haven Palladium*, May 10, 1849.

43. "The Famine in Ireland," *New York Daily Tribune*, Nov. 24, 1845.

44. "Galway Industrial Society," *Daily Picayune* (New Orleans), July 3, 1847.

45. "The Distresses of Ireland," ibid., July 4, 1847.

46. "Letter from England," *Zion's Herald and Wesleyan Journal*, Sept. 16, 1846.

47. "Journal of a Voyage from Liverpool to Boston," *Pilot* (Boston), July 14, 1849.

48. "Letter III, Notes of a Trip to Canada East," *Toronto Globe*, Sept. 1, 1847.

49. "To the Ladies of New York," *Boston Pilot*, Apr. 17, 1847.

50. "Potato Rot," *New Haven Palladium*, Nov. 11, 1847.

51. "The Potato Disease," *Calais Adviser*, Nov. 12, 1846.

52. "Suffering Ireland," ibid., Apr. 8, 1847.

53. "Ireland," *Pennsylvanian* (Philadelphia), Apr. 9, 1847.

54. "Sufferings of Poor Immigrants," *New York Daily Tribune*, Apr. 17, 1847.

55. "Information Wanted of Daniel Marah," *Nova Scotian*, Mar. 6, 1848.

56. "Information Wanted of Joseph Byrne," *Catholic Herald* (Philadelphia), Dec. 7, 1848.

57. "Passage from Londonderry," *Pennsylvanian*, Nov. 18, 1846.

58. "Tapscott's General Emigration and Foreign Exchange Office," *New York Herald*, Jan. 10, 1847.

59. "Roche Brothers & Co. Arrangements," *New York Herald*, Jan. 6, 1847.

60. "Emigrants!" *New York Herald*, June 1, 1848.

61. "Dr. Townsend's Sarsaparilla," *New York Daily Tribune*, Oct. 4, 1847.

62. "Better Government," *New Haven Palladium*, Apr. 11, 1848.

63. "Railroad Agent," *Niagara Mail* (Niagara on the Lake, Ont.), Dec. 22, 1847.

64. "Ireland and the Irish—A Snapping Shot at Passing Events," *Niagara Mail*, Feb. 2, 1848.

65. "Annexation of Ireland," *New York Daily Tribune*, June 18, 1846.

9

Kerby A. Miller

"Revenge for Skibbereen"

Irish Emigration and the Meaning of the Great Famine

IN THE LATE nineteenth and early twentieth centuries, Irish observers as disparate as the nationalist politician John Francis Maguire and the unionist historian W. E. H. Lecky agreed that it was primarily the experiences and memories of the Great Famine that engendered "the savage hatred of England that animates great bodies of Irishmen on either side of the Atlantic"—especially among the Irish in America—inspiring their repeated efforts to destroy the Irish landlord system and free Ireland from British rule.[1] Those efforts, such as the Fenian movement of 1858–67, largely spawned in the Irish ghettoes of New York City, often seemed to be animated at least as much by Irish-American hatred for England as by love of Ireland. Thus, thirty years after the Famine, Michael Flanagan, an Irish farmer in California's Napa Valley, recalled "the rich . . . Devils . . . who drove the [Irish] population into the Poorhouse or across the Atlantic" and dreamed that the Irish in America might pay them "a just reward for their oppression."[2] Likewise in the 1880s, Patrick O'Callaghan, a laborer in Philadelphia, prayed for the "day of retribution," and another immigrant, John Cronin, vowed that the Irish "exiles" in America eagerly awaited an opportunity "to go back [to Ireland] with a double undying vengeance to hurl the Vile Saxon oppressor from the Shores of Erin."[3] Indeed, the Fenian movement was inspired by just such a desire to transport thousands of Irish Americans, ex-soldiers from the American Civil War, back to Ireland so they could reverse the Famine's consequences and reestablish their families on Irish soil. And it was the Fenian movement which inspired the Irish-American ballad, one line of which provides the title of this chapter: "Oh father dear," the song prophesied,

. . . the day will come when vengeance loud will call,
And we will rise with Erin's boys to rally one and all.
I'll be the man to lead the van beneath our flag of green,
And loud and high will raise the cry, "Revenge for Skibbereen!"[4]

Skibbereen was a town in west county Cork whose scenes of Famine suffering gained special notoriety from their published description by Nicholas Cummins, an absentee landlord, who in 1846 discovered to his horror that the cabins on his estate were inhabited by "famished and ghastly skeletons."[5] However, conditions were at least equally awful in other districts, such as west Connacht and the north midlands where, a year later, another visitor "saw sights that will never wholly leave the eyes ·that beheld them, cowering wretches almost naked in the savage weather, prowling in turnip fields, and endeavouring to grub up roots . . . little children . . . their limbs fleshless, . . . their faces bloated yet wrinkled and of a pale greenish hue, . . . who would never, it was too plain, grow up to be men and women."[6] Such personal accounts give terrible meaning to the mere statistical consequences of the Great Famine: between 1.1 and 1.5 million persons dead of starvation or famine-related diseases between 1845 and 1851; at least 500,000 evicted from their homes by landlords and "strong farmers"; some three million people (about 40 percent of the Irish population) on some form of official relief; over a million people crammed into poorhouses designed to hold only a fraction of that number; and, between 1845 and 1855, over 2.1 million Irish (about one-fourth of the island's pre-Famine population) emigrants overseas, nearly 1.9 million of them to North America, of whom perhaps as many as 40,000 died aboard the "coffin ships" or in Canadian and American quarantine hospitals.

NEVERTHELESS, THESE appalling statistics alone cannot explain the "savage hatred" for England that the Famine engendered among the Irish, especially in the New World, and at least one Irish Catholic politician later wondered why what he called "the noble generosity of the English people appears to be forgotten in a frenzy of reproach against the English government."[7] Indeed, one modern scholar, Roger McHugh, who analyzed Irish folklore of the Great Famine, concluded that most Irish country people interpreted that catastrophe as an "act of God" rather than in nationalist terms.[8] Contemporary Irish Catholic clergymen also viewed the Famine as a divine rather than a political phenomenon, as "a calamity

with which God wishes to purify . . . the Irish people," as Archbishop Paul
Cullen put it, and which would "scatter . . . the blessing of the catholic
religion over distant lands," in the words of his arch-enemy, Archbishop
John MacHale.[9] Likewise, visitors to Ireland during the Famine, such as
American missionary Asenath Nicholson, noted that the starving poor
did not curse the government for their suffering but instead thanked God
that the "kind English" sent them food.[10] "[W]ere it not for the English
government that sent all that American Corn," testified one grateful
farmer, "there would not be 100 persons alive."[11] Fatalism and passivity,
the traditional characteristics of the Irish peasantry, seemed to be their
most common responses to the Great Famine: "they have made no battle
for their lives," observed one Quaker relief worker in county Mayo; "They
have presented no resistance to the progress of pinching destitution, except an extraordinary amount of patient endurance."[12] Other observers
noted that most Famine emigrants left Ireland eagerly, expressing "nothing but joy at their escape, as if from a doomed land," "instead of the
sorrow usual on leaving their native country."[13] Indeed, once in America
at least a few emigrants wrote letters full of gratitude toward former
landlords whose financial assistance had enabled them to leave what one
called "the Gulf of Miserary . . . and Ruin." "I am now Employed in the
rail road line earning 5s. a day," wrote Michael Byrne from Vermont to
"your Honour" in Ireland, "And instead of being chained with poverty in
Boughill I am crowned with glory."[14]

What, then, were the sources and causes of the subsequent desire for
"revenge for Skibbereen" that purportedly animated large numbers of
Irishmen and -women on both sides of the Atlantic? First of all, it must
be noted that, despite certain continuities between the pre-Famine and
Famine emigrations, there were significant differences between those
who left Ireland in 1845–55 and their predecessors. In general, the Famine
emigrants were much poorer, less skilled, and more in need of charity
to finance their departures than the pre-Famine emigrants. Some fifty
thousand were "assisted emigrants," whose voyage costs were paid by
their landlords, and in the Famine's latter years, especially, the great majority of the emigrants could pay for their passages only with money sent
by relatives in America. Also, an unusually large proportion of the Famine
emigrants was composed of families, many of whose members, the very
young and the very old, ordinarily did not emigrate and who were often
helpless encumbrances in the New World. In addition, the Famine exodus

was overwhelmingly Catholic, and as many as a third of the emigrants were Irish speakers, Gaelic peasants from far western counties that had sent relatively few emigrants to America prior to 1845. Finally, and perhaps most important, the motives governing most Famine emigrants were qualitatively different from those which had inspired earlier departures. In the pre-Famine decades ambitious emigrants sought what they called "independence," economic advancement, in a land fabled for opportunity and abundance. During the Famine, however, most emigrants aspired merely to survive, and desperate panic and despair fairly screamed from their letters, petitions, and songs. "[P]ity our hard case," wrote Mary Rush of county Sligo to her father in Canada; "For God's sake take us out of poverty, and don't let us die of the hunger." [15]

Second, it is important to note that such panic and despair reflected not only Ireland's food crisis but also the fact that the social and cultural bonds that had held pre-Famine rural society together, despite its dire poverty, were fast dissolving under the Famine's impact. Not only was British government relief inadequate in amount and punitive in its effects, and not only did many Protestant landlords seize the opportunity of their tenants' helplessness by clearing them from their estates, but many Catholics proved equally heartless toward their neighbors and dependents. Indeed, it is likely that a large proportion of evicted farmers and laborers were sublessees dispossessed not by Protestant landowners but by Catholic head tenants, graziers and strong farmers who sought thereby both to rationalize their holdings and to avoid paying local taxes (the poor rates) for the maintenance of their former subtenants. There were other indices of social breakdown as well. Petty rural jealousies, endemic but relatively harmless before the Famine, now had fatal consequences. Even "the bonds of domestic affection were loosening under the pressure of want," testified one relief worker, and reports were common of husbands deserting wives, of grown children turning their parents out on the roads, and of fathers and mothers withholding food from starving offspring. [16] Even the peasants' ancient customs surrounding death, involving communal attendance at wakes and funerals, fell into disuse as the island degenerated into a vast charnal house. In short, Famine Ireland was in a state of social and moral collapse. "[G]azing hopelessly into infinite darkness and despair . . . , stalking by with a fierce but vacant scowl," the famine-stricken Irish, reported one observer, "realized that all this ought not to be, but knew not whom to blame." [17]

Third, it must also be remembered that there was an ancient tradition, woven into the social, religious, and linguistic fabric of Irish Catholic society, that viewed *all* Irish Catholic emigration negatively as involuntary and sorrowful exile; and in addition there was a more recent tradition that attributed all of the tragic dislocations in Irish Catholic history, including emigration-as-exile, to the tyranny of the British government and of the *Sasanaigh*—the Saxons, particularly the Protestant landlord class.[18] In this regard, it is important to note that these beliefs were held most strongly, endlessly repeated in songs and folklore, among precisely those sectors of the Irish Catholic population—the peasantry and especially the Irish-speaking peasantry—who comprised such an unusually large proportion of the Famine emigrants. In addition, for many Irish country people the events of 1845–55 (estate clearances and "assisted" emigration by landlords, parsimonious government relief measures, and mass emigrations by many who, in ordinary circumstances, might not have left Ireland) logically served to corroborate these ancient traditions of emigration as forced banishment caused by English and Protestant oppression. Furthermore, for decades prior to the Famine, Daniel O'Connell and other Catholic nationalist leaders had striven with some success to politicize these ancient resentments in order to mobilize the Catholic masses in their crusades for Catholic Emancipation and Repeal of the Union.

Nevertheless, nationalism's impact on pre-Famine Ireland had been partial and uneven, especially in the western counties, which witnessed so much suffering and emigration after 1845. Also, the early Famine years were so devastating and demoralizing that abstract nationalist slogans had little apparent relevance to people threatened with immediate starvation. Moreover, at first the crisis seemed to obscure Ireland's usual sectarian and political divisions. When the "kind English" sent food that some local Catholic relief committees misappropriated; when Protestant landlords publicly condemned Catholic strong farmers for turning their laborers and servants out on the roads to starve; when Catholic priests denounced as proselytizers the Protestant missionaries who gave soup to starving peasants; and when, in the face of unprecedented human misery, Archbishop Paul Cullen could declare that Ireland's greatest problem was "the schools system"[19]: then the strict distinctions that nationalist politicians tried to draw between the people's "champions" and "enemies" sometimes became dangerously blurred.

Thus, although the Famine and its emigrations did inspire some peasant anger and resistance early on, such emotions were at first imperfectly assimilated to the sharp, ideal dichotomies of modern Irish Catholic nationalism. To be sure, the wholesale clearances of grieving paupers, carried out under British laws and often enforced by British troops, inevitably linked the government to the cruelest actions of the Irish landlord class. However, subtler psychological processes were also at work to politicize the Irish response to the Great Famine. As one historian has noted, the disintegrations of personal relationships and the social dislocations (including panic emigration) that occurred after 1845 reflected not just a failure of the potato crop but "a failure of morale as well."[20] Frightened and demoralized, often able to save themselves only at the expense of neighbors and kinsmen, desperate country folk frequently displayed what one observer called "the most unscrupulous . . . knavery, cunning & falsehood."[21] During and after the Famine, it was natural that those who survived the crisis would feel tremendous shame for such extensive violations of communal mores and that they would seek "explanations" for what had occurred that would project blame and resentment upon "outsiders." It was also natural that the Irish, faced with the failures of traditional beliefs and customs to avert the catastrophe, would turn more attentively to Catholic clerics and nationalist politicians who offered an embracing "explanation" for the crisis that obviated personal guilt, obscured intracommunal conflicts, and generalized the people's individual grievances into a powerful political and cultural weapon against the traditional antagonist. As a result, Catholic Ireland and Irish America emerged from the Famine's terrible crucible more vehemently and unanimously opposed to Protestant England and its Irish representatives than ever before.

However, this is looking ahead, for in the Famine's early years most Irish Catholic politicians and clergy made only muted or confused responses to the crisis: partly because they were paralyzed by its enormity and its apparently divine origins; partly because they hoped that conciliatory words and actions might ensure adequate relief from the government; and partly because they were distracted by the bitter conflicts between Daniel O'Connell and the Young Ireland faction of the Repeal movement. Moreover, some nationalist spokesmen, including both the O'Connellite landlord Sir Thomas Wyse and the Young Ireland leader William Smith O'Brien, initially advocated massive, government-assisted emigration as the best solution to the people's distress. Nevertheless, by

1847–48 Catholic clerics and nationalists of all persuasions were beginning to question, then attack British actions toward Ireland, and to stigmatize Famine emigration as forced exile. During this period, for example, Dublin's leading Catholic newspaper, the *Freeman's Journal,* moved from acquiescence in emigration to near-hysterical hostility. Young Irelanders, such as the Protestant firebrand John Mitchel, were most violent in attributing Famine deaths and departures to British malevolence. In editorials and orations Mitchel and his peers raged at Irishmen so supine as to regard the Famine as "a visitation of Providence" instead of "a visitation of English landlordism"—which was, in Mitchel's words, "as great a curse to Ireland as if it was the archfiend himself had the government of the country." And by the early 1850s Catholic political and clerical opinion was virtually unanimous in blaming the British government for Irish suffering and in denouncing emigration as "a devilish plot" by Ireland's "hereditary oppressors" to "exterminate" the Irish people or "exile" them overseas.[22]

In the light of Catholic Ireland's past sufferings at British and Protestant hands, such criticism was logical and was at least partly justified by contemporary events, particularly when the London *Times,* the mouthpiece of the British establishment, described the Famine as "a great blessing," exulted in Irish evictions and emigration, and gleefully predicted, "In a few years more, a Celtic Irishman will be as rare in Connemara as is the Red Indian on the shores of Manhattan." No wonder that dedicated nationalists such as Mitchel were filled with "a sacred wrath" against England and that ordinary Irishmen and Irish Americans—who first learned of such callous statements through nationalist channels—soon became equally convinced that their sufferings were intentional, their emigration exile.[23] However, as Mitchel and his radical Young Ireland compatriot James Fintan Lalor realized, only far-reaching *social* as well as political revolution, involving the destruction of landlordism itself, could eradicate the root causes of Irish rural distress, and most middle-class Catholic nationalists—wealthy farmers and townsmen—were too conservative to countenance a peasant assault on Irish capitalism. There were still too many landless laborers in Ireland for the Irish bourgeoisie to dare echo Lalor's cry, "the land for the people," since a social upheaval from below would threaten the property of the Catholic middle classes as well as of the Protestant landlords.

Consequently, the gathering nationalist/clerical outcry against England and emigration had sources other than genuine rage, and it may be significant that public criticisms of government policy and emigration became ubiquitous only in the Famine's latter years—*after* decimation of the lower classes—when once-comfortable tenants began to flee en masse from crushing taxation and when the continued flood-tide overseas began to seriously threaten Catholic strong farmers, shopkeepers, and clergymen with a loss of cheap labor, valuable customers, and devout parishioners. Thus, Mitchel, Lalor, and a few dedicated revolutionaries aside, the primary function of Catholic leaders' attacks on British misgovernment and emigration was not to inspire violence, or even to halt the exodus, but to articulate popular outrage in ways that would reunite the remnants of the fractured Catholic "nation" behind bourgeois leadership and reconsolidate Catholic opinion against English "tyranny" to better realize the pragmatic and essentially conservative middle-class and clerical goals (legalization of tenant-right and Church control over Catholic education) that dominated the Irish political agenda in the 1850s.

It was ironic, then, that it was Young Ireland's futile but symbolically crucial revolt in 1848 against British rule—a revolt vehemently opposed both by Catholic clerics and by nearly all Catholic politicians—that ensured the future credibility of the nationalist interpretation of the Famine and of Irish emigration. As revolution, Young Ireland's effort was a pathetic farce, but as Irish revolutionary *theater* it was a grand, if hopeless, gesture, which enshrined its defeated leaders in the pantheon of Irish martyrs to the centuries-old struggle against the *Sasanaigh*. Furthermore, the Young Ireland leaders' subsequent personal experiences gave them special authority to interpret all Irish emigration as political exile, for many of them avoided arrest and fled directly to America, while others, such as John Mitchel himself, escaped in the early 1850s from their Tasmanian penal colony and went to the United States. There they received heroes' welcomes and, along with the earlier refugees, engaged in Irish-American journalism and politics, agitated and plotted for Irish freedom, and dramatically personified their own contention that emigration was forced banishment.

Even before the Famine's end, it may be that Young Ireland's rhetoric influenced the interpretations of contemporary events by some Irish emigrants, such as the young Dublin artisan Thomas Reilly, who sailed in early 1848 to New York praying that "the [A]tlantic ocean be never so deep as the hell which shall belch down the oppressors of my race."[24] Young Ireland's successful politicization of Famine sufferings may also be evident in the occasional accounts of evicted farmers swearing vengeance on the British government and on their landlords as they embarked for America. Such stories may have been apocryphal, but they conformed to nationalist models of experience and emotion that gained increasing credibility and currency after the 1848 rebellion. Moreover, the Young Irelanders' influence on Irish and Irish-American political culture long outlived the crisis that precipitated their revolt. Their bitter interpretations of Famine, evictions, and emigration—enshrined in innumerable speeches, poems, songs, sermons, and a few minor masterpieces such as Mitchel's hate-filled books—provided much of the nationalist catechism for later generations on both sides of the ocean. Thus, subsequent emigrants, who never experienced either the horrors or the ambiguities of the Great Famine, learned from childhood "how Erin's children [were] butchered, starved, and ground by the iron heel of the robber Saxon, till worn and broken, the decimated remnant fled their homes and country, to find peace and a grave in a foreign land." [25]

Young Ireland's greatest influence was on the Irish in America, particularly on the Famine emigrants and their children. Although townsmen such as Thomas Reilly and some evicted tenants may have been politicized before their departures, most of those who left home in 1845–55 needed the perspectives of time and distance before they could translate their personal sufferings into nationalist terms. However, once in the New World the Famine emigrants proved especially receptive to nationalist interpretations of their experiences.

One reason, as suggested earlier, was that so many of those who departed during the crisis were peasants, often Irish speakers, who shared a communal culture that had always discouraged emigration and viewed it as forced banishment: reflections of a deeply conservative worldview which devalued individual initiative and responsibility for innovative actions, such as emigration, and which their helplessness in the face of blight, disease, and ruthless evictions had too clearly corroborated. To be sure, these peasants had escaped death by emigrating, but unlike most pre-Famine emigrants, the Famine refugees had not made calculated, responsible decisions to seek "independence" overseas. Rather, they had merely fled in panicked desperation, compelled by fear and by forces beyond their understanding or powers of resistance. Thus, Irishmen who initially had viewed the Famine as God's chastisement for their sins, who felt guilty for their demoralized and antisocial behavior during the Famine, and who emigrated because customary sanctions temporarily crumbled in the face of death—all these had a cultural and psychological need for the examples and exhortations of the Young Ireland leaders who ceaselessly (and justifiably) blamed England, the perennial enemy, for forcing the Irish to leave their homes and to endure the shame and "degradation into which hunger and want will reduce human nature." [26]

In short, the Young Ireland exiles both validated and modernized traditional perceptions and resentments by "explaining" that the Famine emigrants, like themselves, were in truth "exiles" who had been "driven out of Erin" by political tyranny. Moreover, the Irish-American nationalists offered a redemptive solution as well as an explanation for Irish suffering, for if the Famine emigrants rose above self-pity, renewed communal fealty, and united behind nationalist leadership, then they might expunge their shame, win freedom for Ireland, and take bloody vengeance on those deemed responsible for the Famine graves and the coffin ships: they might, in other words, win "Revenge for Skibbereen."

Finally, it is arguable that the Famine immigrants in America would have been much less receptive to such rhetoric, and the fires of late-nineteenth-century Irish-American nationalism might have burned much less intensely, if those immigrants' overall experiences in the United States had been less impoverished and embittering. To be sure, many Famine immigrants, especially those who succeeded in establishing themselves on American farms, achieved at least modest prosperity. However, after an initial period of rambling about, searching for employment, most lived and died in American cities, industrial towns, mining, lumber, and construction camps, where the great majority—semi- and unskilled laborers and servants—seldom rose from the bottom of American society. Despite regional variations, nearly all studies of the Irish in mid-century America exhibit a deadening and depressing sameness. Whether in large eastern seaports like Boston and New York, in small industrial centers like Lawrence and Poughkeepsie, in midwestern cities like South Bend and Milwaukee, even in frontier towns like Denver and Sacramento: in all these, Irish immigrants were disproportionately concentrated in the lowest-paid, least-skilled, and most dangerous and insecure employment. With few exceptions, they also displayed the highest rates of transience, residential density and segregation, inadequate housing and sanitation, commitments to prisons and charity institutions, and excess mortality. In addition, from Protestant Yankees they encountered a pervasive religious and ethnic prejudice which assumed nationwide political dimensions in the nativist Know-Nothing movement of the 1850s and which often resulted in brutal exploitation by bigoted employers and coworkers. As one out-raged immigrant declared, the life of an Irish laborer in mid-century America was often "despicable, humiliating, [and] slavish," for there "was no love for him—no protection of life—[he] can be shot down, run through, kicked, cuffed, spat on—and no redress, but a response of served the damn son of an Irish b[itch] right, damn him." [27]

Thus, Thomas Doyle, a British spy in the United States, was only partly right when, in the late 1850s, he reported to London that it was the Fam-ine immigrants' old memories of the "horrifying cruelties of the Crowbar Brigade" (that is, of mass evictions) which inspired their loyalty to the nascent Fenian movement and their desire to "wreak vengeance on the persecutors of their race and creed." [28] Perhaps equally important were the Famine immigrants' harsh experiences in the United States, for they often engendered bitter disillusion and profound homesickness among those who once fondly imagined they had escaped from poverty and Protestant prejudice. For example, working-class immigrants such as Daniel Rowntree soon had their fill of the so-called promised land. "I have suffered more than I thought I could endure," Rowntree wrote, "in a strange Country far from a friend, necessitated to go on public works from four oClock of a Summer Morning until Eight at Night, enduring the hardships of a burning Sun, [and] then by Sickness losing what I dearly earned." [29] "We don't like this country very well," wrote the wife of an-other Irish laborer, and "I think as soon as possible we will come home to old Ireland." [30] Indeed, according to many observers, poverty and preju-dice encouraged many Famine immigrants at least to entertain the un-realistic dream of actually returning to Ireland. "So hopelessly irksome do our people find their condition in this country," wrote one Irish-American journalist, "that . . . hundreds of thousands . . . would ask no greater boon from Heaven . . . than an opportunity to Stake their lives to regain a foot-hold on their native soil." [31] Thus, another immigrant confessed that he was merely "a Slave in the land of liberty" and announced his intention of joining an Irish American militia company "preparing . . . to invade Ireland." "Perhaps I will return with the green flag flying above me," he wrote; "I care not if it becomes my shroud. I have no regard for life while I am in exile." [32]

Impoverished Irish laborers and domestic servants who dreamed such dreams and resented poverty and mistreatment in America may have been especially susceptible to the appeals of Irish-American nationalists who characterized emigration as sorrowful "exile," blamed it—and the immigrants' sad condition—on British and landlord oppression, and promised that, by working and sacrificing to liberate Ireland, they could expunge their shame and at least enjoy a vicarious realization of their longings. However, even relatively affluent Irish immigrants were also responsive to—and often employed—nationalist rhetoric: in part because as businessmen, Democratic Party politicians, and Catholic clergy or prominent laymen, they found appeals to Irish nationalism useful in mobilizing their Irish customers, employees, constituents, and parishioners for practical *American* purposes; but also in part because even economically successful Irish Americans often suffered from insecurity and prejudice in Yankee society. Thus, William Lalor, a comfortable farmer in Wisconsin, never forgot or forgave the "Yankee tricks" that native Americans had played upon him during his first, difficult years in the United States, and in middle age was prone to indulge the fantasy of returning to Ireland in the ranks of the "Fenian army."[33]

However, many Irish Americans who supported the nationalist cause, especially the upwardly mobile, were less concerned to free Ireland from British rule than to free Irish Americans from nativist scorn and proscription: for only if Ireland were independent and prosperous, editorialized one New York Irish newspaper in the 1850s, would her "exiled children [be] honored or respected"; only then, declared another Irish-American journalist, could they meet native Americans "without being inflamed with feelings of . . . shame" for their heritage.[34] Likewise, for Famine immigrants such as Patrick Ford, who came to America as a child and, as he wrote, had "brought nothing with me from Ireland . . . to make me what I am," as well as for Irish Americans born in the United States, Irish-American nationalism could help resolve their identity crises as well as their problematic status in native society. Hence, Ford, who became Irish America's most influential journalist in the late nineteenth century, readily concluded that "it was necessary for everyone of Irish blood to do all in his power" to elevate the Irish in America by liberating the Irish in Ireland.[35] In short, Irish-American nationalism—and its recurrent theme of emigration-as-exile caused by British oppression—could appeal to those who aspired to full assimilation in American society, as well as to the impoverished masses of Famine immigrants for whom such a goal was unattainable.

Thus, in terms of mass involvement and its avowed goal to transport thousands of disaffected, armed emigrants back to Ireland, the Fenian movement of the 1860s was unique in the history of Irish-American nationalism, for later generations of Irish Americans were less alienated than the Famine immigrants, more successful economically, and integrated into political, religious, and social institutions that promoted security and contentment. Nevertheless, the Famine exodus and its nationalist fervor left an indelible mark on Irish as well as Irish-American society, influencing future developments on both sides of the Atlantic. In Ireland, beginning with the Fenian movement, all future Irish nationalist movements were heavily dependent on Irish-American approval and funds. On the American side, nationalist interpretations of the Great Famine enshrined a now-permanent model for Irish emigration, to which all emigrants, present and future, had to conform. The shoemaker John Burke, who left his native Westmeath in 1847, for example, did so not on compulsion but from "disgust" at Ireland's inadequate economic opportunities; like his pre-Famine predecessors, he was eager to reach "the land of plenty" and he prospered here. However, when Burke completed his memoirs, he asserted that his own migration, like that of his fellow "exiles," had been caused by the Famine and by British oppression; forty years afterward, he had tailored his story to communal traditions and Irish-American rhetoric.[36] In addition, the Famine emigrants and their nationalist spokesmen passed down a legacy of lasting bitterness and unfulfilled dreams to their American-born offspring. "Keep bright in your mind the story of Ireland," demanded one ex-Fenian of his young son, "and should God send the opportunity during your life [to] aid by voice or means the great struggle which is but postponed, then I charge you in your manhood to act as becometh your race."[37]

"Revenge for Skibbereen"—for "the tears your mothers shed"—was a terrible burden for American-born innocents to bear. However, for their immigrant fathers neither time nor success had dulled recollections of the years "when gaunt hunger and death stalked abroad"[38] and when thousands of evicted peasants had perished on the roads or sailed in disease-ridden "coffin ships" to a not-so-promised land. Thirty years after such events had caused his own emigration, an Irishman in Minnesota still remembered and hated "the cursed government" of Ireland, and in a letter home he asked his cousin, "Why don't you, in the name of God, just shake the dust from your feet and leave your curse upon the system that exiled . . . all . . . good honest and faithful Irishmen from their native land?"[39]

Notes

1. W. E. H. Lecky, quoted in J. C. Beckett, *The Making of Modern Ireland* (New York: Knopf, 1966), 349–50. To conserve space, only direct quotations in this essay will be cited. For full citations to the published secondary and primary sources on which this essay is based, see the endnotes to chap. 7 of the author's *Emigrants and Exiles: Ireland and the Irish Exodus to North America* (New York: Oxford University Press, 1985).

2. M. Flanagan, Apr. 14, 1877 (Flanagan Family Letters, courtesy of Peter and Mary Flanagan, Tubbertoby, Clogherhead, co. Louth).

3. P. O'Callaghan, Aug. 17, 1883 (O'Callaghan Family Letters, courtesy of Eugene O'Callaghan and Mary Flynn, Fallagh, Kilmacthomas, co. Waterford); J. Cronin's letter printed in D. Ryan and W. O'Brien, eds., *Devoy's Post Bag*, vol. 1 (Dublin: C. J. Fallon, 1948), 195–96.

4. R. L. Wright, *Irish Emigrant Ballads and Songs* (Bowling Green, Ohio: Bowling Green University Press, 1975), 54.

5. J. S. Donnelly, Jr., *The Land and the People of 19th-Century Cork* (London: Routledge & Kegan Paul, 1975), 76.

6. Quoted in S. MacManus, *Story of the Irish Race* (New York: Devon-Adair, 1944), 607.

7. A. M. Sullivan, *New Ireland: Political Sketches and Personal Reminiscences of Thirty Years of Irish Public Life* (London, 1882 ed.), 58.

8. R. J. McHugh, "The Famine in Irish Oral Tradition," in *The Great Famine*, ed. R. D. Edwards and T. D. Williams (Dublin: Browne and Nolan, 1956), 391–436.

9. P. MacSuibhne, *Paul Cullen and His Contemporaries, with Their Letters from 1820–1902*, vol. 2 (Maynooth: St. Patrick's College, 1962), 23; Archbishop MacHale cited in O. MacDonagh, "The Irish Catholic Clergy and Emigration during the Great Famine," *Irish Historical Studies* 5, no. 20 (Sept. 1947): 293.

10. A. Nicholson, *Lights and Shades of Ireland* (London: Houlston and Stoneman, 1850), 8–9.

11. J. Nowlan, Sept. 30, 1847 (Nowlan Mss., MC24 I127, Public Archives of Canada, Ottawa).

12. R. D. Webb, "Narrative of a Tour through Erris in 1848" (ms. in the Library of the Society of Friends, Friends' House, London).

13. W. S. Balch, *Ireland As I Saw It: The Character, Condition, and Prospects of the People* (New York: G. P. Putnam, 1850), 136–37, 201–2.

14. Michael Byrne's 1848 letter printed in E. Ellis, ed., "Letters from the Quit Rent Office, The Four Courts, Dublin," *Analecta Hibernica* 22 (1960): 390–93.

15. M. and M. Rush, Sept. 6, 1846, printed in "Further Papers Relative to Emigration to the British Provinces in North America [June 1847]," in the *British Parliamentary Papers, 1847* [824], xxix, 70–77.

16. *Transactions of the Central Relief Committee of the Society of Friends during the Famine in Ireland in 1846 and 1847* (Dublin: Hodges and Smith, 1852), 254; W. Bennett, *Narrative of a Recent Journey of Six Weeks in Ireland* (London, 1847), 130.

17. MacManus, *Story of the Irish Race,* 607.

18. See Miller, *Emigrants and Exiles,* especially chap. 3.

19. MacSuibhne, *Paul Cullen and His Contemporaries,* vol. 3 (1965), 98–101.

20. O. MacDonagh, "Irish Emigration to the United States of America and the British Colonies during the Famine," in Edwards and Williams, *Great Famine,* 329.

21. Webb, "Narrative."

22. John Mitchel et al., cited in R. Kee, *The Green Flag: The Turbulent History of the Irish Nationalist Movement* (New York: Delacorte Press, 1972), 243–55; and M. Brown, *The Politics of Irish Literature: From Thomas Davis to W. B. Yeats* (Seattle: University of Washington Press, 1973), 105.

23. *Times* (London) and Mitchel's reaction cited in Brown, *Politics of Irish Literature,* 105; and A. M. Sullivan, *New Ireland* (1877 ed.): 118–19, 136.

24. T. Reilly, July 19, 1848 (ms. 10,511, National Library of Ireland, Dublin).

25. Miller, *Emigrants and Exiles,* 311.

26. J. O'Donovan Rossa, *Rossa's Recollections* (Mariner's Harbor, N.Y.: The author, 1899), 110.

27. M. J. Adams, letter in *Cork Examiner,* Aug. 10, 1860 (ref. courtesy of Prof. Arnold Schrier, University of Cincinnati).

28. Subinspector T. Doyle, Report #40, Aug. 26, 1859 (Fenian Movement Records, Carton #62, formerly in the Irish State Paper Office, now in the Irish National Archives, Dublin). Also see Summary, Doyle Reports (Sir Thomas A. Larcom Papers, Ms. 7697, 4–6, in the National Library of Ireland).

29. D. Rowntree, Mar. 23, 1853 (collection of Prof. Arnold Schrier, University of Cincinnati).

30. J. Reford, July 15, 1849 (T. 3028/B5, Public Record Office of Northern Ireland, Belfast).

31. P. K. Walsh, letter in *Cork Examiner,* June 11, 1860.

32. T. Reilly, Apr. 24, 1848.

33. W. Lalor, May 12, 1843, July 4, 1867, and Feb. 10, 1868 (Ms. 8567, National Library of Ireland).

34. New York *Irish News,* Apr. 17, 1858; New York *Phoenix,* undated clipping in Subinspector T. Doyle, Report #47, Oct. 28, 1859.

35. Patrick Ford cited in T. N. Brown, *Irish-American Nationalism, 1870–1890* (Philadelphia: J. B. Lippincott, 1966), 21–22; and J. P. Rodechko, *Patrick Ford and*

His Search for America: A Case Study of Irish-American Journalism, 1870–1913 (New York: ARNO Press, 1976), 56.

36. J. Burke, Reminiscences ca. 1888. (New-York Historical Society, New York City).

37. J. P. Carbery, book inscription (June 25, 1870), in *Catalogue of the Everett D. Graff Collection of Western Americana*, ed. S. Storm (Chicago: University of Chicago Press, 1968), 388.

38. M. McAuley, letter in *Fermanagh Reporter*, Apr. 5, 1878 (from the collection of the late Prof. E. R. R. Green, Queen's University, Belfast).

39. L. Doyle letter, 1880, printed in "Letters from America (II)," *Carloviana: Journal of the Old Carlow Society* 1, no. 2 (Jan. 1948): 87.

10

KERBY A. MILLER AND BRUCE D. BOLING

The Pauper and the Politician

A Tale of Two Immigrants and the
Construction of Irish-American Society

T HE LIVES AND correspondence of few Famine immigrants were as
disparate as those of Mary Rush, a poor peasant woman from county
Sligo, and Richard O'Gorman, an affluent lawyer from Dublin.[1] Their
stories and letters, detailed below, are interesting in their own right and
illustrate the diversity of the Irish immigrant experience. Moreover, Mary
Rush and Richard O'Gorman were linked, not only by a shared Catholicism and by the terrible famine which, directly or indirectly, spurred their
separate flights to America, but also through the symbiotic relationships
between the Irish-American bourgeoisie and proletariat. Much later the
Italian Marxist Antonio Gramsci would define such class relationships in
terms of "cultural hegemony." In the middle and later decades of the
nineteenth century, the process described by Gramsci created an Irish-
American political culture that was shaped by the interaction between
the imperatives of the ethnic bourgeoisie and the sensibilities of the immigrant masses. This Irish-American political culture was dominated by politicians, businessmen, clerics, and other professionals such as O'Gorman,
but it could not flourish without the conscious or unconscious acquiescence of poor immigrants such as Mary Rush. As a result, it expressed
and inculcated a new and comprehensive sense of Irish-American identity
that largely obscured or controlled the considerable socioeconomic differences and conflicts among Irish immigrants and united them in loyalty
to a Democratic Party and a Catholic church that institutionalized
"Irishness" and assimilated it to bourgeois American norms.[2]

The Pauper's Plight

Mary Rush and her husband, Michael, were typical Famine emigrants to North America—at least three-fourths of whom were poor laborers and servants—except in one respect. Whereas the vast majority left no written records of their travails, a single letter from Mary Rush, sent from county Sligo to her father, Thomas Barrett in Quebec, survived because it entered the public domain as evidence in the contemporary debates over British policies concerning Ireland and Irish emigration. Penned in early September 1846, the letter passed from Canadian to London officials and was published the following year in the *British Parliamentary Papers.* Rush's remarkable testament and its accompanying documents illustrate both the panic that impelled much Famine emigration, particularly among the rural poor who faced destitution and death if they remained at home, and the failure of British officialdom to respond adequately either to the Famine itself or to the Irish peasantry's desperate need for financial assistance to emigrate overseas.[3]

Sometime in the early 1820s, Thomas Barrett emigrated from the townland of Dromore, in Kilmacshalgan parish, Tireragh barony, in west county Sligo in the province of Connacht. He was accompanied by his wife, Bridget O'Doherty, and several of their children, but he left behind his daughter, Mary, who later married Michael Rush, a cottier in nearby Ardnaglass. During this period, Irish departures for the New World averaged between fifteen and twenty thousand annually. Most of these emigrants went to British North America and primarily sailed from Ulster ports such as Belfast and Londonderry, but about one to two thousand per year embarked from Sligo harbor, usually aboard small timber ships bound for Quebec or the Maritime Provinces. In the 1820s most of the emigrants who took ship at Sligo port had left homes in southwest Ulster, as prior to the Famine relatively few of county Sligo's Catholic inhabitants emigrated. Most were still insulated from North America's published attractions by their poverty and illiteracy and by the prevalence of the Irish language.

IN 1831 NEARLY 97 percent of the heads of households in Tireragh barony were either laborers, cottiers, or farmers too poor to hire laborers themselves; and in 1841 over 90 percent of the families in Kilmacshalgan parish lived in one- or two-room thatched cabins made of mud or dry stones. Thus, although later Canadian censuses recorded Thomas Barrett and his wife as illiterate, they could not have been among Sligo's very poorest inhabitants, for passages to Quebec still cost four to six pounds per adult, plus other expenses. Probably they were small farmers of five to ten acres who had grazed a few livestock and raised oats and potatoes on soil reclaimed from the mountainy bog that dominated the landscape, and who had paid rents largely from the proceeds of spinning and weaving linen before the depression of the 1820s virtually destroyed north Connacht's once-flourishing cottage industries. Probably they left county Sligo to avoid a decline in status, a descent into landless poverty which apparently befell the daughter they left behind. Between 1821 and 1841 the proportion of Kilmacshalgan's parishioners working in industry and other nonfarm pursuits fell from 57 percent to merely 18 percent. Yet, as Sligo's poor became almost exclusively dependent on the land and the potato for employment and sustenance, the county's population continued to increase, from 146,000 in 1821 to nearly 200,000 by the Famine's eve.[4]

Most Irish immigrants who landed at Quebec City during the early nineteenth century either pushed on to Ontario, if they had sufficient capital to purchase land and begin farming, or migrated southward to the United States, if they sought employment as artisans or laborers. Only a small minority remained in the former French colony, most visibly in cities such as Quebec and Montreal where by 1845 the Irish comprised the largest English-speaking minorities. However, most of the Irish who stayed in Quebec province settled on farms, often after several years of saving wages earned by working on urban waterfronts, in canal construction, or for timber companies. By the Famine's eve discrete Irish Catholic (and Protestant) farming communities were scattered from the Gaspé to the Eastern Townships. Unfortunately, farming the richest soils along the St. Lawrence was precluded by prior French settlement, so Irish immigrants turned to marginal, uncleared lands such as those on the hilly slopes of the Laurentian Shield north of the St. Lawrence. There, in the early and mid-1820s, along the banks of the small Rivière du Nord, Thomas Barrett and other Irish Catholic families settled what became known as the parish of St. Columban.[5]

St. Columban was part of the Lac des Deux-Montagnes region. In 1717 the French crown had granted the area, under the seigneurial system, to the missionary Order of St. Sulpice. However, it was not until the early

1800s that the order, headquartered in Montreal, devised a plan for the area's survey and settlement, and the first grants were not made until 1819. Although most immigrants to British North America, such as the Loyalist refugees from the American Revolution, rejected both the seigneurial system and French Catholicism and settled elsewhere than Quebec, at least some poor Irish Catholics apparently found seigneurial fees and clerical paternalism unobjectionable. Thus, in the early 1820s Irish-born Sulpician priests in Montreal succeeded in persuading many of the Irish in Montreal's Griffintown slum to leave the city and colonize the Rivière du Nord. In 1825 the order formally granted the northernmost portion of the seigneurie to the Irish, and in 1830 the settlers were formally organized into the separate parish of St. Columban.

Among the Irish colonists were Thomas Barrett and his family, as well as a William Barrett, also from Sligo, who may have been the former's brother or cousin. On February 27, 1826, Thomas Barrett received a *concession* or grant of Lot 183, containing about 70 to 75 acres in a long, narrow strip, one end of which fronted the river on the Côte St. Paul. Sometime in the 1850s, Barrett also acquired adjacent Lot 184 from another early Irish settler, and by 1861 the Canadian agricultural census recorded his possession of 130 acres.

At first St. Columban grew rapidly, from merely 219 inhabitants in 1825 to 1,015 in 1846. Nearly all were Irish Catholics, mostly from counties in Leinster and north Munster. However, the settlement never flourished economically; instead, St. Columban became the poorest parish in Deux-Montagnes County. The settlers could not even persuade a priest to remain among them until 1840; nor could they afford to build a permanent church until 1860. In many respects, life for the Irish in St. Columban was little different from what it had been at home. The farms were considerably larger than those left behind in Ireland, but once cleared of dense forests most of St. Columban's soils proved thin and stony, which ensured that potatoes and oats, raised for subsistence, were the farmers' primary crops. Most of the settlers had so little capital that the government had to supply them with farm implements as well as blankets and house utensils. Potash, made from the ashes of cleared trees, long remained the farmers' major income source, yet roads were so poor and the weather so severe that markets were often inaccessible. At first, farm animals were few and needed constant protection from wolves, although between 1842 and 1851 the numbers of livestock, especially cattle and sheep "of an inferior quality," increased as the danger from predators declined and as the shallow soils became too exhausted for tillage crops. Only a handful of St. Columbans held nonfarm occupations, such as artisans or as laborers in the parish's few grist- or sawmills, but many farmers had to work on the Beauharnois canal and other public works to earn the cash needed to purchase necessities and pay seigneurial fees.

Thomas Barrett's economic condition was no better than that of most St. Columbans. As late as 1861 his family still lived in a one-story log house; only 16 of his 130 acres were cleared for tillage or pasture; and the total value of his agricultural produce, livestock, and farm implements was merely $128. Moreover, neither Thomas nor William Barrett's names appear prominently in local records, for example as contributors to the parish church or as petitioners to the bishop in Montreal, and it appears that families from more commercially developed mid-Ulster and south Leinster counties such as Tyrone and Kilkenny predominated socially and politically over their less literate, Irish-speaking neighbors from Munster and Connacht.[6]

St. Columban's straitened situation may explain why Barrett's daughter and son-in-law, Mary and Michael Rush, did not leave county Sligo to join her father before potato blight and famine struck Ireland in 1845–46. Either Barrett had sent them remittances insufficient to pay their passages, or the information they had received from the Rivière du Nord suggested they would scarcely improve their condition by exchanging Sligo for Quebec. However, by early September 1846 even the forests and snows of St. Columban seemed preferable to unprecedented misery and almost certain death in Ireland. In August the Irish potato crop failed for the second year in a row and, unlike that of 1845, the failure of 1846 was nearly total, which presaged economic ruin, probable eviction, and dire starvation for poor farmers and laborers alike. Since the overwhelming majority of both men and women in the barony of Tireragh were illiterate, many of them monolingual Irish speakers, it is uncertain whether either Mary or Michael Rush actually penned or merely dictated the following letter, which no doubt was edited before its eventual publication in London. However, the document's authenticity seems unquestionable. Panic and despair; resentment against local landlords and rich graziers, whose cattle throve while children starved; and anger at a relief system that was already proving tragically inadequate: all these emotions of the Irish poor fairly scream from the lines addressed to Thomas Barrett.

Ardnaglass, 6th September 1846

Dear Father and Mother,

I received your kind and affectionate letter dated 24th May, which gave us great pleasure to hear of your being in good health as it leaves us at present; thank God for his mercies to us. Dear father and mother, pen cannot dictate the poverty of this country at present, the potato crop is quite done away all over Ireland and we are told prevailing all over Europe. There is nothing expected here, only an immediate famine. The labouring class getting only two stone of Indian meal for each days labour, and only three days given out of each week, to prolong the little money sent out by Government, to keep the people from going out to the fields; to prevent slaughtering the cattle, which they are threatening very hard they will do before they starve. I think you will have all this account by public print before this letter comes to hand. Now, my dear parents, pity our hard case, and do not leave us on the number of the starving poor, and if it be your wish to keep us until we earn at any labour you wish to put us to we will feel happy in doing so. When we had not the good fortune of going there the different times ye sent us money; but alas, we had not that good fortune. Now, my dear father and mother, if you knew what danger we and our fellow countrymen are suffering, if you were ever so much distressed, you would take us out of this poverty Isle. We can only say, the scourge of God fell down in Ireland, in taking away the potatoes, they being the only support of the people. Not like countries that has a supply of wheat and other grain. So, dear father and mother, if you don't endeavour to take us out of it, it will be the first news you will hear by some friend of me and my little family to be lost by hunger, and there are thousands dread they will share the same fate. Do not think there is one word of untruth in this; you will see it in every letter and of course in the public prints. Those that have oats, they have some chance, for they say they will die before they part any of it to pay rent. So the landlord is in a bad way too. Sicily Boyers and family are well: Michael Barrett is confined to his bed by rheumatism. The last market, oatmeal went from 1£ to 1£.1s. per cwt. As for potatoes there was none at market. Butter 5£ per cwt., pork 2£.8s. per cwt., and every thing in provision way expected to get higher. The Lord is merciful, he fed the 5000 men with five loaves and two small fishes. Hugh Hart's mother is dead; he is in good health. So I conclude with my blessings to you both and remain your affectionate son and daughter.

Michael and Mary Rush

For God's sake take us out of poverty, and don't let us die with the hunger.

Too poor himself to pay the passages of his daughter's family, Barrett appealed for aid to the Hon. C. J. Forbes, Deux-Montagnes County's representative to the Canadian Parliament. After consulting with Fr. John

Falvey, St. Columban's Irish-born priest, Forbes proposed to Lord Elgin, Canada's governor general, that relief funds from the British Treasury be used to bring out from Ireland not only Thomas Barrett's poor relations but also those of St. Columban's other Irish inhabitants. In turn, the latter promised to feed, house, and employ the newcomers. Unfortunately, however, both Lord Elgin and his superior in London, Earl Grey, secretary of state for the colonies, rejected Forbes's and others' proposals for government-assisted emigration from Ireland. Like most Whig statesmen a firm disciple of laissez-faire, Elgin feared that government subsidization of emigration would not only prove expensive and compete with private enterprise, but would also discourage individual industry, thrift, and prudence among Irish Canadians, thereby causing a reduction in the flow of *private* remittances from Canada to Ireland. Lord Grey was equally concerned to minimize government expenditures, and although in 1847 the Whig administration appropriated an additional ten thousand British pounds for the relief of sick emigrants who managed to reach British North America without government aid, he warned the Canadian authorities to "in no degree . . . relax . . . the strictness of their economy" or "their vigilance in resisting ill-founded claims to assistance. . . ."

Sadly, the same spirit of cold, calculating, and niggardly charity characterized the British government's relief efforts in Ireland as in Canada, with especially fatal results in poor western counties like Sligo, where an unusually large proportion of the population depended on potatoes for subsistence. Thus, between 1841 and 1851 the county's population fell 29 percent, and in the barony of Tireragh, where over half the families lived in one-room mud cabins, the population declined by 34 percent due to deaths and emigration. The Barretts' parish of Kilmacshalgan fared slightly better, but still lost 28 percent of its inhabitants.

Despite their poverty and the lack of government aid, apparently the Rush family succeeded in escaping starvation and plague, for on May 15, 1847, the ship *Garrick* from Liverpool disembarked at New York City a veritable tribe of thirteen related Rush and Barrett kin, ranged in age from one to sixty and led by Michael Rush, recorded in the passenger lists as a "laborer," age forty. Perhaps they received financial assistance from other American relatives, from their landlord, or from local charities which enabled them to emigrate; or perhaps they were not quite as destitute as Mary and Michael Rush's letter indicated. In any event, the Rush family cannot be traced beyond the docks of New York. However, it is

virtually certain they did not join Thomas Barrett and settle in St. Columban, for there is no trace of them in the parish's detailed records. Like
most Famine immigrants, the Rushes no doubt chose to explore the more
dynamic economy of urban-industrial America.[7]

Perhaps the Rushes settled in New York City, the hub of America's
commercial, financial, and transportation systems, alongside thousands
of other impoverished refugees from the "great hunger." By 1855 New
York City contained nearly 176,000 Irish-born inhabitants, about 28 percent of the total population, and it was during this era that the tip of
Manhattan Island became the socioeconomic, political, and cultural capital of a new social entity called Irish America, a development that was
due not only to the sheer numbers of Famine Irish settlers, but also to the
influence of a few, more affluent newcomers such as Richard O'Gorman.

The Politician's Progress

In the early nineteenth century, the United Irishmen who had fled to New
York City after the failed Irish rebellion of 1798 found sanctuary in a
Jeffersonian political culture that invited Irish immigration and supported
Irish nationalism. However, by mid-century American urban society was
less confident and more fragmented along socioeconomic, ethnic, and
religious lines. Increasingly fearful of pauper immigrants, organized labor, and the Catholic church, many Protestant Americans—especially the
Whig merchant elite who had long dominated New York's social and political systems—no longer welcomed either Irish Catholic immigrants at
home or the prospect of Irish revolution abroad. Consequently, the fugi-
tive leaders of the Young Ireland revolution of 1848 (and of the Fenian
revolt of 1867) often had to choose between careers as single-minded and
radical Irish-American *nationalists*, thereby marginalizing their personal
prospects in the conservative mainstreams of both Irish-American and
native American societies, and as Irish-American *politicians*, capitalizing
on Irish rhetoric and reputations to unite Irish immigrants, under their
leadership, into a formidable political force, in the process winning approval from the Irish-American Catholic hierarchy, grudging respect
from the native American establishment, and money and power for
themselves.

Richard O'Gorman was a supreme example of an idealistic Irish revolutionary turned pragmatic American politico.[8] The son of a prosperous

woolen merchant and Catholic politician, O'Gorman was born in Dublin in 1821, educated at Trinity College, and trained in London to become a barrister. In 1844 he joined Daniel O'Connell's Repeal Association and soon became a secondary leader of the Association's so-called Young Ireland faction, composed primarily of young Trinity-educated Protestant and Catholic intellectuals such as Thomas Davis, John Mitchel, and John Blake Dillon. Despite his later scholarly reputation, O'Gorman's primary value to this band of Romantic nationalists lay in his social status and in his powerful and florid oratory. Ironically in view of his subsequent American political career, O'Gorman and other Young Irelanders criticized O'Connell and his followers for their alleged demagoguery, political opportunism, place-hunting, mismanagement of Repeal funds, and subservience to the Catholic clergy, especially concerning the issue of interdenominational or "mixed" education, which the Young Irelanders favored and which O'Connell and most bishops strenuously opposed.

Shortly before and during the Great Famine, the Young Irelanders' disagreements with O'Connell and their increasing disaffection from Britain split the Repeal movement and precipitated their abortive "revolution" of 1848. The government arrested the rebellion's reluctant leader, the Protestant landlord William Smith O'Brien, as well as Mitchel, Thomas Francis Meagher, and several others, and sentenced them to exile in Van Diemen's Land (Tasmania). However, many of the Young Irelanders, including Dillon and Michael Doheny, eluded arrest and fled to America. Despite a £300 reward for his capture, O'Gorman, who had attempted to raise the farmers of Limerick and Clare in revolt, escaped to Europe from whence he sailed to New York on June 1, 1849. Ten days earlier, from his temporary refuge in Belgium, O'Gorman wrote Smith O'Brien a letter which declared his ambitions and prefigured his American career: "I am determined," he wrote, "to . . . win some higher character than that of an Irish agitator—I think the keeping up an *Irish party* in America is a fatal mistake, and if I chance to gain any influence over my countrymen, I will seek to induce them rather to blend and fuse their interests with American parties . . ." (May 21, 1849).[9]

On arrival in the United States, O'Gorman first settled in St. Louis, but in 1850 he returned to New York City, where he resided for the rest of his life. Through the patronage of Robert Emmet, scion of 1798 exile Thomas Addis Emmet, O'Gorman and Dillon joined the elite Society of the Friendly Sons of St. Patrick, were admitted to the New York bar, and formed a successful legal partnership which lasted until Dillon's return to Ireland in 1855.[10] Both were cynical about the future prospects of Irish nationalism ("I will believe in the resurrection of Irish nationality when I see dead men rising from their graves," Dillon wrote) and dissociated themselves from most of the other Young Ireland exiles in New York. Thus, in another letter to Smith O'Brien, O'Gorman ridiculed his former comrade (and future Fenian leader) Michael Doheny for the futility of his "warlike and choleric" efforts to stoke the fires of Irish revolution among New York's immigrants (December 12, 1852).

Despite growing American nativism during the mid-1850s, neither O'Gorman nor Dillon had great difficulty, as the latter put it, "in making ourselves quite at home in [this] heretical society," as they prospered in both their legal practice and their business investments. Now married and domesticated in Brooklyn, O'Gorman was more than reconciled to spending the rest of his life amidst the "rush and progress" of New York: "Commercial cosmopolitan and a[d]venturous," he wrote to Smith O'Brien of his adopted city; "I like it extremely, because I suppose, it likes me." Very occasionally, he acknowledged, "I remember my old Home and their comes sometimes, a sting, and I dream of old times But I shake it off soon Its all useless—There is no going back for me—I have staked too much here to think of another change—For the rest of my life, I am American." Indeed, by 1857 O'Gorman was convinced that the "Destiny of our Race" lay not in Ireland but in the United States, for "The moment it touches this soil, it seems to be embued with miraculous energy . . ." The eventual result, he believed, was that "this northern continent will fall into the hands of Men whose composition will be four fifths Celtic" (May 17, 1857).

In 1849 O'Gorman had rationalized his assimilation to American political life as a way "to serve Ireland"—winning "the American mind . . . for her cause" not by "foolish boasting . . . but by silently working on American society and guiding its sights to that island, which was once home of so many of its citizens." However, as Dillon had recognized, Irish-American politics could easily descend into "a mere piece of acting" for "financial speculations," and although Dillon declared himself "not sufficiently yankeefied to be reconciled to the notion of converting sham patriotism into dollars," O'Gorman and many other self-styled Irish "exiles" readily embraced the heady temptations he described in his 1859 letter to Smith O'Brien, by now released from captivity and residing in Ireland.

January 1, 1859

Dear friend,

I heard some ten days ago, from home, that you proposed paying a visit to the United States, and I determined to write you by the next mail Other matters drove this out of my head, and now while I sit recalling my various sins of commission and omission during the year 1858, my conscience disturbs me about you—I hope you will come—and whenever you do come, be sure that you will find one friend at least to welcome you. Indeed the chances are that you will find more friends here, and a more affectionate welcome than you desire.[11]

Every man that can, should see the United States—although from such seeing, as a passing traveller Can get—no very reliable information can be obtained,—However, you have by this time learned the art of seeing—for it is an art—and will not be satisfied with the mere surface At this time too, when Bright[12] and Cobden[13] are talking up American Institutions, it is well to understand something about their working—Cobden and Bright, I think would be the better of a little more Knowledge on that Score—It is quite easy to be an enthusiastic admirer of the United States and its style of government—

The progress of the country in all matters of material wealth is miraculous—There is in the Yankee—wondrous energy—self reliance—power of combination—readiness in the use of all his powers—He has rough and ready work to do, and he does it—The business of the day is to till land—cut down timber—drain swamps—get rid of Indians—build railways, cities, states—and our Yankee does it with surprising speed—and what he can't do himself, he knows how to get others to do for him—This, I suppose, is all that is to be expected—all that is wanting—and we should be satisfied—

And yet, there is another side to the picture—not quite so agreeable to look at—not on bread alone, does man live—Railways and steam ploughs are great—but not the greatest—

The tone of Political morality—in some respects of social morality—is not high—As to Politics, and government, I firmly believe that American progress is *in spite* of the government and the Politicians. I am not perhaps quite entitled to consideration in my opinion on this point—I feel myself intolerant and violent in my contempt for the Diplomacy—government—governors and politicians of the United States—The whole thing seems to me a filthy pool of shabbiness falsehood and corruption. It has grown worse in ten years—I have watched—Ten years ago, we had great men in high places—Webster—Clay Calhoun—Benton[14]—each in his own way, a strong man—They are gone, and we have *adroit* men in their place—*smart* men.

New York is the head Quarters of political corruption—It is here organized—a sort of University for educating the rising generation in the endless variety of means of cheating the public out of their votes and places of Emolument—Here, and for the present, no one can say that Universal suffrage works well—There is only the name in fact—a few leaders—and a few subordinates rule—choose candidates—bring up their armies of voters—and the thing is somehow done as they command—Respectability fears for its eyes and the integrity of its nose, and keeps away from the Polls—For some of our leading politicians are men of Science and strike from the shoulder—and wealth, meekly stays away and consents to be taxed—

There have been various most energetic efforts at Reform made during my time—the results were funny—great struggle—infinite speechmaking—denunciation—detection &c great victory—virtue triumphant at last—new men rule us—and when we come to look at the bills for the year, we are robbed and Cheated and taxed worse than before—I am told this is the boiling and effervescing of the vat—the wine will come in time—I hope so—Time will tell—For the present however—the thing is neither pleasant nor good—It is refreshing however to find that in this effervescing process, our Countrymen have their share—in all political proceedings—primary Elections—smashing Ballot boxes—[im]personating citizens—filling minor offices of all Kinds, and plundering the Public for the Public good—in readiness to gull others or be gulled themselves—the children of our Native Land are Eminently successful. The astuteness of these Citizens in grasping at any man or anything that can serve their end is surprising—

The honest fellow, I left behind me in Ireland a "cheque clerk" on the road, is now owner of a corner grocery in new York and covets the post of alderman, and scents plunder from afar—When you arrive, this potentate will get up a meeting in his own house—thereby securing—1st the sale of unlimited Drinks—2nd the position of an original and creative genius—The seed thus sown will germinate—You will be invited by the city fathers to a reception in the City Hall—Nay, if you choose it—they will have you conveyed thereto in a coach with six white horses—the same poor Kossuth[15] was shown in to an admiring multitude—People will shake you by the hand—the form is settled by long usage—and there's an end of it. I saw the thing done to Kossuth and Meagher[16] and Mitchell[17] and I abhor the ghastly operation—

New York itself will be in 50 years the finest City on this Earth—barring Paris—if even that exels it—It is only *being* built now—yet, its situation is glorious—As to "*society*" here, I have had no concern with it for some years past—I had worn out my taste for it, before I came and never sought much of it—But I Know it nevertheless—It is an unsettled—eager—unsatisfied sort of thing—There is no position permanent here—wealth is all fairy gold—and turns to slate in due course—There is scarcely any family pride or recollection—If you chance to sit at any good mans feast—and he warms into Communicativeness, he tells you that he came into the City of new York twenty years ago, without a shoe to his foot—got on by his *own* exertions owes *no one* any help he; and you begin to think at last—the man grew up out of the Earth and never had a father or mother—so utterly is *self* the leading idea.

These men however are most generous—liberal—while the money comes, it goes—we don't hoard—we are too young to be misers yet—of course, in all I write—I write of classes—There are of course here, noble fellows—genial households—pleasant Clubs—a generous manly scorn for all that is base around us—all that you find here—I would not give up my own friends here for any I have ever met—But the general tone of society is not very high—or very refined. The value of gentlemen is in some places, perhaps, overrated—it may be—but it might not hurt America if its system allowed of some hereditary certainty of position—some class that could sit on the benches and look on at the dust & din and sweat and passion of the arena—

And now I have written you a stupid letter I am sure—nothing in it that you did not Know before. It will let you Know in what mood you may expect to find me—I want you to write me at once—say when you are coming—Don't come till April at all Events—There will be no travelling unless in the south until then—I propose going over in July—Good by my dear friend—

I am yours faithfully
Rich^d O'Gorman

Perhaps when writing to Smith O'Brien, a gentleman of noble lineage and formidable integrity, or in his 1867 oration on the death of his old comrade, Meagher, O'Gorman could pay fleeting tributes to his own former idealism. Otherwise, as the old Fenian John O'Leary later observed, "O'Gorman seems to have exhausted his whole stock of [Irish] patriotism in '48" and took "little part in Irish [nationalist] affairs" thereafter, "save in what may be called the ornamental, oratorical [St.] Patrick's day line of business."[18] However, that "line of business" paid very well. As O'Gorman's career attested, the opportunities in New York politics were boundless for a man who could trade on his nationalist past and oratory to win the allegiance of his fellow immigrants, curry the favor of the local Irish-American Catholic hierarchy—privately, over dinners with Archbishop Hughes, and politically, by championing Church interests, as in public support for parochial education—and yet mix confidently with the city's wealthiest merchants and lawyers, gratifying their need for "culture" with

erudite addresses on Shakespeare and Goldsmith while exalting their patriotism in more bombastic speeches on the Fourth of July.[19]

Thus, despite his disclaimers to the fastidious Smith O'Brien, O'Gorman had already plunged headlong into the "filthy pool" of New York
City politics. Before 1859 O'Gorman had joined Tammany Hall, the city's
chief Democratic Party organization, and had begun his political career
as the Hall's chief "ornamental Irishman." Thanks to the Famine, by 1855
over one fifth of New York City's voters were Irish-born, and during the
next two decades Tammany naturalized (often illegally) thousands more
immigrant voters—over 41,000 in 1868 alone! Moreover, the collapse of
the nation's party system in the 1850s created unprecedented political flu-
idity and opportunities. The local Democrats themselves were divided
between rival "machine" politicians Fernando Wood and William Tweed,
each of whom angled for Irish support, while the party's "Swallowtails"—
the wealthy merchants, bankers, and developers who financed the Democracy—looked askance at both and demanded low taxes, social peace,
and a city government favoring their business interests. In addition, New
York's skilled and unskilled laborers (many of the former, and most of the
latter, Irish-born) were mobilizing, formally and informally: organizing
unions and third-party movements; striking for higher wages and shorter
workdays; demanding favorable legislation; and, in times of depression,
petitioning the city government for "work or bread" in mass meetings
that frightened all men of property, both native- and Irish-born. Finally,
the advent of Civil War threatened a loyalty crisis in the city, especially
within the Democratic Party, many of whose leaders (Wood, for example)
and Irish adherents opposed the war itself, as well as the Republican administration, wartime conscription, and the abolition of slavery. The horrific Irish-led Draft Riots of July 1863 only epitomized the political, class,
and ethnic conflicts that rent New York City in the 1850s and 1860s—
and made Richard O'Gorman a valuable component in the Democratic
coalition, based largely on Irish votes, that Tweed put together to rule
the city between 1865 and 1871.[20]

During the Civil War, O'Gorman echoed Tammany policy by rallying
the Irish to fight for the Union while criticizing Republican policies, especially emancipation. The vigorously anti-Irish *New York Times* called
O'Gorman's public criticisms of the Lincoln administration "Copperhead
speeches," but in fact they were designed to divert Irish immigrant frus-

trations away from violence and into safe, Democratic channels. O'Gorman's reward came in late 1865, when all the city's Democratic factions, plus the elite reformers in the Citizens Association, secured his election to the first of two terms as corporation counsel. Despite his promises to the reformers, O'Gorman soon became a pivotal figure in the infamous "Tweed Ring" which looted the city's finances during the next six years. As New York's chief law officer, O'Gorman allegedly authorized payment to Ring henchmen of at least a million dollars in fraudulent claims against the city, while charging the taxpayers over five hundred dollars a day for his and his associates' legal services. O'Gorman also was intimately involved in lucrative frauds involving the opening, widening, and improving of city streets, and he intentionally mismanaged city lawsuits against influential Democrats, even foiling the prosecutions of many Ring leaders after the *Times's* revelations of fraud, the subsequent collapse of the city's bond market, and public outrage over the 1871 Irish-Orange riot caused Tweed's fall from power that year.

Apparently, O'Gorman's close relations with leading Swallowtail Democrats, such as Samuel Tilden and Charles O'Conor, saved him from Tweed's disgrace. Although no longer corporation counsel, he remained president of the state's immigration commissioners, expanded his lucrative private law practice, and, ironically, by 1876 had become a leading spokesman for one of the city Democracy's anti-Tammany or "reform" factions. The *New York Times's* personal hostility continued, but neither its frequent reiteration of old scandals, nor its new charge in 1877 that he swindled orphans whose estate he managed, prevented his nomination by all Democratic factions for a superior court judgeship and his election in 1882. O'Gorman's elevation to the bench, bastion of property and order during the class conflict–ridden 1880s, evidently stifled even the *Times's* virulent criticisms—perhaps especially after 1886, when O'Gorman helped elect as mayor the wealthy Swallowtail and Tammany nominee, Abram S. Hewitt, by persuading at least some Irish Catholics not to support the independent candidacy of Henry George, radical reformer and hero to class-conscious Irish workers.

In any case, after 1882 and until his death, the *Times* reported only the "society" weddings of O'Gorman's children and the lavish testimonial dinners at Delmonico's and the Lotos Club occasioned by his retirement from the superior court in 1890. By the time of O'Gorman's death in 1895, the *Times* recalled only his "patriotism" during the Civil War and described him as a "distinguished jurist and orator." Even after the panic of 1893 and the distribution of much of his wealth to his four married children, O'Gorman's estate at death still amounted to over $75,000. His funeral at fashionable St. Francis Xavier Church, like his children's weddings and his testimonial dinners, was attended by a cross-section of the city's native and Irish-American political, social, and religious leaders, including Archbishop Michael Corrigan, banker Eugene Kelly, Judge Charles P. Daly, and William R. Grace, shipping magnate and New York's first Irish Catholic mayor, as well as a host of lesser politicians, the trustees of the Irish Emigrant Industrial Savings Bank, and representatives from Irish-American societies ranging from the elite Friendly Sons of St. Patrick to more plebeian veterans' and militia companies.[21] In 1858 his old Young Ireland comrade, Michael Doheny, had described O'Gorman as "sharp as a chisel and equally keen in his race for money."[22] Financially as well as politically, O'Gorman had won his race. To be sure, the course had turned out to be much more devious than he had imagined as an idealistic and rebellious youth, but, as he wrote to Smith O'Brien in 1859, he had left that "honest fellow . . . behind [him] in Ireland."

The O'Gormans and the Rushes in the Making of Irish America

Ordinary Irish immigrants, especially western peasants such as Mary and Michael Rush, brought to America a culture that was in rapid, even traumatic transition between tradition and modernity. On one hand, their sense of identity was profoundly localistic and familial, bound to specific communities, landscapes, and folkways that were expressed primarily in the Irish language and were often pre-Christian in origin. On the other hand, since the late eighteenth century even the townlands of western Ireland were increasingly assimilated into an international capitalist economy and a cosmopolitan religious and political culture. The steady commercialization of Irish agriculture and the spread of markets, fairs, shops, branch banks, and cottage industries had all made Irish country folk more dependent on a cash economy; the growing influence of the Catholic clergy had begun to formalize and institutionalize rural religious practices and beliefs; and the political agitations of the United Irishmen (1790s), Daniel O'Connell (1820s–1847), and Young Ireland (1842–48) had broadened and sharpened the peasants' archaic resentments against Protestant landlords and British officials.

Yet the results of change were mixed and often contradictory. The violent activities of the Whiteboys and other secret agrarian societies stemmed primarily from the growing socioeconomic conflict over land use *within* the rural Catholic community: a conflict which ranged poor subsistence cultivators and landless laborers like Michael Rush against relatively affluent, profit-seeking strong farmers, graziers, and their middle-class urban and clerical allies—many of whom, like Richard O'Gorman, were active Irish nationalists. By contrast, although nationalist rhetoric played upon the peasants' material grievances, as well as on their tribal resentments against Protestants, bourgeois nationalists and their clerical auxiliaries sought to unite all Irish Catholics across class lines and under bourgeois leadership. Indeed, Young Irelanders such as O'Gorman tried to assimilate Catholics and Protestants in a comprehensive Irish identity that would suppress sectarian as well as class conflicts.

Popular attitudes toward emigration, even to the "promised land" of the United States, were equally diverse. Thomas Barrett's departure in the early 1820s indicates that many rural Catholics, like their Ulster Protestant predecessors, were beginning to accept the imperatives of an international labor market and coming to view emigration to the New World as escape or opportunity. Likewise, despite the political circumstances that compelled his own voyage overseas, clearly Richard O'Gorman—like most middle-class Irish—viewed emigration in positive, materialistic terms. By contrast, Mary Rush's long hesitation may have reflected the peasantry's traditional belief that Irish emigration was unwilling exile, forced by cruel fate or English oppression, which would result only in communal tragedy and personal sorrow. During the Great Famine, rural Irish experiences of mass evictions and starvation and of inadequate or injurious British government policies easily corroborated the old popular conviction that Irish emigration was tantamount to political banishment. Also, the high mortality rates and the poverty and prejudice the Famine Irish suffered in New York and elsewhere in America threatened to confirm their worst fears and alienate the newcomers from the land of their adoption—or at least from its Protestant ruling classes—while in turn the transplanted peasants' customs, religion, even their very appearance only fueled American nativist prejudices and political movements.

In a sense, the dilemma of the Irish immigrant bourgeoisie was similar to the one they had encountered in Ireland. In the face of Protestant prejudice and exclusion, middle-class Irish Americans discovered they could not gain status in American society until they had both mobilized the immigrant masses, to demonstrate their political leverage, and imposed bourgeois norms on them, to reassure the host society's governing classes that the Irish as a group were sufficiently "civilized" to be accepted and entrusted with opportunities and influence. Likewise, only the reality or at least the prospect of such acceptance would enable the Irish-American bourgeoisie to establish their cultural authority over the immigrant masses by providing "successful" models for lower-class immigrant emulation, as well as material benefits trickling downward to the Irish working classes in the forms of employment, minor offices, charity, and other kinds of economic and political patronage.

Thus, the project of bourgeois Irish Americans such as Richard O'Gorman was to break the cycle of alienation and conflict: to both mobilize and "tame" the Mary and Michael Rushes by uniting them politically behind middle-class leadership and by "uplifting" them socially and culturally according to middle-class norms. In these respects, Richard O'Gorman was an ideal ethnic leader for a people in transition. As a figure of inherited Irish status, he could command the residual deference of transplanted peasants, and as a lawyer and politician he could command the legal knowledge and the sources of patronage that the immigrants needed to survive in a hostile environment. As a corrupt opportunist, O'Gorman not only reflected his own complete assimilation to the social mores of Gilded Age America, but he also demonstrated to poor but ambitious immigrants a way to adapt to nineteenth-century capitalism so as to exploit in New York the economic and political opportunities denied them in Ireland.

Perhaps most important, as a real political exile, he could symbolize and speak to the poor Famine immigrants' resentments against England and the American Protestant establishment alike, while demonstrating through his achievements that the legacy of English oppression and the burden of nativist hostility could be surmounted. For despite his literal banishment, and unlike fellow fugitives such as Doheny, O'Gorman was typical of most middle-class Irish Americans who desired upward mobility and assimilation to American bourgeois society, and who, like the Irish-American Catholic clergy, regarded radical manifestations of Irish-American nationalism—as well as class conflict and traditional peasant customs—with aversion, aware as they were that such practices offended Anglo-American sensibilities and, by association, impeded their own prospects for advancement. Consequently, O'Gorman's function was to utilize traditional tribal, peasant symbols to mobilize ordinary immigrants for distinctly modern and ultimately assimilative ends. Ideally, in return Mary Rush and other members of the Irish-American working classes would gain, materially at best or vicariously at least, from the social and political ascent of the bourgeoisie and from the entire group's consequent integration into native American society and culture. Redefined and sanitized, "Irishness" would be reaffirmed yet made fully compatible with being "American."

To be sure, the difficulties the immigrant bourgeoisie faced in creating a self-conscious Irish America while winning acceptance in native society were great. On one hand, their initial success under Boss Tweed collapsed in ruin and increased group opprobrium which threatened even O'Gorman's status. On the other hand, the Draft and Orange-Green riots, as well as continued class conflict, demonstrated the dangers of group mobilization and the fragility of middle-class hegemony over New York's Irish-American proletariat. However, formal political organizations, such as Tammany Hall, increasingly institutionalized and tempered ethnic conflicts; in 1886 Henry George's failed mayoralty campaign was the last major Irish working-class challenge to bourgeois and clerical hegemony; and by the time of O'Gorman's death in 1895 the Irish-American middle class had succeeded in safely assimilating Irish symbols and interests to the imperatives of the American socioeconomic and political order and, more specifically, of the Democratic Party and the Catholic church, which represented that order to the immigrant masses. In turn, the growing influence of those increasingly Irish-dominated institutions channeled Irish working-class aspirations, nationalist dreams, and residual customs into forms that most native Americans considered legitimate, harmless, or quaint. We may speculate as to the implications of O'Gorman's devious example of successful dishonesty for the deeper meanings of both native and Irish-American culture and identity, but his eulogy by the *New York Times*, and the gathering at his funeral by representatives of the native Protestant and Irish-American elites alike, clearly indicated that by the century's end the despised children of the Famine had become, at least by association, whatever it meant to be called "good Americans."

Notes

1. This article is an expanded version of two essays that will appear in a collection of Irish immigrants' letters and memoirs, edited by the authors in collaboration with Arnold Schrier and David N. Doyle, to be published by Oxford University Press. The authors wish to thank Professor David Fitzpatrick of Trinity College, Dublin, and Marianna O'Gallagher of Québec City for their advice and encouragement.

2. On cultural hegemony theory generally, see: A. Gramsci, *The Modern Prince and Other Writings* (New York: International Publishers, 1957); Q. Hoare and G. N. Smith, eds., *Selections from the Prison Notebooks of Antonio Gramsci* (New York: International Publishers, 1971); J. V. Femia, *Gramsci's Political Thought: Hegemony, Consciousness, and the Revolutionary Process* (Oxford: Clarendon Press, 1981); R. Williams, "Base and Superstructure in Marxist Cultural Theory," *New Left Review* 82 (Nov.–Dec., 1983); and T. J. Jackson Lears, "The Concept of Cultural Hegemony: Problems and Possibilities," *American Historical Review* 90 (June 1985). For a more comprehensive application of hegemony theory to the formation of Irish and Irish-American culture and identities, see K. A. Miller, "Class, Culture, and Immigrant Group Identity in the United States: The Case of Irish-American Ethnicity," in *Immigration Reconsidered: History, Sociology, and Politics*, ed. V. Yans-McLaughlin (New York: Oxford University Press, 1990).

3. The Rush letter and accompanying petitions, letters, and memoranda by C. J. Forbes, Fr. John Falvey, Lord Elgin, and Earl Grey are printed in "Further Papers Relative to Emigration to the British Provinces in North America [June 1847]," in *British Parliamentary Papers*, 1847 (824), xxix, 70–77.

4. Demographic and socioeconomic data on Kilmacshalgan parish and Tireragh barony, co. Sligo, are taken from the Irish censuses of 1821, 1841, and 1851, and from the Irish Poor Law Commission Reports (1836), vols. 30–33, both also in the *British Parliamentary Papers*. The authors wish to thank John C. McTernon of the Sligo County Library for demographic and other data on the Barrett-Rush families and their townlands from co. Sligo's parish, tithe, land, and other records.

For general surveys of Irish emigration to British North America in the 1820s and during the Famine, see: W. F. Adams, *Ireland and the Irish Emigration to the New World* (New Haven: Yale University Press, 1932); K. A. Miller, *Emigrants and Exiles: Ireland and the Irish Exodus to North America* (New York: Oxford University Press, 1985), esp. chaps. 6–7; C. J. Houston and W. J. Smyth, *Irish Emigration and Canadian Settlement: Patterns, Links, and Letters* (Toronto: University of Toronto Press, 1990); and D. McKay, *Flight from Famine: The Coming of the Irish to Canada* (Toronto: McClelland & Stewart, 1990).

5. On Irish settlement in Quebec, see: Houston and Smyth, *Irish Emigration*; and the essays by M. O'Gallagher and by D. A. McQuillan in vol. 1 of *The Untold Story: The Irish in Canada*, ed. R. O'Driscoll and L. Reynolds (Toronto: Celtic Arts of Canada, 1988).

6. On the Irish settlement of St. Columban, see: C. Bourguignon, *Saint Colum-ban: Une épopée irlandaise au piédmont des Laurentides* (Chambly, Qué.: Editions Passé Présent and the Author, 1988). The authors wish to thank Claude Bourguig-non for his generosity in sharing data on the Barretts from his research in St. Columban's land, tax, census, and church records.

7. On the Rush family's 1847 voyage to New York, see I. A. Glazer and M. H. Tepper, *The Famine Immigrants: Lists of Irish Immigrants Arriving at the Port of New York, 1846–1851*, vol. 1 (Baltimore: Genealogical Publishing Co., 1983), 492–93.

The Rush family's decision to avoid Quebec was a sound one, for the Irish settlement on the Rivière du Nord was already in economic and demographic decline. Indeed, its ability to absorb new immigrants had been exhausted by the late 1830s, when many of the sons of the original settlers began to abandon St. Columban and seek employment in Montreal and, increasingly, in American cities like Boston—their emigration merging indistinguishably with the general exodus of French Canadians to the United States in the late nineteenth and early twentieth centuries. As a result, St. Columban's population fell from about 1,000 in 1850 to merely 324 in 1901. Among those who disappeared from the banks of the Rivière du Nord were the Barretts, for between 1898 and 1903 the last of the line, Michael, a day laborer in Montreal and probably the nephew of Thomas Barrett, sold to French Canadian farmers what remained of his family's concessions.

8. On Richard O'Gorman and the Young Irelanders in Ireland and America, see C. G. Duffy, *Young Ireland* (New York: D. Appleton, 1881); R. Pigott, *Personal Recollections of an Irish National Journalist* (Dublin: Hodges, Figgis, 1883); T. F. O'Sullivan, *The Young Irelanders* (Tralee, Co. Kerry: The Kerryman, 1945); K. B. Nowlan, *The Politics of Repeal* (London: Routledge & Kegan Paul, 1965); B. M. Touhill, *William Smith O'Brien and His Revolutionary Companions in Penal Exile* (Co-lumbia: University of Missouri Press, 1981); R. O'Conner, *Jenny Mitchel: Young Irelander* (Dublin: O'Conner Trust, 1988); R. Davis, *The Young Ireland Movement* (Dublin: Gill & Macmillan, 1987); and B. O'Cathaoir, *John Blake Dillon, Young Ire-lander* (Dublin: Irish Academic Press, 1990), which makes extensive use of the Dillon Letters at Trinity College, Dublin, quoted in this essay.

9. The Richard O'Gorman letters published and quoted in this essay are lo-cated in the William Smith O'Brien Papers (Mss. 443–47, National Library of Ire-land, Dublin).

10. On O'Gorman, see D. McAdam et al., *History of the Bench and Bar of New York*, vol. I (New York: New York History Co., 1897), 437–38; R. C. Murphy and L. J. Mannion, *History of the Society of the Friendly Sons of Saint Patrick in the City of New York* (New York: The Society, 1962); and J. K. Sharp, *History of the Diocese of Brooklyn, 1853–1953*, vol. 1 (New York: Fordham University Press, 1954), 215.

11. In 1859 Smith O'Brien made an extensive tour of the United States; he later described his impressions in *Lectures on America . . . delivered in the Mechanics Institute, Dublin, November 1859* (Dublin: A. M. Sullivan, 1860).

12. John Bright (1811–1889). British statesman, orator, and radical land, tax, and political reformer; leader of the Anti–Corn Law League (1838–46); fervent

admirer of American institutions and supporter of the Union during the Civil War; advocated Protestant disestablishment and peasant proprietorship in Ireland, but opposed Gladstone's Irish Home Rule Bill of 1886.

13. Richard Cobden (1804–1865). British statesman, political economist, and radical reformer; advocate of free trade and foremost leader of the movement to repeal the Corn Laws, 1838–46; visited the United States in 1835 and 1859; like his close friend, John Bright, a staunch supporter of the United States during the Civil War.

14. Senators Daniel Webster of Massachusetts (1782–1852), Henry Clay of Kentucky (1777–1852), John C. Calhoun of South Carolina (1782–1850), and Thomas Hart Benton of Missouri (1782–1858) were the acknowledged giants of antebellum American politics.

15. Lajos Kossuth (1802–1894). Radical Hungarian nationalist and fiery orator; leader of Hungarian revolution against Austria in 1848; after defeat and exile, in 1851 he visited the United States seeking support; was lionized by Democratic politicians but denounced as an "infidel" and "red republican" by Catholic clergy.

16. Thomas Francis Meagher (1822–1867). Young Ireland journalist and orator, noted for the vapid bellicosity of his speeches; transported to Tasmania after the July 1848 rising; escaped to the United States in 1853 and became a popular lecturer, Irish-American newspaper editor, and Democratic Party politician; in the Civil War he became brigadier general of the New York Irish Brigade, which suffered heavy casualties at the battles of Fredericksburg and Chancellorsville; after the war, was appointed acting governor of Montana Territory, where he died in mysterious circumstances.

17. John Mitchel (1815–1875). Radical Young Ireland journalist, although an Ulster Protestant. Arrested for treason-felony and sentenced to exile in Tasmania in May 1848, before the July rising. Escaped to the United States in 1853 and published and edited radical Irish-American nationalist newspapers that outraged conservative Irish-American Catholic clergy. Espoused slavery, Southern secession, and the Confederacy during the Civil War; after the war he served as Fenian agent in Paris. Returned to Ireland in 1874 and was twice elected member of Parliament for north Tipperary on an uncompromisingly nationalist platform.

18. J. O'Leary, *Recollections of Fenians and Fenianism* (Dublin: Downey & Co., 1896), vol. I, 95.

19. O'Gorman's political and social career can be followed most easily in the indexed, albeit usually hostile, articles and editorials in the *New York Times*.

20. On the Irish in mid- and late-nineteenth-century New York City politics, see R. Ernst, *Immigrant Life in New York City, 1825–1863* (New York: Columbia University Press, 1949); F. E. Gibson, *The Attitudes of the New York Irish toward State and National Affairs, 1848–1892* (New York: Columbia University Press, 1951); A. B. Callow, *The Tweed Ring* (New York: Oxford University Press, 1965), esp. pp. 135–43 on O'Gorman; J. Mushkat, *Tammany: The Evolution of a Political Machine, 1789–1865* (Syracuse: Syracuse University Press, 1971), and *Fernando Wood* (Kent, Ohio: Kent State University Press, 1990); D. C. Hammack, *Power and Society: Greater New York at the Turn of the Century* (New York: Columbia University Press, 1982); Amy Brid-

ges, *A City in the Republic: Antebellum New York and the Origins of Machine Politics* (Ithaca, N.Y.: Cornell University Press, 1987); S. P. Erie, *Rainbow's End: Irish-Americans and the Dilemmas of Urban Machine Politics, 1840–1985* (Berkeley: University of California Press, 1988); and I. Bernstein, *The New York City Draft Riots: Their Significance for American Society and Politics in the Age of the Civil War* (New York: Oxford University Press, 1990).

21. For O'Gorman's obituary and a description of his funeral, see *The New York Times*, March 2 and 5, 1895.

22. Michael Doheny, Aug. 20, 1858 (Ms. 446, no. 3058, William Smith O'Brien Papers, National Library of Ireland).

11

MICK MULCRONE

The Famine And
Collective Memory

The Role of the Irish-American Press
in the Early Twentieth Century

Introduction

THE GREAT FAMINE of 1845–1850 was a seminal event in the course of modern Irish history and the defining episode in the history of the Irish in the United States. The Famine set in motion a tradition of sustained emigration on a scale unmatched in the modern world.[1] In the decades following the Famine, the population of Ireland plunged from an estimated 8.5 million in 1845 to less than half that number by 1914.

The Great Famine decimated Ireland. An estimated one million died of starvation or fever, with massive concentrations in the poorer districts of the west.[2] Between 1845 and 1855, another 1.6 million fled from hunger and mass evictions, mostly to North America.[3] Britain, the wealthiest, most industrialized nation in the mid-nineteenth-century world, offered little assistance. Instead, policy makers chose to use the Famine as an opportunity to rationalize the Irish system of landholding by clearing crowded estates of their tenants. Sir Charles Trevelyan, the official in charge of relief, attributed Ireland's plight not to the "physical evil of famine" but to the "moral evil of the selfish, perverse and turbulent character of the people."[4] Adherence to free-market economic principles was deemed more important than providing humanitarian assistance.

Those who survived the ocean crossing were cast exhausted and ill equipped upon the shores of North America. The cities along the East

219

Coast afforded scant sympathy or assistance to the destitute Irish, who brought little with them but bewilderment, poverty, and disease. The hostile reception that greeted them only exacerbated their confusion and shame. The Irish were despised because they were poor, foreign, and Roman Catholic. To civic leaders, the hordes of ignorant Irish that swarmed into tenements or spilled out into shantytowns posed an imminent threat to the social order. One Bostonian complained of "the ravenous dregs of anarchy and crime, the tainted swarms of pauperism and vice Europe shakes on our shores from her diseased robes."[5] The *Chicago Tribune* observed, "who does not know that the most depraved, debased, worthless and irredeemable drunkards and sots which curse the community are Irish Catholics?"[6]

Nativist attacks lost some of their shrillness after the 1870s. By some accounts the Irish were by then "generally well-regarded" as they pulled themselves out of poverty and became more like native-born Americans in speech and manner.[7] But the memory of past indignities and present insecurities nourished a lingering sense of unease. The horror of the "Great Hunger" and the shame and humiliation of its American aftermath were seared into folk memory to survive down the generations. In the collective mythos, England "'had crippled the Irish deliberately,' unfitting them for success abroad while obliging their exodus."[8]

Famine memories and the unresolved trauma of the immigration experience continued to resonate through Irish-American consciousness well into the twentieth century. The Famine experience remained central to the immigrants' conception of themselves as involuntary exiles, informing attitudes about their identity and their relationship to the dominant culture. It also served as a wellspring for their obsessive and often corrosive antipathy toward Great Britain. In 1915 an Irish member of the British Parliament acknowledged the enduring legacy of the Famine:

> There is almost no part in the world where anti-English influences worked so powerfully as in the United States. Almost every Irishman there is the son or grandson of an evicted tenant—evicted in all the horrors of the black 40's. And most of them have heard stories of these wrongs at their mothers' knees.[9]

The primary role of the Irish-American press in the first decades of the twentieth century was to make sense of the insecurities and aspirations of the American Irish and to devise comprehensible strategies by which respectability and acceptance might be won. An examination of the discourse in Irish-American newspapers of 1913–18 reveals the degree to which the Famine experience continued to shape Irish-American sensibilities during a critical phase in the development of the national Irish-American community. The press was a powerful coalescing force. Irish-American consciousness was both forged in and reflected through its prism. The Irish-American press also reinforced a sense of shared experience and connectedness to a larger national and international Irish community.[10] This impulse found secular expression in Irish-American nationalism, which was orchestrated by the press and directed as much to American circumstances as to concern for conditions in Ireland. Michael Davitt articulated the psychological appeal of Irish-American nationalism in a speech at Cooper's Union in 1880:

> You want to be honored among the elements that constitute this nation, as a people not coming from a paupered land . . . you want to be regarded with the respect due you . . . aid us in Ireland to remove the stain of degradation and in America you will get the respect you deserve.[11]

But if the press was the primary agent of nationalist aspirations, it was also a product of those forces that gave rise to the nationalist impulse. The Irish-American press of 1914–18 mirrored an Irish-Catholic mind shaped by a legacy of colonial subjugation and tempered by the post-Famine experience of immigration and adjustment to the conditions of the New World. To the peasant Irish, the Famine was the product of powerful, implacable forces over which the individual could exercise little control. Emigration thus became a form of involuntary exile, and those who sailed for America blamed Britain for their leaving.[12] The mythos of emigration as involuntary exile was galvanized by the Famine into the folk memory of the American Irish.

This "culture of despair" survived in the Irish imagination and in many forms of popular expression until well into the twentieth century.[13] The post-Famine emigration experience generated an entire genre of ballads of which thousands survive in the living tradition. Most express anger and a sense of irreconcilable loss at having been forced to leave Ireland. Many—those most popular in the Irish-American press—end with ringing cries for revenge against the foreign tyrant, Britain.[14]

Irish America on the Eve of World War I

In 1914, Irish America remained a nation in exile. Irish immigrants and their first-generation American-born children numbered 4.5 million, surpassing even the population of Ireland. In all, between fifteen and twenty million Americans could claim at least partial Irish ancestry. And although the Irish had scattered throughout the United States, 60 percent of the national Irish community was concentrated in the six states of the Northeast, where the post-Famine trauma was most severe and the legacy of anti-Irish nativism remained strongest.[15]

Immigration continued, but the numbers were in decline. The exodus from Ireland to the United States, one of the largest folk migrations in recorded history, had fallen from a peak of 219,000 in the post-Famine year of 1851 to less than 50,000 by 1910. The American-born now outnumbered their immigrant Irish parents two-to-one.[16] The diaspora had begun to abate: Irish America was coming of age.

The Irish could look to many examples of their rising status. As Boling and Miller demonstrate earlier in this volume, the Irish were a powerful presence in politics, organized labor, and the Catholic church. Their knowledge of English and their skill at organization enabled the Irish to rise to positions of leadership in the labor movement. Irish clerics dominated the hierarchy of the Catholic church and edited the vast majority of Catholic newspapers. The Irish, by seizing control of urban political machines across the nation, became arbitrators between immigrant America and the old-guard elites. In New York City—the capital of immigrant America—the Irish would run the Tammany machine, with its rich network of political influence and patronage, as an Irish fiefdom for more than half a century.

In the economic arena, the Irish had achieved relative occupational parity with native white Americans. The prospect of social mobility, denied in the old country, had awakened a hunger for achievement in the new. A higher proportion of Irish children than those of WASP parentage was attending college. In northern cities, one fifth of all public school teachers were Irish Catholic. Irish pugilists would dominate professional boxing from the 1880s until 1937, when Joe Louis knocked out James J. Braddock to win the world heavyweight crown. And although most Irish were still members of the working class, because of their dominance of the American Federation of Labor they enjoyed a disproportionate share of the best-paid union jobs.

But not everyone shared in the spoils of economic achievement. Despite advancements, many were left behind by the rising tide of upward mobility. In 1900, one quarter of Irish-born males and one seventh of American-born males of Irish descent still labored in low-paying, unskilled occupations. Irish females continued to scrub clothes and scour floors in the homes of the urban elite and to labor in the sweat shops of the textile industry.[17] As late as 1915, the early death rate among the Irish was the highest in New York City and twice that of contemporary Ireland.[18] The Irish died in such numbers from tuberculosis that it was commonly known as "the Irish disease."[19] Schizophrenia and the ravages of chronic drinking sent a disproportionate number of Irish immigrants to public mental asylums.[20]

The level of Irish achievement was determined in part by local conditions. In San Francisco, where the Irish encountered little discrimination or alienation, they responded with confidence and quickly rose to positions of authority in all areas of public and private life. San Francisco, however, was an exception. Along the Eastern Seaboard where most of the Famine Irish settled, the Irish experienced more nativist discrimination and developed a "defensive ghetto mentality dominated by an inferiority complex."[21]

Insult seemed to follow achievement. When an upstart Irishman, Hugh O'Brien, was elected mayor of Boston in 1885, the Yankee-controlled state legislature responded by seizing control of the city police department. The Boston police force would remain under control of the state legislature until 1962, two years after John F. Kennedy, grandson of another Boston Irish mayor, was elected president of the United States. In 1888, the mayor of New York insulted Irish sensibilities by refusing to review the annual St. Patrick's Day Parade. When the Irish of Boston built a grand cathedral a decade later, Yankee city planners showed their contempt by raising an elevated rail trestle a few yards away, casting a perpetual pall of darkness, clamor, and soot upon the city's most visible symbol of Irish achievement and subjecting the mass and its celebrants to the regular roar of rail traffic.[22]

Irish political successes attracted the ire of Progressive reformers.[23] As "proletarian pioneers" of the urban ghetto, the Famine Irish of the mid–

nineteenth century were the first to challenge Anglo-Saxon political and cultural hegemony.[24] One contemporary observer complained that Irish political machines had transformed American cities into "the worst governed cities in the civilized world . . . these Irish immigrants had neither the temper nor the training to make a success of popular government. They were totally without experience of the kind Americans had acquired in the working of democratic institutions."[25]

A few voices among the Anglo-Saxon elite championed Irish contributions to the American social fabric. But the cumulative weight of insults regarding Irish achievements coupled with the attacks upon Irish capacities to participate in American political and institutional life bruised Irish sensibilities and heightened their sense of insecurity. The conflicting realities of their collective status offered mixed signals to the Irish. And none were more aware of their insecurity or more sensitive to snubs from Anglo-Saxon America than the rising middle class, whose "influence in public life increased all out of proportion to their status in public life."[26]

The resurgence of a strain of nativism based upon the inherent superiority of the Anglo-Saxon race added an additional burden. Despite their achievements the Irish remained, by the measure of America's ruling elite, obstacles to all that was proper and progressive. The *Atlantic Monthly* warned:

> The only hope for the Irish lies in the mingling of their blood with that of native Americans. Even those who move up, rise to the level of saloon keepers. When they enter politics, they leave honesty behind, perhaps because they have always thought of governments as oppressors. They pose a danger of turning the United States away from its friendly, close ties to the English.[27]

The American Irish in the first years of the twentieth century were in a state of transformation. As the elite of immigrant America and role models for more recent immigrant groups, the Irish middle class stood at the doors of acceptance into American society. But those doors remained closed. America was still a Protestant nation, and the top positions in government, business, and intellectual life—the inner sanctums of true power—remained the domain of the WASP. The Irish in America were stuck in the ambiguous position of being "the group closest to being in while still being out."[28]

The Irish-American press responded to the improved but still insecure status of the Irish and to indignities both real and imagined by sounding the ancestral cry—often to the point of shrillness—and placing blame on the Anglo-Saxon. If some Irish were ill equipped for life in urban America, it was due to past deprivations under British colonial rule. If they suffered discrimination and slander in some parts of the United States, it was because of Anglo-Saxon influence. Many factors contributed to Irish insecurity, but "most important, WASP non-recognition of Irish-American accomplishments embittered the Irish middle class and kept old inherited wounds fresh." [29]

Collective Memory and the Press

The Irish-American antipathy toward Great Britain was sustained by a collective memory and an oral tradition that nourished a profoundly telescoped sense of historical time. The past wielded mythic power over the present. The Famine held such sway over the collective memory of the American Irish that T. P. O'Connor, a moderate nationalist leader in Ireland, delivered this warning to the British Parliament in 1918:

> The Irish in America live in 1846. The things they heard from their mothers or grandmothers of the reactionary policy in Ireland send these Americans of Irish blood back to 1846, and when they get there, there is no reasoning but the frenzied and justifiable resentment against the treatment to which their forefathers had been subjected. . . . there is only one permanent factor in the minds of men of Irish blood and that is the famine and emigration of 1846.[30]

Elizabeth Gurley Flynn, a labor organizer who grew up in New England in the 1890s, acknowledged the relationship between identity and folk memory:

> The awareness of being Irish came to us as small children, through plaintive song and heroic story. . . . As children we drew in a burning hatred of British rule with our mother's milk. Until my father died, at over 80, he never said "England" without adding, "God damn her!"[31]

Thomas Flynn bequeathed his hatred of England to his daughter despite the fact that he was born in America and had never set foot upon Irish soil. The power of collective memory to obliterate the tempering influence of time prompted British consul Frederick Leahy to issue this complaint about Irish Americans in 1917: "Their minds hark back to the past, and their mental picture is based upon an Ireland of 75 to 100 years ago."[32]

The Irish-American press of 1914–18 served as a virtual repository for the collective memory of the American Irish. At a time when most Irish and American history was written by Anglo-Saxons and formal alternative institutions such as the Irish-American Historical Society were in their infancy, serialized features in the Irish-American press offered alternative and oppositional interpretations of the Irish experience—interpretations that both drew upon and sustained the collective memory of oral tradition. This attention to the past served two purposes: it reinforced a sense of common identity by depicting the Irish in America as a nation of exiles who were forced to flee Ireland because of British oppression; and it cast suspicion upon present Anglo-Saxon intentions in the United States as well as Ireland.

In the *San Francisco Leader*, "Duffy's Irish History" presented a weekly litany of past British atrocities. Time and again, the series returned to the Famine. Similar features appeared in other Irish-American papers. In the New York *Irish World*, Famine tales were retold in the language of a shared nightmare:

> an appalling picture springs up from memory. . . . ghosts walk the land. . . . great giant figures reduced to skeletons by hunger, shake in their clothes. . . . those who have managed to escape this dread visitation are flying panic-stricken to the seaports. . . . to famine ships and fever.[33]

Religion and politics were important priorities within the Irish-American community. But the notion of the Irish as involuntary exiles was central to the emigrant experience as defined by the press. The *Leader* complained that British misrule had left the Irish race ". . . scattered all over the world."[34] The *Irish World* argued that the post-Famine Irish diaspora was a consequence of British policies:

> In 1840 the population of Ireland was 8 million. Today it is 4.39. It is the only country in Europe that has had its population diminish by one half in the course of two generations. . . . Irish exiles did not leave their land of birth of their own free will. They were forced to do so. . . . The emigrant ship was their only refuge. . . . They who should have enriched the land of their birth. . . . have contributed to the upbuilding of the United States, Canada, New Zealand.[35]

The *Irish World* blamed England not only for the depopulation of Ireland but also for the dissolute state of Irish industry.

> A depopulated Ireland is England's stern accuser. . . . Ireland alone, among all the nations of the world, is a land whose population has been more than cut in two: whose industries have been killed; whose cities and towns are dying of dry rot and whose fertile fields have been turned into grazing grounds for bullocks. . . . [36]

The press enlisted the post-Famine experience in America as additional evidence of British injustice and as justification for continued resentment.[37] And if the Irish press was guardian of the collective memory and rage, the exiled Irish would be agents of its revenge. According to the *Chicago Citizen*, the consequences of British colonial policies provoked ". . . a legitimate anger which shall never be calmed until our common enemy shall have made reparations for the sufferings, the extinction and the massacre of the unoffending children of the Gael."[38] "It's hard to forget," the *Leader* advised. "Is it possible to forgive?"[39] For the New York *Gaelic-American*, the answer was clear: "The exiles who were driven out everywhere on the lone highways of the world have everywhere risen up like armed avengers to demand an accounting. . . ."[40]

Anglophobia and Irish-American Identity

Anglophobia was a defining feature of the post-Famine Irish-American experience. A combination of ancestral hatred of Britain that survived from the old country and a fear of Anglo-Saxon influence in the new, Anglophobia provided a framework through which attitudes could be defined and events made comprehensible. The Anglophobic imperative overwhelmed differences based on class, region, and levels of adjustment. It bound the scattered Irish together in a sense of community and common purpose, and found its most coherent expression in a number of recurring themes in the Irish-American press.

The movement in favor of closer United States ties with Great Britain, which had begun to gather momentum before the turn of the twentieth century, caused great concern. That movement paralleled the push toward Anglo-conformity, a well-orchestrated campaign to advance the Anglo-Saxon dimension of American identity. The rationale in support of

Anglo-conformity was based on the assumption of Anglo-Saxon genetic and cultural superiority and upon the belief that Americans—despite the swelling numbers of new immigrants—were still overwhelmingly of English stock.

Irish newspapers condemned the thaw in Anglo-American relations. The *Irish World* dismissed the advocates of Anglo-American cooperation as "Anglomaniacs."[41] The *Chicago Citizen* scoffed at assertions that the United States was an Anglo-Saxon nation and insisted upon a hybrid conception of America's racial identity.[42] The *Gaelic-American* argued: "[the idea] that the American people are overwhelmingly of English blood will soon have to be dropped. . . . [it is] an impudent claim, repeated at every opportunity by Anglomaniacs and echoed by fools who know no better."[43] The *Leader* suggested that the "Celtic spirit" supplemented that of the Saxon. With the melting pot simmering for two generations, it was "not improbable," according to the *Leader*, that one third of all Americans had Irish blood flowing in their veins.[44]

Fired by ancestral loyalties and emboldened by their rising if still insecure status, Irish Americans challenged the Anglo onslaught in every available forum. The Irish constructed a Celtic interpretation of history as a "defensive weapon against anglophile historians."[45] The resulting "literature of justification"—a mark of rising respectability and continued insecurity—became a staple of the Irish-American press.[46]

Evidence of the Anglo infestation was everywhere. Minor incidents swelled into portents of great alarm. For the *Gaelic-American*, a student performance of the English national anthem at a New York convent school became an act of disloyalty: girls of Irish descent were being ". . . taught to reverence the traditions of the hereditary enemy of their race and religion."[47] A proposal to reorganize the United States Army in regional regiments like the British Army was ridiculed as an attempt by "Anglomaniac toadies" to anglicize the American armed forces.[48] Irish leaders even damned Rhodes scholarships as part of a British plot to reconquer America.[49]

Irish papers condemned the growing fascination with Anglo-Saxonism as a betrayal of American traditions. A Carnegie-sponsored campaign to commemorate a century of peace with Great Britain inspired particular scorn. The *Irish World* criticized a decision to issue two special U.S. postage stamps to commemorate Anglo-American friendship as tantamount to ". . . placing our country in the false and humiliating position of being junior partner in the firm of John Bull and Company."[50] The *World* suggested that the burning of the nation's capitol in 1812 was an event more worthy of official commemoration. The *Leader* was even more dismissive of the "100 Years of Peace":

> Feeble editorials have appeared . . . urging their readers to get in line and whoop things up for the dear, old "step-mother" country. . . . the celebration will be a failure. Americans are not to be fooled even by Carnegie millions. They recognize Britain as their bitterest enemy.[51]

Irish-American newspapers framed their arguments against closer ties with Great Britain in hyper-patriotic terms in an attempt to equate Irish Anglophobia with American interests. The *Irish World* denounced Irish-American politicians who exhibited insufficient resolve in condemning pro-British tendencies as ". . . worse than renegades in Ireland, for not only do they betray Ireland, but the U.S. as well. . . . Judas, who went and hanged himself, was noble in comparison to this rotten crew."[52] The *Gaelic-American* stretched even further in its vilification of church leaders in Ireland—the "mitred imperialists"—who failed to denounce British colonial policies: "those who are taking their stand on the side of the Scarlet Harlet [*sic*] will be placed in the same category as the Tories of the American revolution . . . the stain of national treachery will follow their kindred to the seventh generation."[53] Each demonstration of sympathy toward Britain, whether in Ireland or in the United States, constituted an affront to both countries. Thus Irish devotion to both Ireland and the United States could be perfectly reconciled: if anti-British sentiment was the hallmark of American patriotism, then Irish and American interests were one and the same.

Self-Image: Inferiority and Pride

The assertive self-confidence of Irish-American Anglophobia was tempered by a nagging undercurrent of insecurity and inferiority—inheritances of the post-Famine experience. This hunger for respect found expression in the Irish-American press through an often obsessive attention to real and imagined insults.[54] In the 1880s, the Irish were still generally regarded as the most disruptive element in the nation. The mainstream press reinforced and promoted a stereotypical image of the Irish as "socially troublesome and inferior—a lower order of mankind."[55] Negative portrayals of the Irish became a regular feature of late-nineteenth-century graphic humor.[56] The popular stereotype of Irish "Paddy," a drunken, childlike, often truculent oaf, was a creation of early Victorian imagination. "Paddy" made his first appearance in American periodicals after the Civil War and became a staple figure in *Puck* and *Harper's Weekly* until well after the turn of the century.[57]

The Anglo-Saxon dimension was unmistakable. In many caricatures, "Paddy" is a riotous, reckless fanatic, "eternally hostile to Great Britain."[58] In others, he is a drunken, priest-ridden fool, more content to wallow in squalor and indolence than to embrace the more proper Yankee (i.e., Anglo-Saxon) virtues of sobriety and thrift. Irish women fared little better. The stereotype Irish-American female was "Queen of the Kitchen," a "funny, disorderly, hardworking but unpredictable servant girl" who squandered her hard-earned wages in support of squalling children, dissolute husbands, and lazy, feckless relatives.[59]

By the turn of the century, the image of the Irish in graphic humor was in transition. "Paddy," the bomb-wielding fanatic and booze-gorged gorilla, was giving way to less strident portrayals. In the Hearst papers "Happy Houligan," a whimsical shanty Irishman, began to share the comic pages with "Jiggs" and "Maggie," an upwardly mobile lace-curtain couple.

But an element of condescension remained. Houligan, along with Mickey Dugan and his gang of Irish street urchins of "Hogan's Alley," stood as prototypical urban slum dwellers. Jiggs and Maggie, who had escaped the slums, were objects of bemused contempt: Jiggs because of his pugnacity, his fondness for drink, and his lingering attachment—despite his wife's objections—to the saloon and his old working-class pals; Maggie for her social pretensions and her relentlessly unsuccessful efforts to ingratiate herself with the native-born elite. By the eve of World War I, the post-Famine days of "No Irish Need Apply" had passed. Yet discrimination survived in more subtle ways, and the stereotypes of the nineteenth century continued to taunt the Irish well beyond the turn of the century.[60]

Irish-American newspapers relentlessly condemned the anti-Irish caricatures that appeared in the mainstream press. The *Leader* accused Scripps' *San Francisco Daily News* of Anglo-Saxon sympathies because of its portrayal of Irish immigrants. In reaction to "Confessions of a Wife," a *Daily News* fiction serial that included a depiction of an Irish domestic servant, the *Leader* observed:

> This Alexandrine indecency written by some anonymous hack with the mind of a slut and the pen of a pander portrays the Irish servant girl before her high-brow employer as the usual soft, slushy, ignorant, untidy and half-witted slattern of the anti-Irish stage . . . [61]

Old stereotypes gained new life in the emerging medium of motion pictures.[62] The *Irish World* condemned motion pictures—a popular form of mass entertainment among immigrants—for distorted portrayals of the Irish. The so-called Hogan movies, which were filled with Irish gangsters, prompted real-life hoodlums to adopt Irish names, according to the *Irish World*, thereby heaping a double slander upon the Irish.[63] Other movies defamed Irish women by depicting them as frequenting dances and partaking in other equally dubious "debaucheries."[64] The *Irish World* argued: "We have succeeded in driving the stage Irish from the theatres. We should not permit moving picture shows to perpetuate the foul anti-Irish calumnies the defunct 'stage Irishman' sought to perpetuate."[65]

The campaign against the stage Irishman sometimes descended into reaction and self-loathing. When John Millington Synge's *Playboy of the Western World* came to America in 1911–1912, the Ancient Order of Hibernians, the United Irish Societies, and the Irish-American press orchestrated a national campaign of public protests and legal injunctions in an attempt to drive the play from the stage. The campaign also targeted the "vile so-called Irish plays" of Lady Gregory.[66] Ironically, Synge and Gregory were two of the guiding lights of the Gaelic renaissance, a flowering of the arts that arose around the turn of the century to win worldwide critical acclaim. Synge and Gregory drew upon Irish folkways and the lyrical cadences of Irish peasant speech as sources of inspiration. For the Irish-American press, however, theatrical celebrations of Irish rural life inspired more shame and indignation than pride. This willingness to engage in symbolic self-annihilation as a means of securing status gave testimony to the lingering post-Famine insecurities of the American Irish.

Irish papers also stood the line against anti-Catholic discrimination. The *Chicago Citizen* called the governor of Florida a "bigoted barbarian" for allegedly barring Catholics from teaching in public schools.[67] The *Leader* charged that a wartime proposal to ration meat on Tuesdays was an attempt to double the sacrifice of Catholics who already refrained from eating meat on Fridays.[68]

All the while it challenged negative depictions, the Irish-American press labored to instill a sense of ethnic pride among the American Irish. Newspapers regularly featured examples of Irish-American success stories and promoted social mobility as a strategy to achieve respectability. The *Irish World* advocated education and cooperation with other ethnic groups. Socioeconomic advancement would achieve two goals. It would confer status upon the Irish in America and aid in the effort to free Ireland:

> Those Irish out here who forget or want to forget they are Irish or of Irish extraction forget a great deal more, the remembrance of which would ennoble them among their peers. You have nothing to be ashamed of in the history of your country or your race. . . . [carry] yourselves in this land . . . as equals of any and all the various races.[69]

The Irish press labored to buttress the self-confidence of its readers by glorifying Irish culture and accomplishments while disparaging those of the English. The press challenged an underlying premise of Britain's imperial mission—that Anglo-Saxon superiority gave Britain a mandate to rule and civilize the less advanced peoples of the earth. Much like African American newspapers of a later period, Irish newspapers sought to invert the relationship between colonizer and colonized by insisting that Irish civilization predated that of the English. The *Chicago Citizen* claimed that Irish scholars brought religion and culture to English "cave-men [who] subsisted on wild berries and dwelt under the ground in dug-outs."[70] The *Leader* insisted that the English were aboriginal hunter-gatherers at a time when poetry and high culture flourished in Ireland: the Irish "were a civilized race when the English were digging acorns in the forested wilds."[71]

Another strategy was to portray Irish racial characteristics as superior to those of the English. Celtic "spirituality" and "love of justice" stood in contrast to English "hypocrisy" and "blind, stupid materialism."[72] This tactic challenged one of the staple justifications of British colonial rule—that the Irish were unfit to govern themselves. In America, the Progressive campaign for "good government" carried equally powerful implications of Anglo-Saxon ascendancy. The Irish press challenged the assumption that old-guard elites were better equipped to run American cities than Irish machine politicians.

Irish-American support for racial and social equality, however, did not always translate into support for other subordinate groups. The contradictions articulated in the Irish-American press mirrored the warring insecurities that festered within the Irish-American psyche. The *Chicago Citizen*, for example, attacked the Guardians of Liberty for refusing to endorse any Irish Catholics or Jews in a judicial election.[73] Yet the *Citizen* also condemned Bolsheviks as anti-Christian Jews who possessed little talent for government.[74] The *Citizen* promoted social mobility for the Irish but expressed alarm when upwardly mobile blacks began to move into white neighborhoods in Chicago.[75] On the West Coast, the *Leader* lambasted anti-Catholic and anti-Irish discrimination. Yet for all its proclaimed belief in tolerance and fair treatment, the *Leader* lobbied against Chinese and Japanese immigration and decried "the utter uselessness of the Protestant religion." Ironically, the attitudes of the Irish-American press on the issue of race gave implicit endorsement to the Anglo-Saxon racial hierarchy it claimed to abhor.

The Irish-American press blamed Britain not only for the despoliation of Ireland and the scattering of her people through famine, but also for the low self-esteem of the Irish or what the press called the "slave mentality." If the Irish peasant was lazy and unproductive, it was because of British policies "which would have destroyed industry among the Dutch or the Chinese."[76] If the Irish were ashamed of their language, the oldest written vernacular north of the Alps, it was because Britain had characterized the Celts as "barbarous and illiterate from the beginning of time."[77]

The "slave mind," according to the Irish-American press, was a debilitating affliction of the spirit, a vestige of colonialism which robbed the Irish of their self-confidence, dignity, and direction. One manifestation of the slave mind was the belief that England had done its best to provide relief during the Famine. Other manifestations included Irish doubts about their ability to govern themselves, and the lingering desire to be "lorded over" by the English.[78] The *Gaelic-American* feared that the slave mind had destroyed the "moral courage" of the Irish people.[79] The *Irish World* despaired that the affliction of the spirit lingered in America despite Irish successes:

What then is the source of the racial weakness which torments us. . . . We have retained our physical courage, but long subjugation to foreign rule . . . sapped our moral vitality. . . . Here in this free land the restoration to perfect moral health should have begun earlier and should have progressed further than in Ireland.[80]

The Irish-American press of 1914–18 offered two mutually reinforcing strategies to resolve this crisis of the spirit: social mobility in America and freedom for Ireland through the dissolution of the British Empire. The defeat of Great Britain—"the harlot of nations, the modern Babylon"—and Ireland's consequent entry into the community of nations would vindicate the Irish in America. The "world will be sweeter when the British Empire is burned up," the *Irish World* promised.[81] The *Leader* declared: "Forever blessed be the boot that administers that glorious kick."[82]

Conclusion

By the eve of World War I, most of the survivors of the Famine had passed on. But the legacy of the Famine continued, fed by fresh infusions of immigrants, folk memories, and rising rumblings of Anglo-Saxon ascendancy. Although the status of the American Irish was much improved, the awareness of past indignities and present insecurities kept old wounds festering and nourished an ancestral hatred of all things Anglo-Saxon.

Ireland was emerging from its long colonial past. In America, the immigrants and their offspring remained a nation of uneasy exiles in search of a secure self-definition. The Irish-American press provided that definition in an American context and—as war descended upon Europe and rebellion stirred in Ireland—served as a lightning rod for their collective discontent.

Irish-American newspapers would use the Famine as a clarion call to rally support for the independence struggle in Ireland, especially following the 1916 Easter Rising. They would point to the Famine record in a failed attempt to keep the United States from entering World War I as Britain's ally. The memory of the Famine would also inspire fierce opposition in 1918 to a British plan to impose military conscription on Ireland. Irish-American newspapers feared that conscription would plunge the Irish nation into a final episode of irreversible decline: what starvation and emigration had failed to accomplish in 1845–1852 would be brought to grim fruition on the battlefields of France.

The power of the Famine began to wane in the 1920s as increasing numbers of Irish Americans scrambled upward into middle-class respectability. The founding of the Irish Free State and Irish-American bewilderment over the Irish Civil War did much to diminish anti-British sentiment, and with it the emotive resonance of the Famine. As the decades advanced and self-confidence increased, the catastrophe would recede in popular memory. Yet despite assimilation, the passage of time, and the election in 1960 of John Fitzgerald Kennedy—a descendant of post-Famine immigrants—as president of the United States, the Famine still remains in the mind of many Irish Americans. Generations after the appearance of the potato blight in 1845, Famine stories are a recurring feature of the Irish-American press and a motivating force among political and civic organizations. The experience of 1845–52 endures as a cornerstone of Irish-American identity. The memory of the Great Hunger has faded, but a powerful residue remains.

Notes

1. The character and scale of emigration changed dramatically with the Famine. Most pre-Famine immigrants to the United States were Protestants from prosperous commercialized districts. Famine immigrants came in huge numbers from the poor regions of the west. Most were Catholics. Donald E. Jordan, *Land and Popular Politics in Ireland: County Mayo from the Plantation to the Land War* (Cambridge: Cambridge University Press, 1994), 109. Some historians suggest that the Famine emigration was a continuation of earlier trends. See Mary Daly, *The Famine in Ireland* (Dundalk: Dundalgan Press, 1986), 34.

2. Some revisionist historians put the number of deaths as low as half a million. See, for example, Daly, *The Famine in Ireland*, 99–100. The generally accepted number of famine deaths, however, is one million. See Cormac Ó'Gráda, *Ireland before and after the Famine: Explorations in Economic History 1800–1930* (Manchester: Manchester University Press, 1988), 49; Christine Kinealy, *This Great Calamity: The Irish Famine 1845–52* (Dublin: Gill and McMillan, 1994), 168; and Cathal Póirtéir, ed., "Introduction," *The Great Irish Famine* (Dublin: Mercier, 1995), 9.

3. See R. D. Edwards and T. D. Williams, eds., *The Great Famine* (New York: New York University Press, 1957), 388; Ó'Gráda, *Ireland before and after the Famine*, 55; Kinealy, *This Great Calamity*, 297–300. As many as two million emigrated in the decade following the first appearance of the potato blight. See David Fitzpatrick, "Flight from Famine," in Póirtéir, *Great Irish Famine*, 175.

4. Quoted in Andrew M. Greeley, *That Most Distressful Nation: The Taming of the American Irish* (Chicago: Quadrangle Books, 1972), 36.

5. Boston school board member quoted in Anthony J. Lukas, *Common Ground* (New York: Vintage Books, 1986), 121.

6. *Chicago Tribune*, 1855. Quoted in Ellen Skerrett, "The Catholic Dimension,"

in *The Irish in Chicago,* ed. Skerrett, Lawrence J. McCaffrey, Michael F. Funchion, and Charles Fanning (Urbana: University of Illinois, 1987), 26.

7. John Higham, *Strangers in the Land 1860–1925: Patterns of American Nativism* (New York: Atheneum, 1963), 26.

8. Kerby A. Miller, *Emigrants and Exiles: Ireland and the Irish Exodus to North America* (New York: Oxford University Press, 1985), 550.

9. *New York Times,* Mar. 17, 1915, 2.

10. In 1914 at least twenty-five newspapers exclusively devoted to Irish issues were published in the United States. A sample of four weekly papers is cited in this monograph. Two were published in New York: The *Irish World,* founded in 1870, was the largest and most successful Irish paper in America. The *Irish World* promoted middle-class values and moderate nationalist agenda; the *Gaelic-American,* founded in 1903 by John Devoy, was the most uncompromising voice of Irish nationalism in the United States. The *Chicago Citizen,* founded in 1882, took a moderate position on the Irish national question. The *San Francisco Leader* was founded in 1902 by Fr. Peter Yorke, an Irish-born priest. The *Leader* embraced conservative Catholic values and a strident form of nationalism.

11. Quoted in Thomas N. Brown, "Origins and Character of Irish-American Nationalism," *Review of Politics* 18 (1956): 334.

12. This is a major theme of Kerby Miller's *Emigrants and Exiles.*

13. Robert S. Fortner, "The Culture of Hope and the Culture of Despair: The Print Media and 19th Century Irish Imagination," *Eire/Ireland* 13 (Fall 1978): 38.

14. See Arnold Schrier, *Ireland and the American Emigration 1850–1900* (Minneapolis: University of Minnesota Press, 1958), 94–100.

15. A. J. Ward, "America and the Irish Problem, 1899–1921," *Irish Historical Studies* (Mar. 1968): 64. Joel Perlman, *Ethnic Differences: Schooling and Social Structure among Irish, Italians, Jews and Blacks in an American City, 1880–1935* (Cambridge: Cambridge University Press, 1988), 43.

16. Schrier, *Ireland and the American Emigration,* 9.

17. Miller, *Emigrants and Exiles,* 499, 506.

18. Ibid., 506.

19. Elizabeth Gurley Flynn, *The Rebel Girl* (New York: International Publishers, 1955), 25; Mark Tierney, *Modern Ireland 1850–1950* (Dublin: Gill and MacMillan, 1972), 91.

20. Miller, *Emigrants and Exiles,* 506.

21. Timothy J. Sarbaugh, "Exiles of Confidence: The Irish-American Community of San Francisco 1880–1920," in *From Paddy to Studs: Irish-American Communities in the Turn of the Century Era 1880 to 1920,* ed. Timothy J. Meagher (New York: Greenwood, 1987), 173–75.

22. Lukas, *Common Ground,* 459, 377.

23. See George Mowry, *California Progressives* (Berkeley: University of California Press, 1951), 88–89; Paul Glad, *The Trumpet Soundeth: William Jennings Bryan, 1896–1912* (Lincoln: University of Nebraska Press, 1960), 114.

24. Lawrence J. McCaffrey, "The Irish Dimension," in Skerret et al., *The Irish in Chicago,* 2, 4.

25. Edward E. Ross, *The Old World in the New* (New York: Century, 1914), 261–62.

26. Thomas N. Brown, *Irish-American Nationalism 1870–1890* (Philadelphia: Lippincott, 1966), 180.

27. *Atlantic Monthly*, Mar. 1896, quoted in Rita J. Simon, *Public Opinion and the Immigrant: Print Media Coverage 1880–1980* (Lexington, Mass.: Lexington Books, 1986), 140.

28. William Shannon, *The American Irish* (New York: Macmillan, 1963), 132.

29. Miller, *Emigrants and Exiles*, 498.

30. *Chicago Citizen*, Oct. 4, 1918, 2.

31. Flynn, *Rebel Girl*, 23.

32. Quoted in Miller, *Emigrants and Exiles*, 551.

33. *Irish World*, July 10, 1915, 2.

34. *San Francisco Leader*, Apr. 17, 1915, 1.

35. *Irish World*, Oct. 3, 1914, 4.

36. Ibid., Mar. 11, 1916, 4.

37. The collective memory suffered occasional bouts of amnesia. The *Chicago Citizen* claimed, for example, that the United States "threw open the portals of her hospitality and welcomed the exile" after the Famine. "America-Ireland Orange and Green," *Chicago Citizen*, May 3, 1918, 1. In fact the Irish encountered much hostility.

38. *Chicago Citizen*, Jan. 31, 1914, 1.

39. *San Francisco Leader*, July 10, 1915, 2.

40. *Gaelic-American*, Jan. 12, 1918, 4.

41. *Irish World*, Mar. 11, 1914, 4.

42. *Chicago Citizen*, Sept. 21, 1917, 4; May 2, 1914, 4.

43. *Gaelic-American*, May 16, 1914, 4.

44. *San Francisco Leader*, Oct. 13, 1917, 4.

45. Brown, "Origins of Irish Nationalism," 343–45.

46. Edward Wakin, *Enter the Irish-American* (New York: Thomas Crowell, 1976): 164.

47. *Gaelic-American*, Apr. 25, 1914, 8.

48. Ibid., Sept. 23, 1916, 4.

49. Carl Wittke, *Irish in America* (Baton Rouge: Louisiana University Press, 1956), 163.

50. *Irish World*, Aug. 8, 1914, 4.

51. *San Francisco Leader*, Feb. 21, 1914, 4.

52. *Irish World*, Oct. 21, 1916, 2.

53. *Gaelic-American*, Mar. 20, 1915, 4.

54. Brown observed that the Irish-American experience was characterized by "a pervasive sense of inferiority, an intense longing for acceptance and respect, and an acute sensitivity to criticism." Thomas Brown, *Irish American Nationalism*, 23.

55. M. R. Fallows, *Irish-Americans: Identity and Assimilation* (Englewood Cliffs, N.J.: Prentice-Hall, 1979), 35.

56. See John J. Appel, "From Shanties to Lace Curtains: The Irish Image in *Puck*, 1876–1910," *Comparative Studies in Sociology and History* 13 (1971): 375.

57. *Puck's* circulation peaked in the late 1890s. The average readers of *Puck* were middle- or lower-middle-class whites of Anglo-Saxon ancestry. Appel, "From Shanties," 365, 374.

58. Ibid., 367.

59. Ibid.

60. A widely circulated book on immigration published in 1914 echoed the nineteenth-century Irish stereotypes. The Irish were described as profligate, improvident, prone to abuse drink, and likely to have too many children. Ross, *Old World in the New*, 24–45.

61. *San Francisco Leader*, Feb. 13, 1915, 4.

62. Dennis Clark, *Hibernia America: The Irish and Regional Cultures* (New York: Greenwood, 1986), 153.

63. *Irish World*, Jan. 24, 1914, 4.

64. Ibid., Apr. 18, 1914, 4.

65. Ibid., Jan. 24, 1914, 4.

66. Mary McWhorter, Ladies Auxiliary of the Ancient Order of Hibernians, "Gross Libel to the Irish Race," letter to the editor, *Irish World*, Dec. 25, 1915, 5.

67. *Chicago Citizen*, Oct. 4, 1918, 4.

68. *San Francisco Leader*, Nov. 17, 1917, 4.

69. *Irish World*, Aug. 7, 1915, 7.

70. *Chicago Citizen*, Nov. 22, 1918, 4.

71. *San Francisco Leader*, May 24, 1913, 4.

72. *Irish World*, Aug. 12, 1916, 4; "Ireland's Past and Future," editorial, *Irish World*, Jan. 24, 1914, 4; "Acme of Hypocrisy," editorial, *Gaelic-American*, Oct. 31, 1914, 4.

73. *Chicago Citizen*, Nov. 16, 1918, 4.

74. Ibid., Feb. 15, 1918, 4.

75. Ibid., Feb. 28, 1914, 4. The *Irish World*, whose founder learned the newspaper trade on the staff of the abolitionist *Liberator*, offered the most egalitarian line on the issue of race.

76. *San Francisco Leader*, Jan. 24, 1914, 4.

77. *Irish World*, Apr. 8, 1916, 7.

78. Ibid., June 3, 1916, 4; "Woodrow Wilson Wins Pyrrhic Victory," *Gaelic-American*, Nov. 18, 1916, 8; "John Stuart Mill on Ireland," editorial, *Irish World*, July 1, 1916, 1.

79. *Gaelic-American*, Oct. 3, 1914, 8.

80. *Irish World*, Mar. 10, 1917, 4.

81. Ibid., June 3, 1916, 4.

82. *San Francisco Leader*, Aug. 7, 1915, 1.

12

CHRISTINE KINEALY

The Great Irish Famine—
A Dangerous Memory?

THE 150TH ANNIVERSARY of the Great Irish Famine has produced a
feast of commemorative events and activities. These have included
public and private ceremonies, remembrance and memorial services,
publications, paintings and plays, television documentaries and debates,
symphonies and statues, exhibitions and conferences, famine walks and
wakes, and even a proposed tribunal at which the British government will
be indicted for genocide.[1] The interest in these events has been broad,
extending beyond the reach of professional historians. Government ministers and presidents, politicians and journalists, Famine committees and
heritage consultants indicate a wide popular interest. Collectively, they
have been named "faminists." The geographic range of interest has also
been broad, reflecting the international impact of the tragedy, largely as
a result of the emigration that occurred both during and after the Famine.
This has been helped by the sensitive approach of the former President
Mary Robinson to the Irish diaspora and their ongoing ties with Ireland.

The interest in the Famine during this commemoration is particularly
surprising in light of the long silence which was evident regarding this
event, especially among Irish historians. Within the recent commemorations, the involvement of the Irish government has been significant with
the appointment of a Famine Committee in 1994, responsible to a designated government minister, and with the appropriation of a quarter of a
million pounds, partly to fund new historical research. It was disbanded
in 1997. Shortly afterwards a new committee was appointed to commemorate the 1798 uprising. As a consequence of government funding, a
number of in-depth local studies of the impact of the Famine have been

undertaken. However, these varied activities raise questions about the rediscovery of the Famine. Will the new research enlighten or obfuscate many of the key issues regarding the Famine, or will it result in a re-statement of the traditional arguments? While there is undoubted scope for more local studies, some of the larger defining issues of the Famine remain underexplored, and a number of archives in both Ireland and Britain remain underused.

The question of remembrance itself requires careful thought. Are we aware of what we are remembering? How should it be remembered? And even *when* it should be remembered? After the summer of 1997—which was officially designated the end of the commemoration by the Irish government—will the Famine be consigned to a further 150 years of silence, until the next anniversary? Furthermore, why did the official commemorations end in 1997? In 1847, there was a further four years of the great tragedy still to run!

Famine or Starvation?

The memory of the Famine is not uniform but operates on a variety of levels, including the private and public, the personal and political. A number of issues are highly controversial and reflect the approach and values of the people who are remembering. For example, even the descriptor "Famine" has been an area of debate. The titles "The Great Famine," "*An Gorta Mor,*" "The Great Starvation," "God's Visitation," "The Great Calamity," "The Great Hunger," and "The Irish Holocaust" are all ways of describing the same event, but they reflect a variety of interpretations and approaches. The use of the term "Famine," for example, is disliked by a number of nationalist commentators on the grounds that during the years 1845–52 large amounts of food continued to be exported from Ireland, mostly to Britain. Instead, they prefer to use "starvation" or the traditional Irish designation "*An Gorta Mor*" (The Great Hunger). For others, the words "holocaust" and "genocide" are too emotive and ascribe to the British government a malignant intent which they believe was not the case. Also, these words are more generally associated with a recent crime against humanity in the twentieth century. Nevertheless, a number of nineteenth-century commentators, including Michael Davitt, did use the word "holocaust" to describe the Famine.[2] More recently, the historian Roy Foster referred to the Famine as the "Irish holocaust."[3]

How to Remember?

The passage of 150 years has created a country that is vastly different from the Ireland of the 1840s. Apart from the obvious political division of Ireland and the creation of a separate independent state, mass democracy is now in place. Moreover, the social, economic, linguistic, demographic, industrial, financial, and cultural basis of the society has changed. The unprecedented scale and pace of change in the last 150 years (much of which was expedited by the Famine) makes it difficult to gain a full appreciation of the nature and context of the tragedy of the Great Famine. Yet the echoes and ripples of that grotesque turning point in Irish history remain in the consciousness of the Irish people, and subtle reminders of it are still apparent on the Irish landscape.

Whose Famine?

The memory and, therefore, the commemoration of the Famine, is not the exclusive preserve of the Irish people who live on the island of Ireland. Although there had been emigration from Ireland before the 1840s, the Famine gave it a new scale and urgency. Those who left were not the strongest, brightest, and most ambitious members of the old society (as many earlier emigrants had been), but many of them were economic refugees, who were impoverished, disease-ridden, and lacking in skills, and who were seeking an alternative to death at home. Subsequent generations of emigrants left to ensure the financial solvency of the families who remained behind.[4] Inevitably, the memories of the Famine among post-Famine emigrants were colored by their reasons for leaving Ireland, and it is no coincidence that some of the most radical nationalist writings of the late nineteenth century came from people whose families had left Ireland, either directly or indirectly, as a result of the Famine. As a consequence, the "ownership" and the commemoration of the Famine extends far beyond the shores of Ireland.

Within the international Irish community, virtually all of the Famine commemorations have been located within the Catholic sector of the Irish population and Irish diaspora. Yet the impact of the Famine was not confined to the Catholic community. Nor indeed was the short-lived but generous response to the suffering in Ireland. Fund-raising during the Famine was a truly ecumenical affair, cutting across religious, national, social, and cultural barriers. Individual donations were given by such diverse personalities as the pope, the queen of England, the tsar of Russia, and the sultan of Turkey. Contributions were also received from poorer groups in society, including dock workers in New York, ex-slaves from the Caribbean, convicts in England, and groups of Native American Indians.[5] A number of religious groups were also involved in the distribution of relief. While the involvement of the Society of Friends has been widely recognized and praised, the fine contributions of members of the Church of Ireland and the Catholic church—a number of whom lost their lives—have sometimes been overlooked.

The impact of the Famine was also broader than has sometimes been depicted. The effect of the potato blight on Ulster has largely been ignored. However, rural poverty in Ulster had many parallels with poverty in the southwest of the country. The decline of the domestic linen industry in Ulster after 1815 created much economic hardship and further increased dependence on a single crop—the potato. Also, in the early nineteenth century, population growth was rapid and competition for land intense. By the 1840s, Armagh was the most densely populated county in Ireland and had become a flashpoint for sectarian rivalry over land. The potato blight appeared in parts of Ulster as early as September 1845. It returned even more virulently in 1846, coinciding with a depression in the linen industry and a poor oats harvest. Contemporary reports from Ulster revealed destitution and suffering that mirrored the experience of more notorious places in the west of the country. During the Famine years, mortality in Ulster doubled, the population dropped by an average of 20 percent, and the number of evictions quadrupled. These events affected the Presbyterian and Protestant poor as much as the Catholic poor, and local research has revealed that in a number of areas mortality was highest among non-Catholics.[6] Mortality, evictions, and emigration, it appears, cut across religious divides.

Nonetheless, the truly national extent of the Famine has been marginalized, and within Ulster, much of the commemoration has been confined to Catholic communities. In this way, the selective memory of the Famine has been largely sectarian. Yet the Famine in many ways was a major blow to the Act of Union of 1800. The Union, which created the United Kingdom, had been based partly on promises of economic benefits to the Irish economy. But the United Kingdom was confronted with economic collapse in one of its component parts in less than fifty years of its inception. The issue of imperial responsibility was abandoned after 1847, when the financial basis of Famine relief was moved from the central government onto local Irish taxation. This abandonment of the Irish Protestant Ascendancy by the British establishment could have been the death knell of Unionist aspirations. Yet the opposite occurred. While the radical nationalist tradition adopted the Famine as a symbol of the failure of the Union, the Protestant elite in the north maintained their faith in the Union and used the Famine as an opportunity to display increased sectarianism. The language of sectarianism was evident as early as 1849. Following the introduction of an additional tax on Ireland to support the areas in the west of the country where the Famine was still raging, a massive campaign opposing the new tax was mobilized in the northeast, led by wealthy Protestants. They argued that if this money was paid, they would be "keeping up an army of beggars, fed out of the industry of Ulster."[7] One local landlord suggested that the Famine was relatively absent in the north because

> the Northerners are a hardworking, industrious people, and the blessing of God is upon their labours. If the people in the South had been as industrious as those in the North, they would not be in the condition they are in.[8]

Religious, cultural, and economic separateness fused as papism, the potato, and poverty became intertwined. This myth has been perpetuated, and poverty and Famine have been appropriated as the preserve of Irish Catholics.

How to Remember

This raises the central question of how a human tragedy of the dimension of the Famine should be commemorated. The problem of representation is common to all commemorations, but, with the exception of the Jewish Holocaust, few have to deal with such horrendous subject matter. Commemoration is an emotional experience. As such, it holds the potential to illuminate a process of self-discovery or to confirm and heighten a prejudice. It can be a healing process or it can reopen old wounds. The latter was evident in the numerous demands for an apology from the British government for the Famine, coming from a diverse range of people and not exclusively from republican nationalists. While the Conservative government led by John Major refused to have any direct involvement with the Famine commemorations, one of the first acts of Tony Blair's government was to acknowledge and express regret for the role of the British government during the Famine years.[9] This acknowledgment was widely criticized in both England and Ireland as being unnecessary and setting a dangerous precedent.[10]

To what extent, however, are the politicians of today accountable for the failures of a former government—a government, moreover, which was controlled by a small undemocratic clique, and which frequently acted with the support of Irish landlords, including Daniel O'Connell?[11] In the nineteenth century, paupers throughout the British Isles were treated harshly, and poverty was regarded as the fault of the individual. The writings of Charles Dickens, among others, provide a contemporary insight into the condition of the poor in England.[12] In 1846–47, there were also widespread food shortages in the Highlands of Scotland, which was sometimes refered to as "The Scottish Famine."[13] But while evictions and emigration increased, and birth rates and marriages fell, there was no excess mortality. Within the United Kingdom, Ireland was unique in undergoing such an ordeal.[14]

The recovery of the past can be painful, and to some extent this can account for the long silence regarding the Famine. The Famine did not end with the return of good potato harvests in 1852, as mortality, evictions, disease, and emigration all continued to be higher than the pre-Famine levels. Even 150 years later, Ireland has not recovered from the demographic shock of the Famine years, and today it is the only European country with a population smaller than in 1841. Furthermore, it is only beginning to be realized that scars left by such tragedies are deep and enduring. It is only as Ireland emerges with a distinctive and positive cultural identity within Europe that Irish people throughout the world are able to come to terms with the impact of the Famine years and to confront the ghosts of their tragic past. The outcome of this confrontation can be positive and it can be part of a "healing process" for Ireland and the Irish diaspora.[15] Inevitably, this throws a great responsibility on historians and researchers, especially those who have admitted that they have allowed current political events to constrain and shape their interpretation of the past.

Representing the Famine

The fact that there are few contemporary photographs means that many images of the Famine are retrospective or re-created. The contemporary images that have survived are mostly sketches or prints commissioned by the British press to inform a middle-class audience in Britain. Ironically, some of these images became a tool that was used against the Irish victims, eliciting disdain rather than sympathy. In the immediate aftermath of the Famine, the visible reminders of the Famine largely disappeared— Famine graveyards, workhouses, and soup kitchens for example became representations of the failure of Irish society and were abandoned and left to disintegrate from the landscape and dissipate from memory. Retrieving the buried experience of the Famine was made more difficult by the fact that, with the exception of a few nationalists, many of whom resided outside Ireland, the experience of the Famine years appeared to disappear from the public arena in the immediate aftermath of the event. Survivors of the calamity perhaps felt a mixture of pain and guilt which made retrieval difficult. The cultural revival at the end of the nineteenth century had no place for a recent memory based on pain and suffering and ignominy, in a country that was rediscovering its golden past. Not surprisingly, no national monument was erected to the Famine of 1845–50 for 150 years, while the lesser known, but no less deadly Famine of 1740–41 had two monuments. Yet, in spite of this collective silence, at a personal and individual level, the Famine was not forgotten. The creation of a folk archive in 1945, based on a questionnaire of Famine memories (an initiative by Eamon de Valera's government), showed that there were numerous enduring and powerful private recollections of the Famine.[16]

The Silence of Historians

The current explosion of interest in the Famine is remarkable given the silence of the previous 150 years. This silence has been most evident among the academic community. From 1900 to the 1980s, only two major publications on this topic were produced. This was in spite of a renewed interest in historical research and methodology, and the emergence of a number of influential Irish historians (notably R. Dudley Edwards, Theo Moody, F. S. L. Lyons, and David Quinn, among others). Astonishingly, only one of these books was produced by Irish academics, and even that was not the initiative of the professional historians but was written at the instigation of the *Taoiseach*, Eamon de Valera, who did not want the one hundredth anniversary of the Famine to pass unnoticed, despite its coinciding with the ending of the Second World War (known as the "Emergency" in Ireland).

In 1944, de Valera commissioned a comprehensive academic publication on the Famine which he hoped would be ready for 1945. It was envisaged that the book would be about one thousand pages in length and would incorporate the most up-to-date research on the Famine. The government contributed funding for the publication which was intended to provide a subvention toward publishing costs and a fee for some of the authors. The initial editors of the publication were Professor Theodore Moody, Professor Robert Dudley Edwards, and Dr. David Quinn, although Dr. Quinn pulled out when he moved to an academic position in England and Moody was eventually replaced by T. D. Williams.[17] Before this appointment, however, none of these academics had shown any particular interest in the Famine, and this did not change following publication. Moody, Edwards, and Quinn had all received training between 1929 and 1932 at the Institute of Historical Research in London—a pioneer of the new historical approach, which stated that historical research should be value-free, scientific, and "past-centered."[18] This early leaning toward "value-free" history laid the foundations for the influential "revisionist" interpretations that dominated Irish historiography from the 1960s to the 1990s. It was also evident in the dry and detached approach of the editors to the Famine publication.

The publication commissioned by de Valera took almost twelve years to materialize and in its final form was far shorter and less comprehensive than had been envisaged by the *Taoiseach*. The subtitle of the publication, *Studies in Irish History*, provided an indication that the book was not the complete overview that had been intended. Moreover, certain key issues, such as mortality, were deliberately omitted or sidetracked. Both the editors and de Valera were disappointed in the final product, although the Irish academic community, perhaps in a spirit of self-defense, rallied around in support of the publication.[19] Less professional generosity was evident a few years later when Cecil Woodham-Smith's classic, *The Great Hunger*, was published. While Woodham-Smith's book captured the public imagination, for the most part the Irish academic establishment derided or ignored her publication. She was particularly criticized for presenting what was alleged to be an overemotive view of the Famine, which was in sharp contrast to the sanitized approach of Edwards and Williams. Outside Ireland, however, Woodham-Smith was widely praised, propelling her book into the best-seller league, and within Ireland, despite academic hostility, her book enormously outsold *Studies in Irish History*.[20]

The early divisions that emerged over interpretations of the Famine highlighted an important divide in Famine historiography; that is, the split between the popular and the professional memory of the Famine. While the folk memory of the Famine held on to the horrors of the Famine—coffin ships, mass graves, large-scale evictions, greedy landlords, food leaving a country devastated by Famine, and a society turned upside down by such unrelenting suffering—academic interpretations (until recently) have tended to be dominated by claims of continuity, inevitability, and ignorance.

Although the revisionist interpretation of the Famine is being successfully challenged, a number of core issues are still in dispute. The question of suffering is still debated. In the language of more recent revisionist interpretation, the terms "oppressed" and "oppressors," "victims" and "perpetrators" are replaced with the more upbeat description of "winners" and "losers." In a tragedy of the dimension of the Famine, the "winners" are few—perhaps merchants, solicitors, solvent landlords, large farmers, and ships' captains. The "losers" are many. The aggregate, and appalling, statistic that at least one million people died during the Famine years disguises a more awful truth. The namelessness and anonymity of the Famine victims renders them invisible and masks the real human tragedy of the loss. Even compared with contemporary famines, the Irish Famine was the most lethal in modern history. Also, unlike today's famines, the Irish Famine occurred within the jurisdiction of, and a stone's throw away from, the capital of the richest empire in the world. Furthermore, in addition to those who died in their own country, approximately 10 percent of emigrants died shortly after leaving Ireland. Even for those who survived the horrors of the journey, their life span in the new country was short and the quality of life (for the first generation anyway) was poor. Few of them ever returned to the country of their birth. For these people, economic refugees rather than emigrants, the description "winner" hardly seems appropriate.

Confronting Unpleasant Realities

In addition to the large number of commemorative events, the 150th anniversary has resulted in an outpouring of books and articles on the Famine. As a consequence, a more textured and diverse view of the Famine is emerging. More work remains to be done, partly to make up for the long dearth of serious research. Much of the current writings are helping to provide a solid basis of fact and interpretation which, in turn, will help to shape any future commemorations. However, as the old myths about the Famine are gradually discarded, it is important that they are not replaced with a new set of myths or crude antimyth statements. Also, the more unpleasant truths about the Famine have to be confronted and not avoided. For example, the ships that left Ireland laden with food during the Famine were doing so largely for the financial benefit of *Irish* merchants and traders. The large farmers who benefited from the availability and sale of cheap land toward the latter end of the Famine were also Irish and, sometimes, Catholic. Furthermore, there is a danger that the commemorations can be sanitized and the more obscene aspects of the Famine—all famines—forgotten. Corruption, stealing, hoarding, and even cannibalism are part of the darker reality of the Famine years, and should not be forgotten in an attempt to make the Famine a simplistic morality tale about the "goodies" (the Irish people en masse) and the "baddies" (the whole of the British people).

When Was the Famine?

The timing of the Famine commemoration has been confusing. Unlike many historical anniversaries or commemorations, there is no one day that marks the start of the Famine, nor is it clear when the Famine ceased. The Famine was a process rather than a single event, and it was its longevity which made it unique. Also, the impact of the Famine varied over time and geographic area, making it even more difficult to pinpoint a key date. For example, in Skibbereen in county Cork, suffering was most intense in the early part of 1847, when it attracted so much international attention; for areas in county Clare, the impact of the Famine was cumulative, and mortality was proportionately higher in 1849 than it had been in earlier years.

Commemorations of the Famine commenced early in terms of the unfolding of events 150 years earlier. Even before the end of 1994, preparations were being made for a series of events and activities. By the beginning of 1995, the Famine commemoration was in full swing, and a latent public memory appeared to be unleashed as the demand for "Famine memorabilia" got under way. The early and sustained interest in the Famine took most people, including historians, by surprise. How accurate are these activities historically?

Although the autumn of 1845 marked the first appearance of the potato blight in Ireland, there was no excess mortality in the twelve months that followed. Through a combination of good fortune (the blight was localized and mostly confined to the east of the country) and a swift and traditional response by the ruling Tory government, there was no famine in Ireland in the year following the first failure of the potato crop. In the summer of 1846, even nationalist newspapers in Ireland such as *The Freeman's Journal* were congratulating the prime minister, Sir Robert Peel, on his successful handling of the crisis.

The Irish Famine only commenced in the wake of the *second* failure of the potato crop in the harvest of 1846. Following this, the devastation was rapid and extensive. By this stage, a new Whig-Liberal government was in place, led by Lord John Russell (a traditional ally of Daniel O'Connell). The new government responded to the second year of shortages with a change of policy that made entitlement to relief dependent on hard physical labor on the public works. The inadequacy and inefficiency of the public works, combined with low wages paid in a period of famine prices, resulted in a swift, sharp increase in mortality. It was in the winter of 1846–47 that the Irish Famine—replete with deaths, disease, mortality, evictions, and emigration—really began.

In recognition of the failure of the public works, the government again changed its policy on Famine relief. In the summer of 1847, soup kitchens were opened throughout Ireland for the distribution of free food. As a consequence, for the first—and only—time during the Famine, the problem of hunger was tackled directly. At its peak in the summer of 1847, over three million people were receiving free rations of soup daily. This amazing logistic feat demonstrated the ability of the British government to provide large-scale relief in the midst of a crisis. The soup kitchen scheme was short-lived. It was terminated in the autumn of 1847, following which the Irish Poor Law (based on the workhouse system and financed from local taxation) was made responsible for providing all Famine relief.

Significantly, in the summer of 1847, a senior government official—Sir Charles Trevelyan—declared that the Irish Famine was over and that the British government was no longer morally responsible for any future destitution. Subsequent events proved that the Famine was far from over. In 1848, despite the stringent conditions attached to obtaining relief, over 1 1/2 million people were in receipt of workhouse relief. Moreover, in some parts of the country, mortality was higher in 1849 than it had been in "Black '47." The abnormally high rates of mortality continued well into the 1850s, long after the potato blight had disappeared from Ireland. The demographic decline also continued, and 150 years later Ireland has still not recovered from the shock of the Famine years. Demonstrably, the Famine did not end in 1847.

Yet the Irish government, in a gesture redolent of the actions of the British government 150 years earlier, decided that the summer of 1997 should mark the official end of the Famine commemoration. The commemoration closed with a musical festival with which it was intended to "bury the ghost of the Famine."[21] At the same time, the government wanted to have time to prepare a further commemoration for the two hundredth anniversary of the 1798 uprising in 1998. A number of people and organizations expressed concern at the commercial and flamboyant nature of the proposed Famine festival and the focus on big-name attractions rather than the nature of the event being remembered.[22] Joe Murray of the aid agency AFRI described the affair as "dancing on the graves of the famine dead." John Waters of the *Irish Times* detected a more sinister motive, commenting that the "Famine dead are offered at the alter of Tourism."[23] The ending of the Famine in 1997, as was the case in 1847, appears to have been chosen to suit a political and commercial convenience rather than to reflect the reality of the situation. Or is the desire to bury the ghost of the Famine a new way of reimposing a silence on the Famine?

Conclusion

The anniversary of the Great Famine has demonstrated a massive interest in that defining event in Irish history. Apart from historians—who ignored the Famine for so long—the Famine has started to attract the interest of folklorists, geographers, demographers, linguists, political activists, and Third World specialists. The Irish government has also become a significant force in supporting the various events and activities, including the funding of new research on the Famine. However, one of the most positive features of the recent commemorations is that the memory and the "ownership" of the Famine have been taken out of the hands of the government and of professional academics. It has also been remembered and honored in many private and personal ways.[24] It is to be hoped that ordinary people—both within Ireland and elsewhere—will not follow the Irish government and stop commemorating the Famine in 1997 but will continue to remember and honor the victims of the Famine beyond that date.

The Famine commemoration has had far-reaching effects. For example, Third World groups have used the memory of the Famine to inform and remind people of famine and suffering in the world today. They have also drawn parallels between the (inadequate) response of the British government in the 1840s and the (still inadequate) response of many contemporary Western governments. The anniversary of the Famine has also helped to build bridges between various groups. In August 1995, a Famine ceremony was held at the Botanic Gardens in Dublin (where the blight was first observed in 1845). Representatives and ambassadors from countries that had sent money to Ireland during the Famine were invited to attend the commemoration.[25] Close links have also been forged between the Choctaw Indians (who sent $170 to Ireland during the Famine) and the Irish people, culminating in the Irish president, Mary Robinson, being made an honorary Choctaw chief. Unfortunately, an opportunity to build stronger bridges between Britain and Ireland, and between the various communities in the north of Ireland, appears to have been wasted. The fear of some historians and political commentators that to remember the Famine would only serve to give succor to republican nationalism or "ideological bullets to the IRA" has proved to be groundless. It is clear, however, that the Famine was viewed by some as a dangerous memory that had to be controlled or forgotten.[26] In a recent visit to Ireland, Gary White Deer, a representative of the Choctaw Nation, described the Irish Famine as a "sacred memory." This sacred memory should not be forgotten after 1997 or allowed to become the sole preserve of government officials, political activists, or even academics.

Notes

1. In 1998, the Irish Famine/Genocide Committee in New York intends to put the government of Lord John Russell on trial on a charge of genocide.

2. Davitt described the Famine as "the holocaust of humanity." Michael Davitt, *The Fall of Feudalism* (London: Harper & Brothers, 1904), 50.

3. Roy Foster, *Modern Ireland, 1600–1972* (London: Allen Lane/Penguin, 1988).

4. For more on emigration see Kerby A. Miller, *Emigrants and Exiles: Ireland and the Irish Exodus to North America* (Oxford: Oxford University Press, 1985); and Roger Swift and Sheridan Gilley, *The Irish in Britain 1815–1939* (London: Pinter Publishers, 1984).

5. For more on charitable donations see Christine Kinealy, "The Role of Private Philanthropy during the Famine," in Patrick O'Sullivan, ed., *The Meaning of the Famine* (Leicester: Leicester University Press, 1997).

6. Gerard MacAtasney, "Challenging an Orthodoxy: The Famine in Lurgan, 1845–47" (M.A. thesis, Queen's University, 1995); Christine Kinealy and T. Parkhill, *The Famine in Ulster* (Belfast: Ulster Historical Foundation, 1997).

7. *Hansard's Parliamentary Debates,* (Mar. 1, 1849), col 62.

8. Robert Dolling, landlord in county Armagh, quoted in Gerard MacAtasney, *'This Dreadful Visitation': The Famine in Lurgan/Portadown* (Belfast: Beyond the Pale, 1997).

9. For example, the Famine Committee in Liverpool approached the British government in 1995 for financial support for the erection of a statue commemorating Famine emigrants who had passed through or stayed in Liverpool. The government refused to support the project on the grounds that it had only a local interest. An Early Morning Motion in the British House of Commons in 1995 to commemorate the Famine was defeated.

10. For example, critical articles and editorials appeared in *The Times, The Telegraph,* and *The Independent,* June 2 and 3, 1997, and *The Sunday Tribune,* June 8, 1997.

11. O'Connell welcomed the coming to power of the Whig government in June 1846. He died at the height of the Famine in May 1847. Many of the Young Irelanders criticized his "soft" approach to the policies of the British government.

12. Written in the 1830s by Charles Dickens, *Oliver Twist* was intended as a critique of the "new" Poor Law of 1834 and its harsh treatment of paupers.

13. T. M. Devine, *The Great Highland Famine: Hunger, Emigration and the Scottish Highlands in the Nineteenth Century* (Edinburgh: J. Donaldson, 1988).

14. For more on the impact of the Irish Famine see Christine Kinealy, *'A Death-Dealing Famine': The Great Hunger in Ireland* (London: Pluto Press, 1997).

15. Research on the impact of postcolonial traumatic stress is currently being undertaken by Dr. Garrett O'Connor of the University of California, L.A.

16. This archive is maintained in the Department of Irish Folklore in University College, Dublin.

17. For more on this episode see Cormac Ó'Gráda, "Making History in Ire-

land in the 1940s and 1950s: The Saga of the Great Famine," *Irish Review* 12 (1992): 87–107.

18. Brendan Bradshaw, "Revising Irish History," in Daltún Ó Ceallaigh, *Reconsiderations of Irish History and Culture* (Dublin: "Leithmas," 1994), 30–32.

19. See F. S. L. Lyons's review of Edwards and Williams, eds., *The Great Famine: Studies in Irish History* (New York: New York University Press, 1957), in *Irish Times*, Jan. 21, 1957.

20. For example, in a provocative article, "We Are All Revisionists Now" in *Irish Review* (6 1986): 1–6, historian Roy Foster describes Woodham-Smith as a "zealous convert."

21. *American Irish Newsletter* 21, no. 8 (1996).

22. *The Title*, July 28, 1996.

23. *Irish Times*, May 27, 1997. Also see *The Phoenix* (Dublin), May 23, 1997.

24. For example, in June 1996, I attended a gathering of the Killoran Clan in co. Sligo and joined them when they visited Sligo harbor and threw wildflowers into the sea, in recognition that this would have been the last view of Ireland that many of their ancestors would have had.

25. This event was organized by Don Mullan of Concern, a Third World group.

26. For example, on the "Davis" Show broadcast in February 1995 (by RTE), Eoghan Harris alleged that the Famine Commemoration was a political device by the IRA; Conor Cruise O'Brien made a similar claim on a "Newsnight" program broadcast in Britain in June 1995 (BBC 2). Neither man has any specialist knowledge of the Famine, but their comments are an example of the "politicization" of the Famine commemorations.

Contributors

Bruce D. Boling earned his B.A. and a master's degree from the University of Iowa; a master's in library science from the University of California, Berkeley; and a master's and Ph.D. degree (linguistics, with a speciality in Celtic languages) at Harvard University. He has taught linguistics at Harvard and the University of North Carolina, Chapel Hill, and has been a professional librarian at Brown University, the University of Wyoming, and the Library of Congress. Currently, he is principal cataloger at the library of the University of New Mexico, and he has also held research fellowships at the Dublin Institute for Advanced Studies and the Ulster Folk and Transport Museum. In addition to his own published work on the Irish language, he has collaborated with Kerby Miller on three articles in Irish immigration history and is now engaged with Miller and two other colleagues on a comprehensive edition of Irish immigrants' letters and memoirs. His special interest is the investigation of the English dialects spoken in Ulster, using immigrants' letters and other sources to reconstruct the dialect speech of the eighteenth and nineteenth centuries.

Arthur Gribben is a native of Dundalk, county Louth, Ireland. His academic background is in folklore and mythology as well as in theater arts. In 1988, he was awarded his Ph.D. from UCLA upon completion of his dissertation, *The Role of the Ancient Irish Saga, Táin Bó Cuailnge, in the Sense of Local Cultural Identity in North County Louth, Ireland*. He has taught at UCLA and The Union Institute and currently teaches at California State University, Northridge. His previous publications include *The Irish Cultural Directory for Southern California; Holy Wells & Sacred Water Sources in Britain & Ireland;* and articles and film reviews in academic and professional publications. He has been a consultant for the media division of the

National Endowment for the Humanities; director of The Great Famine Symposium at Loyola Marymount University (1993); film review editor for *Western Folklore;* treasurer for the California Folklore Society; and founder of the UCLA Film & Folklore Society. Gribben is founder and director of Irish America Net (www.irishamericanet.com), a major Internet information resource about Irish America.

WAYNE HALL is the author of a 1980 study, *Shadowy Heroes: Irish Literature of the 1890s* (Syracuse University Press), and of a number of articles on the nineteenth-century Irish literary-political journal the *Dublin University Magazine.* He has recently completed a book-length study of the same journal. Currently, he is director of undergraduate studies in English at the University of Cincinnati.

RUTH-ANN M. HARRIS is the author of *The Nearest Place That Wasn't Ireland: Early Nineteenth Century Irish Labor Migration* (Iowa State University Press) and the editor of the first four volumes of *The Search for Missing Friends: Irish Immigrant Advertisements Placed in the* Boston Pilot (New England Historic Genealogical Society). Since 1993 she has taught Irish and Irish-American migration history at Boston College. In 1994–95 she was a senior research fellow at the Institute of Irish Studies at Queen's University, Belfast. She is currently engaged in preparing a book on the immigrant letters of Irish women in America entitled *'Come You All Courageously Together': Irish Women Write Home.*

NEIL HOGAN is a graduate of St. John Fisher College, Rochester, New York, and a newspaper professional and reporter with the *New Haven Register.* He is cofounder and first president of the Connecticut Irish-American Historical Society and editor of the Society's newsletter. He is the author of four books and numerous articles, and from 1986 to 1991 he wrote a weekly Connecticut history column for the *Sunday New Haven Register.* He is a charter member and former vice president of the Ethnic Heritage Center of New Haven. He holds membership in a number of other associations and societies, among them the Labor History Association of Greater New Haven, the National Parks and Conservation Association, the New Haven Colony Historical Society, the Connecticut Humanities Council, and the Connecticut Historical Society.

DAVID S. JONES was born in Liverpool. He received his Ph.D. in political science at Queen's University of Belfast in 1977. He worked as a lecturer in the Department of Agriculture, Northern Ireland Civil Service, from 1975 to 1978. He then lectured at the University College of Botswana, under the designation of the Overseas Development Administration, before joining the National University of Singapore in 1982, where he is now senior lecturer in the Department of Political Science. He has published articles and essays on Southeast Asia and Southern Africa, as well as on Irish history and politics. His most recent publication on Ireland is his book, *Graziers, Land Reform and Political Conflict in Ireland*, published by Catholic University of America Press in 1995.

CHRISTINE KINEALY was born near Liverpool, England, but her grandparents came from counties Mayo and Tipperary. She is a graduate of Trinity College, Dublin, where she completed her Ph.D. in modern history in 1984. Shortly thereafter she moved to Belfast, where she researched and taught history. Her acclaimed reassessment of the Famine period, *This Great Calamity: The Irish Famine, 1845–52*, was published by Gill and Macmillan in 1994. A follow-up volume, *'A Death-Dealing Famine': The Great Hunger in Ireland*, was published in 1997 by Pluto Press. She is currently engaged in research on international donations to Ireland during the Famine and exports from Ireland, 1846–49. She is a fellow of the University of Liverpool.

PATRICIA LYSAGHT is a native of county Clare, Ireland. Her academic background is in law as well as in Irish language and literature, and comparative folklore and ethnology. Upon completion of her law studies at University College, Dublin, in 1971, she was called to the Irish Bar. In 1982, she was awarded her Ph.D. upon completion of her dissertation, *The Banshee*, which was published in book form in 1986. In 1987–88, she was a Humboldt scholar and research professor at the Westfälische Wilhelms-Universität, Münster, Germany. She is a member of the major international societies for folklore and ethnological research and is currently president of the International Commission for Ethnological Food Research. Her main research interests concern Irish traditional life and identity, narrative forms, repertoire formation and performance, belief and custom, foodways and material culture. She has lectured and published extensively in Ireland, Europe, and North America. She also works with the Irish and international media in the production of programs connected with Irish life and culture. She is currently a lecturer in the Department of Irish Folklore, University College, Dublin.

KERBY A. MILLER received his B.A. degree at Pomona College and his M.A. and Ph.D. degrees in history at the University of California, Berkeley. Since 1978, he has taught Irish and American history at the University of Missouri, Columbia, where he is now professor of history. He has also been senior research fellow at the Institute of Irish Studies at Queen's University, Belfast, and a visiting professor in the Department of History at Queen's. His history of Irish immigration, *Emigrants and Exiles: Ireland and the Irish Exodus to North America* (Oxford University Press, 1985), won the Merle Curti and Theodore Saloutos prizes in U.S. social and immigration history, respectively, and was a finalist for the Pulitzer Prize. His research was the basis for a documentary film, *Out of Ireland,* which was shown on PBS stations nationwide in 1995. With the film's producer, Paul Wagner, he has written a companion volume, *Out of Ireland* (Elliot and Clark, 1994). With Bruce Boling and two other colleagues, he is now preparing an edited collection of Irish immigrants' letters and memoirs for publication by Oxford University Press.

MICK MULCRONE holds a master's in journalism from the University of Oregon and a Ph.D. from the University of Washington, Seattle. His doctoral dissertation explores World War I–era censorship of the Irish American press. He has published articles on Irish American history in *Journalism History* and *Portland Magazine,* and has delivered papers on representations of the Irish in the media at national and international scholarly conferences. Several of his papers have won regional and national awards for excellence. He is presently an assistant professor in the Department of Communication Studies at the University of Portland, Oregon. His father and maternal grandparents emigrated from the west of Ireland.

GEARÓID Ó hALLMHURÁIN was born in Clare and educated at University College, Cork, Université de la Sorbonne, and Queen's University, Belfast, from which he holds a Ph.D. in social anthropology. A former archivist with Comhaltas Ceoltóirí Éireann, he has been researching Irish traditional music and folklore for over twenty years. In 1982, he was awarded a music research bursary by the Irish Arts Council to conduct a series of ethnographic field studies in the west of Ireland as well as in Irish immigrant communities in Canada and the United States. From 1985 to 1990, he studied ethnomusicology with the late John Blacking at Queen's University, Belfast. He has recorded Irish traditional music on uillean pipes and concertina, most recently with the Kilfenora Céilí Band, Ireland's oldest traditional music ensemble. He currently lectures in cross-cultural literature and research methods at the University of San Francisco and is completing a post-Famine history of traditional music making in the west of Ireland.

MICHAEL QUIGLEY did his postgraduate studies at McMaster University, Hamilton, Ontario. His dissertation title is "Farmers, Merchants and Priests: The Rise of the Agrarian Petty Bourgeoisie in Ireland, 1850–85." He is the author of two local histories: a *Centenary History of the Hamilton Philharmonic Orchestra* (1984) and *On the Market: An Illustrated History of the Hamilton Farmers' Market* (1987), and is a contributor to *Canadian Journal of Irish Studies*. He has served as an instructor at the University of Western Ontario and is currently historian and publicist on the executive committee of the Toronto-based Action Grosse Île. The committee was created by Irish community representatives from Metropolitan Toronto, Brampton, Hamilton, and Kingston to ensure that the mass graves of the Irish Famine victims of 1847 are perpetuated as the main theme of the National Historic Park on Grosse Île and as a permanent monument to the Irish role in the building of Canada.

JILLIAN STRANG was born in England and is a graduate of Oxford University. A resident of Massachusetts now, she earned her doctorate in comparative history from Brandeis University and teaches at Bentley College. Her research focuses on nineteenth-century British social history, including Victorian prison reform, philanthropy, and the work of the Salvation Army.

JOYCE TOOMRE is a research fellow at Harvard University's Russian Research Center and Adams House. She earned her A.M. and Ph.D. degrees in Slavic literature from Brown University in 1973 and 1977, respectively, as well as an M.A. (Econ.) in government from the University of Manchester, England, 1960. She has lectured widely in culinary history, especially at Radcliff College, Brown University, and Cambridge School of Culinary Arts. Since 1991, she has been managing editor of *The Culinary Times*. She is the author of many journal articles, and her book *Classic Russian Cooking: Elena Molokhovets' "Gift to Young Housewives"* is an annotated translation of the major prerevolutionary Russian cookbook. Her current research focuses on the foodways of ethnic Boston.

Index

109 SEASONAL HOLIDAYS

114 LAND ORGANIZATION

1432 PARTIAL POTATO FAMINE (IRELAND) P134